ZERO HARM CULTURE

Corporate Journey

Dr Harbans Lal Kaila
Hem Raj

Prints Publications Pvt Ltd
New Delhi

Published by

Prints Publications Pvt Ltd
Viraj Tower, 4259/3, Ansari Road,
Darya Ganj, New Delhi-110002
Tel. : +91-11-45355555
Fax: +91-11-23275542
E-mail : contact@printspublications.com
Website :www.printspublications.com

First Edition : 2024

ISBN: 978-81-199721-7-3

Price: Rs. 1495/-

Published and Printed by Mr. Pranav Gupta (Managing Director) on behalf of Prints Publications Pvt Ltd, New Delhi.

CONTENTS

ABOUT THE AUTHOR

Dr Harbans Lal Kaila

Dr Harbans Lal Kaila, earned Masters' degree in Psychology from Guru Nanak Dev University and PhD from Tata Institute of Social Sciences, Mumbai. Served SNDT Women's University and Central Labour Institute, Mumbai for 28 years. Represented India in Conferences at New York, Berlin, Muscat, Rome, New Zealand, Japan, London, Malaysia, Dubai, Cairo and Sydney. Editor of 'Journal of Psychosocial Research'. With 40-years professional experience, Published books/articles. Founder Director of the Forum of Behavioural Safety, successfully conducted 2000 behavioral safety culture programs and seven national conferences for industry.

Hem Raj

Hem Raj is a Human Resource professional with more than two decades of comprehensive experience, initially with COWI and then with Hindalco Industries Limited. He is a recipient of a Group Study Exchange fellowship to the Netherlands from Rotary International in 2009. Hem Raj has been the recipient of several awards, including the Aditya Birla Chairman's Young Professional Award for 2008 and nominations for the Aditya Birla Chairman's Distinguished Professional Award for 2016 and 2023. Hem Raj is also a proud fellow of the Learning and Performance Institute (UK).

FOREWORD

Mahad Manufacturers Association: A Beacon of Sustainable Development and Social Responsibility.

Shri Sambhaji Pathare, *President, Mahad Manufacturers Association*

In 2005, Mahad Manufacturers Association (MMA) for CETP found itself in the 11th spot in the infamous "World Dirty Thirty" list, highlighting the environmental challenges faced by its member industries. However, under the visionary leadership of its Chairman, Shri. Sambhaji Pathare, MMA embarked on a transformative journey that not only cleansed its own operations but also set a shining example for the entire nation.

The pivotal moment came when Chairman Mr Pathare introduced stage-wise sampling of individual industries' Effluent Treatment Plants (ETP), aiming to understand the true efficacy of effluent treatment. Despite initial resistance from some industries, Chairman Mr Sambhaji Pathare, with the support of the Executive Committee, led by example by initiating stage-wise sampling at his own industry as a unit head. This courageous step proved to be the "Brahmastra" (ultimate weapon), fostering trust and confidence among industry members.

The success of stage-wise sampling catalyzed a paradigm shift. Industries began investing in their ETPs, significantly reducing the pollution load on the Common Effluent Treatment Plant (CETP). Recognizing this monumental achievement, the Government of Maharashtra and the Maharashtra Pollution Control Board bestowed the Vasundhara Award upon MMA CETP in 2017, affirming its commitment to environmental stewardship. Also it set an example as role model CETP in Asia Envirotech International Conference 2017.

With the best support of Executive Committee Members and Industries, Chairman Sambhaji Pathare's leadership extended beyond environmental initiatives. MMA's social responsibility initiatives, such as the free

Mobile Hospital in association with Satya Sai Seva Trust which covered more than 65000 patients till date and the 24-hour MMA Hospital which is now in collaboration with Walavalkar Hospital Chiplun, providing Critical essential healthcare services to thousands of beneficiaries, including nearby villagers, industries, and workers.

During the COVID-19 pandemic, MMA's proactive response was commendable. It was first Industrial association which established a 200-bedded Dedicated COVID Health Center, offering free treatment to indoor and outpatient patients, alleviating the burden on rural communities. It Treated almost 1850 Indoor patients and thousands of outdoor patients not only in the vicinity but from the other districts as well. Former Chief Minister Shri. Uddhavji Thakrey praised MMA's efforts, recognizing their significant impact on public health.

In addition to healthcare initiatives, MMA's contributions to education and skill development are noteworthy. Under his chairmanship MMA started ETP operators course in joint venture with Dr Danav Green Tech Institute and BATU University.

Digitalizing over 160 Zilla Parishad schools and establishing state-of-the-art Skill Development Institute in partnership with renowned universities like Babasaheb Ambedkar Technical University demonstrate MMA's commitment to empowering youth and fostering economic independence.

President Mr Sambhaji Pathare attributes MMA's success to the collective efforts of executive members, industries, government officials, and society. Their collaborative approach has not only transformed Mahad's industrial landscape but has also provided sustainable development and upliftment to the community at large. As MMA continues its journey, it stands as a beacon of hope, proving that with determination and collective action, even the greatest challenges can be overcome for a brighter, more sustainable future.

Dr Kaila (Pioneer of BBS - Behaviour Based Safety) has played great role in the implementation of BBS in Mahad MIDC and in more than 2000 industries in India and abroad which has started developing real safety culture across the organisation. If we all adopt BBS in our life it will definitely help to reduce accidents in Industries and also on road. BBS not only make our life safe but due to reduction in accidents increases our productivity and hence economic growth of organisations and our nation.

We always say prevention is better than cure like that BBS plays same role in our life. I will say BBS is Bramhasra for sustainable development our country and to make our life easier, safe and peaceful .

Zero Harm for People, Plant and Property as broadly defined also need to be understood in terms of not only physical injuries but also emotional injuries which are more frequent. Zero-harm culture from workplace to anyplace is need of the hour as many incidents happen outside workplace.

Supportive Safety Culture is one of the essential pillars for building a progressive and sustainable organisation. Every individual's behaviours as safety ambassador, collaboration and engagement with all levels; encouragement, rewards and recognition for right safety behaviours make a big contribution towards developing and implementing a long term positive safety culture. BBS throws light on various elements that are necessary for implementing a culture of safety and will surely help to understand what is a safety-culture program and how to begin a journey for developing positive safety culture. To achieve zero incidents/ injuries, Behaviour Based Safety (BBS) management assumes greater significance.

This manuscript co-authored by Dr Harbans Lal Kaila and Mr Hem Raj, is a continuous effort of the authors to help organisations build positive safety cultures.

Thanks to Hon. Dr Kaila for his lifetime efforts and great achievement in personal and Industrial Revolution through BBS program in India.

—Sambhaji B. Pathare

"Chief Operating Officer" Calyx Chemicals and Pharmaceutical Ltd (API Drug Manufacturer, USFDA approved), President, Mahad Manufacturers Association, Technical Director on "Sai Industries" at Mahad (M S Epoxy Barrel Manufacturing Company), Chairman-MMA Skill development centre, Mahad.

CHAPTER

1 UNVEILING THE IMPACT

HOW THE CRASH OF CHALLENGER, PIPER ALPHA & FUKUSHIMA TRANSFORMED INDUSTRIAL SAFETY

Industrial safety incidents have long been a grim reminder of the consequences that can arise from overlooking safety measures. These incidents not only result in loss of life and severe injuries but also lead to substantial economic losses and environmental damage. Historically, the field of industrial safety has been shaped by tragic events that have spurred changes in regulations, practices, and technology. The importance of understanding these incidents cannot be overstated, as they serve as pivotal learning moments for industries worldwide. They highlight the need for continuous improvement in safety protocols and the dire consequences of complacency.

Industrial safety is not just a concern for those on the factory floor or at the construction site. It impacts everyone from the CEO to the consumer. The ripple effects of safety incidents can be felt across the globe, as they can disrupt supply chains, damage brand reputation, and erode public trust. Therefore, it is crucial for industries to not only comply with existing safety standards but also to actively participate in the advancement of these protocols. This proactive approach to safety can help prevent disasters and protect lives.

The study of past industrial safety incidents serves as a foundation for understanding the evolution of safety measures. By analyzing these events, industries can identify patterns and underlying issues that need to be addressed. This knowledge is instrumental in shaping safety standards and regulations that aim to mitigate risks and prevent future catastrophes. It is through the lens of history that industries can learn valuable lessons and ensure a safer future for all stakeholders involved.

THE CRASH OF CHALLENGER: BACKGROUND AND OVERVIEW

On January 28, 1986, the world watched in horror as the Space Shuttle Challenger broke apart 73 seconds into its flight, leading to the deaths of all seven crew members. The Challenger disaster became a defining moment in space exploration and industrial safety. The incident was the result of a failure in the shuttle's O-ring seals, which were not designed to handle the unusually cold temperatures on the day of the launch. This technical oversight, compounded by a culture that prioritized schedule over safety, ultimately led to the catastrophe.

The Challenger disaster prompted an extensive investigation, which culminated in the Rogers Commission Report. This report not only detailed the technical causes but also highlighted the organizational and cultural failings that contributed to the accident. The findings revealed a need for better communication, decision-making processes, and risk management within NASA and its contractors. It became a case study in how complex systems can fail and how important it is for all levels of an organization to have a safety-first mindset.

The lessons from the Challenger disaster reached far beyond the aerospace industry. It served as a wake-up call for all sectors that relied on complex technologies and processes. The tragedy underscored the importance of addressing not only the technical aspects of safety but also the human and organizational factors. Industries began to understand that safety could not be an afterthought; it had to be integrated into every facet of operations, from design and development to execution and maintenance.

THE IMPACT OF THE CRASH OF CHALLENGER ON INDUSTRIAL SAFETY

The impact of the Challenger disaster on industrial safety was profound and far-reaching. It brought to light the critical need for comprehensive safety systems that encompass both engineering solutions and human factors. In the wake of the tragedy, industries across the board reevaluated their safety protocols, emphasizing the importance of redundancy, quality control, and thorough testing. The realization that even small components, such as an O-ring, could lead to such catastrophic results changed the way industries approached the design and manufacturing of products.

Risk assessment and management took on a new level of significance after the Challenger disaster. Industries began to implement more rigorous risk analysis techniques, ensuring that potential hazards were identified and mitigated at every stage of a project. This mindset shift also affected the organizational hierarchy, where the input of engineers and technical experts became more valued in decision-making processes, particularly when it came to safety concerns.

The disaster also prompted a reassessment of emergency response strategies. Companies invested in improved training for their employees, developing more robust evacuation and disaster recovery plans. This was not just about being prepared for an incident but creating a mindset where safety was considered everyone's responsibility. Internal reporting systems for safety issues were strengthened, encouraging employees to voice concerns without fear of retribution.

PIPER ALPHA: LESSONS LEARNED AND SAFETY REFORMS

The Piper Alpha disaster, which occurred on July 6, 1988, in the North Sea, stands as one of the worst offshore oil rig disasters in history. The series of explosions and resulting fire claimed the lives of 167 men and led to substantial changes in the way safety is managed in the oil and gas industry. The subsequent Cullen Report identified serious safety management flaws and inadequate emergency response procedures as key factors in the tragedy.

One of the main lessons from Piper Alpha was the need for effective safety management systems. The disaster demonstrated that safety could not be left to chance or ad-hoc measures. Instead, it required a systematic approach that encompassed regular safety training, hazard assessments, and continuous monitoring. As a result, the oil and gas industry implemented Safety Case Regulations, which required companies to demonstrate their ability to operate safely through detailed safety cases.

Another significant reform post-Piper Alpha was the adoption of the 'permit-to-work' system. This system ensures that any hazardous activity is properly planned, authorized, and communicated to all relevant personnel before commencement. The aim was to prevent the kind of confusion and miscommunication that contributed to the Piper Alpha disaster. This approach has since been adopted in various forms across multiple industries, highlighting the influence of the lessons learned from Piper Alpha.

FUKUSHIMA: A TURNING POINT IN NUCLEAR SAFETY

The Fukushima Daiichi nuclear disaster, triggered by the Great East Japan Earthquake and Tsunami on March 11, 2011, had a profound impact on the nuclear industry and industrial safety as a whole. The catastrophic failure of the plant's cooling systems led to meltdowns, hydrogen-air explosions, and the release of radioactive materials. This event forced a global reconsideration of nuclear safety standards and the associated risks of nuclear power.

One of the key outcomes from the Fukushima disaster was the realization of the need for enhanced safety measures to withstand extreme natural events. The nuclear industry worldwide undertook comprehensive assessments to evaluate the resilience of nuclear facilities against earthquakes, tsunamis, and other natural disasters. This led to the strengthening of existing plants and more stringent design requirements for new facilities, ensuring a higher level of built-in safety.

Another turning point was the emphasis on the importance of a strong safety culture within the nuclear industry. Fukushima highlighted that technical safeguards alone were insufficient to prevent a disaster. There needed to be an organizational culture that prioritized safety above all else, with clear and effective communication channels, robust training programs, and a system that empowered every employee to act in the interest of safety without hesitation.

THE LASTING EFFECTS: HOW THESE INCIDENTS TRANSFORMED INDUSTRIAL SAFETY

The cumulative effects of the Challenger, Piper Alpha, and Fukushima disasters have had a lasting impact on the landscape of industrial safety. These events have been catalysts for change, driving the development and implementation of more comprehensive safety regulations and standards. The approach to industrial safety has become more proactive, with a focus on preventing accidents before they occur rather than merely responding to them.

One of the lasting effects is the integration of safety into the corporate governance structure. Boards of directors and senior management now routinely discuss safety performance and strategies, recognizing that safety is integral to the long-term success and sustainability of their operations. This has led to the creation of dedicated safety departments and the appointment of Chief Safety Officers in some organizations, elevating the importance of safety to the highest levels of corporate leadership.

Another lasting effect is the advancement of safety technology. From improved personal protective equipment to sophisticated monitoring and control systems, technology has played a significant role in enhancing safety. Real-time data collection and analysis have become invaluable tools for predicting potential safety issues and responding swiftly to incidents. The development of automated safety systems has also reduced the reliance on human intervention, thereby minimizing the risk of human error.

THE ROLE OF REGULATIONS AND STANDARDS IN SAFETY IMPROVEMENT

Regulations and standards are the backbone of industrial safety improvement. They provide the framework within which industries operate, setting the minimum requirements for safety performance. Post-disaster investigations often lead to revisions and updates to these regulations, ensuring that they reflect the latest understanding of safety best practices and technological advancements.

Regulations serve as a benchmark for industries to measure their safety protocols against. They compel companies to comply with certain safety standards, but they also encourage industries to go beyond compliance and strive for safety excellence. This is achieved through voluntary industry standards and best practices that often exceed regulatory requirements. Organizations that adopt these higher standards not only improve their safety records but also gain a competitive edge by demonstrating their commitment to safety to stakeholders.

Standards also play a critical role in facilitating international cooperation on safety matters. They provide a common language and set of principles that can be adopted across borders, ensuring consistency in safety practices. This is particularly important in industries that operate globally, as it helps to ensure that safety does not vary significantly from one country to another. By harmonizing safety standards, industries can work together to raise the overall level of safety across the board.

THE IMPORTANCE OF SAFETY CULTURE IN INDUSTRIES

Safety culture is the collective mindset and attitudes towards safety within an organization. It is an intangible yet crucial element of industrial safety, as it influences the behavior of every employee, from the boardroom to the shop floor. A strong safety culture is characterized by a shared commitment to safety, open communication, and the willingness to learn from mistakes.

Developing a positive safety culture requires consistent effort and leadership at all levels. Leaders must demonstrate their commitment to safety through their actions and decisions, setting the tone for the rest of the organization. Employees must feel empowered to speak up about safety concerns without fear of retaliation. This level of transparency and trust is essential for identifying and addressing safety issues before they escalate.

The role of ongoing education and training cannot be overstated in fostering a safety culture. Regular safety drills, workshops, and discussions keep safety at the forefront of employees' minds and ensure they are equipped with the knowledge and skills to act safely. By investing in the development of a safety culture, industries not only protect their employees but also enhance their overall performance and resilience.

TECHNOLOGY AND INNOVATION: ADVANCEMENTS IN SAFETY MEASURES

Technological innovation plays a pivotal role in advancing industrial safety measures. The continuous development of new technologies and the innovative application of existing ones have led to significant improvements in safety across various industries. These advancements range from simple ergonomic tools that reduce physical strain to complex systems that monitor and control hazardous processes.

One of the most impactful technological advancements is the use of sensors and automation in safety systems. Sensors can detect changes in environmental conditions, equipment performance, or hazardous substance levels, providing early warnings of potential safety issues. Automation takes this a step further by enabling systems to respond to these warnings without the need for human intervention, thereby reducing the risk of human error and increasing the speed of response.

Another area of innovation is in the field of safety training and education. Virtual reality (VR) and augmented reality (AR) technologies have revolutionized safety training by allowing workers to experience realistic simulations of hazardous situations without any actual risk. This immersive training helps employees better understand the dangers they may face and how to respond effectively, leading to safer behavior in real-world scenarios.

THE ONGOING EFFORTS TO IMPROVE INDUSTRIAL SAFETY

The journey to improve industrial safety is ongoing. While the lessons learned from incidents like the Crash of Challenger, Piper Alpha, and Fukushima have shaped the safety landscape of the industries, the work is never truly complete. Safety is a dynamic field that must evolve with new technologies, processes, and societal expectations. Continuous vigilance and a commitment to learning and adapting are essential to prevent future tragedies.

Industries must keep striving for higher safety standards, not just to comply with regulations but to fulfill their moral obligation to protect their employees and the communities in which they operate. The investments made in safety today will pay dividends in the form of lives saved, injuries prevented, and disasters averted. It is a collective responsibility shared by all stakeholders, from regulators to individual workers, to ensure that the lessons of the past are not forgotten and that the pursuit of safety excellence remains a top priority.

The ongoing efforts to improve industrial safety are a testament to the resilience and dedication of industries worldwide. By embracing the challenges and learning from past mistakes, industries can continue to innovate and enhance their safety practices. It is through this continuous improvement that the safety of workers and the public will be safeguarded for generations to come.

For those interested in contributing to the advancement of industrial safety, we encourage you to stay informed, get involved, and advocate for the highest standards of safety in every industry. Your voice and your actions can make a difference in creating a safer world for all.

REIMAGINING INDUSTRIAL SAFETY: THE IMPACT OF THE CHERNOBYL NUCLEAR ACCIDENT ON THE INDUSTRY'S SAFETY PARADIGM

The Chernobyl nuclear accident, which occurred on April 26, 1986, in the former Soviet Union, is etched in history as one of the most catastrophic industrial disasters of the 20th Century. The explosion and subsequent fire at the Chernobyl Nuclear Power Plant's Reactor 4 released massive quantities of radioactive particles into the atmosphere, contaminating the surrounding environment and exposing countless individuals to dangerous levels of radiation.

The incident not only resulted in immediate health effects and environmental devastation but also sounded a global alarm, leading to an unprecedented introspection into nuclear safety and industrial practices at large. The world suddenly awakened to the stark reality of industrial catastrophes and their potential to transcend national boundaries, impacting global communities and ecosystems.

As the dust settled, it became clear that the disaster was not just a failure of technology but also a failure of systems, processes, and safety culture. This realization would eventually lead to a significant shift in how industries across the board perceived and practiced safety, transforming the safety paradigm in ways that continue to resonate today.

THE IMMEDIATE IMPACT OF THE CHERNOBYL ACCIDENT ON THE SAFETY PARADIGM

In the aftermath of the Chernobyl disaster, the immediate impact on the safety paradigm was one of shock and urgency. The industrial sector, especially the nuclear industry, scrambled to understand what had gone wrong and how similar events could be prevented in the future. It was a period marked by intensive scrutiny, evaluations, and swift changes in safety protocols.

Regulatory bodies tightened their oversight, while operators and engineers revisited safety procedures and emergency response plans. In many cases, this led to the suspension of operations at nuclear facilities around the world for thorough inspections and upgrades, reflecting a newfound prioritization of safety over production or economic considerations.

Furthermore, the accident brought to light the critical need for improved training and education of personnel. It underscored the importance of not only equipping workers with the knowledge to operate complex systems safely but also fostering a culture where safety concerns could be raised and addressed without fear of retribution or dismissal.

LESSONS LEARNED FROM THE CHERNOBYL ACCIDENT

The lessons drawn from the Chernobyl accident were numerous and profound. One of the key takeaways was the concept of 'safety culture' – an organizational mindset that emphasizes safety as a core value and encourages an ongoing commitment to safety improvement. The disaster highlighted that technical safeguards alone were insufficient and that human factors played a crucial role in ensuring safety.

Another lesson was the importance of designing systems with robust safety features that could withstand both human error and unexpected events. The principle of 'defense in depth' gained traction, advocating for multiple layers of protection to prevent accidents or mitigate their consequences.

Additionally, the Chernobyl accident demonstrated the need for comprehensive disaster management plans that included not only prevention but also preparedness, response, and recovery strategies. The international community recognized the importance of collaboration and the sharing of best practices in enhancing global safety standards.

THE LONG-TERM EFFECTS OF THE CHERNOBYL ACCIDENT ON THE INDUSTRY'S SAFETY PRACTICES

As years passed, the Chernobyl accident continued to influence industry safety practices in lasting ways. One of the most significant changes was the integration of risk assessment into the lifecycle of industrial operations. Industries began to systematically identify potential hazards, assess the likelihood and impact of incidents, and implement measures to reduce risks to acceptable levels.

The disaster also spurred the development of advanced monitoring and diagnostic technologies. Real-time surveillance systems became more sophisticated, allowing operators to detect and address anomalies before they escalated into serious problems.

The focus on safety extended beyond the confines of individual facilities to encompass the entire supply chain. Companies started to evaluate the safety practices of their partners and vendors, recognizing that a chain is only as strong as its weakest link. This holistic approach to safety reinforced the interconnectivity of industries and the collective responsibility for preventing accidents.

REIMAGINING INDUSTRIAL SAFETY: HOW THE CHERNOBYL ACCIDENT CHANGED THE INDUSTRY'S APPROACH

The Chernobyl accident served as a catalyst for reimagining industrial safety. It prompted a shift from a reactive stance—responding to accidents after they occurred—to a proactive one, where prevention is paramount. Safety became an integral part of organizational strategy, with leadership roles dedicated to overseeing safety performance and fostering a positive safety culture.

Industries also began to appreciate the value of transparency and open communication. The initial secrecy surrounding the Chernobyl disaster and its consequences had exacerbated the situation, leading to a call for greater openness about risks and incidents. This transparency not only builds public trust but also facilitates learning and the continuous improvement of safety practices.

The concept of 'sustainable safety' emerged, integrating safety with broader environmental and social considerations. The goal was not just to prevent accidents but to do so in a way that was sustainable for people, the planet, and business operations over the long term.

THE ROLE OF REGULATIONS AND INTERNATIONAL ORGANIZATIONS IN REDEFINING SAFETY STANDARDS

Regulations and international organizations have played a pivotal role in redefining safety standards post-Chernobyl. Governments around the world enacted stricter regulations, requiring industries to meet higher safety benchmarks and undergo regular inspections. These regulations were not static; they evolved based on scientific advancements, technological changes, and lessons learned from subsequent incidents.

International organizations, such as the International Atomic Energy Agency (IAEA) and the World Association of Nuclear Operators (WANO), stepped up their efforts to facilitate cooperation and information sharing among nations. They established guidelines and safety standards that transcended national borders, recognizing the global implications of industrial accidents.

These entities also provided a platform for peer reviews and audits, enabling industries to learn from each other's experiences and adopt best practices. The collective action fostered by these organizations has been instrumental in raising safety standards worldwide.

CASE STUDIES OF INDUSTRIES THAT HAVE IMPLEMENTED CHANGES IN THEIR SAFETY PRACTICES POST-CHERNOBYL

Several industries serve as case studies for the implementation of changed safety practices in the wake of the Chernobyl disaster. The nuclear industry, for instance, has dramatically overhauled its approach to safety. New reactor designs now incorporate passive safety features that rely on natural forces like gravity and convection for cooling, reducing the dependence on human intervention and complex machinery.

The chemical industry, similarly, has strengthened its commitment to process safety, focusing on the prevention of chemical releases and explosions. Initiatives like Responsible Care® have encouraged companies to improve their environmental, health, safety, and security performance.

The aviation industry, too, has seen significant advancements in safety. Enhanced training programs, the adoption of Crew Resource Management (CRM), and improvements in aircraft design and maintenance practices have all contributed to making air travel one of the safest modes of transportation.

THE FUTURE OF INDUSTRIAL SAFETY: ANTICIPATING AND PREVENTING ACCIDENTS

Looking to the future, the emphasis on industrial safety is increasingly geared towards anticipating and preventing accidents before they occur. Predictive analytics and artificial intelligence are being leveraged to identify potential risks based on historical data and current conditions. This forward-thinking approach aims to stay one step ahead of

FROM TRAGEDY TO TRANSFORMATION

The Evolution of India's Safety Attitude After the Bhopal Gas Incident

I still remember the day I first heard about the Bhopal Gas incident. It was one of those moments that leave an indelible mark on your consciousness. The tragedy that unfolded on the night of December 2, 1984, at the Union Carbide India Limited (UCIL) pesticide plant in Bhopal, Madhya Pradesh, is etched in the memory of Indians as one of the darkest chapters in our industrial history. A deadly cloud of methyl isocyanate (MIC) gas enveloped the surrounding areas, leading to unprecedented loss of life and long-term health consequences for thousands.

The incident didn't just shock the nation; it sent ripples across the globe, raising serious questions about industrial safety and corporate negligence. As a writer and a concerned citizen, I believe it's crucial to revisit this catastrophe and comprehend its magnitude. The UCIL disaster was not merely an industrial accident; it was a wake-up call that highlighted the catastrophic consequences of overlooking safety protocols.

In the immediate aftermath, there was chaos and confusion. The city of Bhopal was thrown into a state of emergency, with hospitals overwhelmed and people scrambling for safety. The gas leak didn't just cause immediate fatalities; it resulted in chronic health issues and a lingering sense of insecurity among the survivors. The repercussions of that night continue to be felt even decades later, and it has had a profound impact on how safety is perceived in India.

The Immediate Aftermath of the Bhopal Gas Incident

In the days following the Bhopal Gas incident, the city resembled a war zone. Over 500,000 people were exposed to the toxic gas, and the immediate death toll was in the thousands. The exact number of casualties has been a matter of debate, but one thing was clear: the tragedy was of an unprecedented scale. Hospitals were inundated with victims suffering from eye irritation, respiratory issues, and other symptoms of MIC exposure.

I recall images in the media of panic-stricken faces and mass funerals, which were heartbreaking. The local government, along with various agencies, scrambled to provide immediate relief, but the scale of the disaster was overwhelming. There was a palpable sense of helplessness among the people, and the government's response was criticized for being inadequate and slow.

The incident also exposed the lack of preparedness for such disasters in India. There was a dearth of information on MIC, its potential impact on human health, and how to treat exposure. The medical community struggled to manage the crisis, and the lack of specific antidotes or treatment protocols compounded the problem. This immediate aftermath laid the groundwork for a transformed perspective on the importance of industrial safety in India.

Impact on Public Perception of Safety in India

The Bhopal Gas tragedy was a turning point in how safety was viewed in India. Prior to this incident, there was a general complacency about industrial hazards. The scale of the disaster, however, brought the issue of safety to the forefront of public consciousness. There was a newfound awareness that such an event could happen anywhere, and that existing safety measures were grossly insufficient.

The public outcry was loud and clear. People demanded justice for the victims and stricter safety regulations to prevent such incidents in the future. This was a period of transformation in the Indian psyche; safety was no longer an afterthought but a fundamental right. The Bhopal disaster became a symbol of the potential cost of neglect, and the need for a proactive approach to safety became a central theme in public discourse.

This shift in perception also led to greater scrutiny of other industries and their safety practices. Communities living in the vicinity of industrial plants became more vigilant, and the media played a crucial role in highlighting safety lapses. The tragedy had instilled a fear that galvanized the public, activists, and the government to take action towards ensuring a safer future for all.

Changes in government regulations and policies

In response to the public outcry, the Indian government was compelled to reevaluate and strengthen its approach to industrial safety. One of the key outcomes was the enactment of the Environment (Protection) Act of 1986, which provided the framework for regulating environmental pollutants and handling hazardous substances. This act was a significant step forward in India's environmental legislation and was directly influenced by the events in Bhopal.

Subsequent amendments and new regulations also emerged, aimed at enhancing safety in industrial operations. The Factories Act was amended to include stricter safety guidelines and measures to protect workers. The government also established the National Disaster Management Authority (NDMA) in 2005, with the mandate to develop policies, plans, and guidelines for disaster management to ensure a timely and effective response.

These regulatory changes marked a shift from a reactive to a proactive stance on safety. The government's role expanded from mere compliance checks to actively promoting a culture of safety. Audits, inspections, and training programs became more rigorous and frequent. The legal framework also evolved to hold industries accountable for lapses in safety, leading to a more responsible industrial environment.

THE ROLE OF NGOS AND ACTIVISTS IN ADVOCATING FOR SAFETY

The aftermath of the Bhopal Gas tragedy saw a surge in activism and the rise of non-governmental organizations (NGOs) dedicated to the cause of industrial safety and environmental protection. These groups played a pivotal role in keeping the issue alive in public memory and advocating for the rights of the affected individuals.

Activists worked tirelessly to ensure that the victims received proper compensation and medical care. They also campaigned for the cleanup of the contaminated site and the surrounding areas. The relentless efforts of these organizations not only provided support to the affected communities but also put pressure on the government and industries to improve safety standards.

NGOs like the Bhopal Medical Appeal and Sambhavna Trust have been instrumental in providing ongoing healthcare and rehabilitation to the survivors. These organizations have also been at the forefront of research into the long-term effects of MIC exposure. Their advocacy has helped to shape policies and influence public opinion on the need for robust safety measures.

The engagement of civil society has been crucial in ensuring that the lessons of Bhopal were not forgotten. The collaborative efforts of activists, NGOs, and the affected communities have been essential in driving change and promoting a culture of safety across industries in India.

Corporate Responsibility and Accountability Post-Bhopal Gas Incident

The Bhopal Gas tragedy underscored the need for corporate responsibility and accountability in a way that no other event had before. It became clear that businesses could no longer operate with impunity, and that they had a moral and legal obligation to ensure the safety and well-being of their workers and the communities in which they operated.

The concept of 'Corporate Social Responsibility' (CSR) gained prominence, and companies began to integrate safety and environmental sustainability into their business models. The legal framework also changed to reflect this new reality. The Companies Act of 2013 included CSR provisions, mandating that companies of a certain size spend a percentage of their profits on social and environmental initiatives.

Moreover, the disaster led to a reevaluation of the 'polluter pays' principle, which holds that those responsible for pollution should bear the costs of managing it to prevent damage to human health or the environment. The principle was reinforced within Indian jurisprudence, and companies were now held to higher standards of liability for any lapses that led to accidents or environmental damage.

This shift was not just a matter of legal compliance; it represented a fundamental change in the ethos of corporate India. The tragedy served as a constant reminder that the true cost of negligence could be immeasurable, and that responsible business practices were not just good ethics but also good business.

THE EVOLUTION OF SAFETY PRACTICES IN INDUSTRIES

The Bhopal Gas tragedy served as a catalyst for the evolution of safety practices in industries across India. There was a collective realization that safety protocols cannot be mere formalities; they must be an integral part of the industrial process. As a result, safety management systems became more sophisticated, with a focus on risk assessment, prevention, and continuous improvement.

Industries began adopting international safety standards, such as ISO 45001 for occupational health and safety management systems. These standards provided a framework for organizations to identify, control, and reduce workplace risks, thereby enhancing employee safety. There was also a greater emphasis on emergency response planning, ensuring that both employees and the surrounding communities were better prepared for potential incidents.

Additionally, companies started investing in state-of-the-art safety equipment and technologies. Regular safety drills became routine, and employees received extensive training on safety protocols and emergency procedures. This proactive approach to safety was a marked departure from the past and indicated a significant shift in how industries perceived and managed risks.

Case Studies of Industries that have Implemented Significant Safety Measures

To illustrate the transformation in safety practices post-Bhopal, let's examine a few case studies of industries that have taken significant steps to enhance safety measures.

One such example is the chemical industry, which was closely scrutinized after the Bhopal incident. Companies like Tata Chemicals have implemented rigorous safety management systems and have been recognized for their high safety standards. They conduct regular audits, safety training, and have established transparent reporting mechanisms for accidents and near-misses.

Another example is the oil and gas sector, where companies like Reliance Industries have invested heavily in safety infrastructure. Reliance's Jamnagar refinery, one of the largest in the world, has an exemplary safety record, thanks to its advanced control and safety systems, regular maintenance protocols, and a strong culture of safety among its workforce.

These case studies reflect a broader trend across various industries in India, where safety has become a core value. The implementation of advanced safety measures and a commitment to continuous improvement have become benchmarks for success and competitiveness in the industry.

THE ROLE OF EDUCATION AND AWARENESS IN CHANGING SAFETY ATTITUDES

Education and awareness have played a crucial role in changing safety attitudes in India post-Bhopal. There has been a concerted effort to incorporate safety education into the curriculum of schools and professional institutions. By teaching the principles of safety and environmental stewardship at an early age, we are creating a generation that is more cognizant of these issues.

Professional training programs have also been revamped to include comprehensive safety modules. For example, engineering courses now often contain subjects on industrial safety and risk management, which were not as emphasized before the Bhopal tragedy. This has led to a workforce that is better equipped to identify and mitigate risks in the workplace.

Public awareness campaigns have also been instrumental in changing attitudes towards safety. Government initiatives, along with NGO efforts, have worked to keep the importance of safety in the public eye. These campaigns have been effective in promoting a culture of safety and encouraging individuals to be proactive in ensuring their own safety and the safety of those around them.

THE LASTING IMPACT OF THE BHOPAL GAS INCIDENT ON INDIA'S SAFETY ATTITUDE

The Bhopal Gas tragedy was a watershed moment in the history of industrial safety in India. The catastrophic event served as a stark reminder of the importance of safety and the dire consequences of negligence. In the years that followed, we have witnessed a paradigm shift in how safety is perceived and practiced in India.

The transformation has been multifaceted, involving changes in government regulations, corporate practices, and public attitudes. The collective efforts of the government, NGOs, activists, and the corporate sector have contributed to a more robust safety culture. While the scars of Bhopal will always remain, the incident has also been a catalyst for positive change, ensuring that the lessons learned are not forgotten.

As we continue to work towards a safer future, it is imperative that we maintain this momentum and commitment to safety. The evolution of India's safety attitude after the Bhopal Gas tragedy is a testament to the resilience and determination of a nation to learn from its past and build a safer and more responsible future for all its citizens.

UNDERSTANDING THE FACTORS BEHIND INDIA'S BEHAVIORAL-BASED SAFETY RECORDS IN ROAD AND WORKPLACE ACCIDENTS

In my years of working with safety programs across various industries, I've come to understand the pivotal role of Behavioral-Based Safety (BBS) in creating secure working environments. BBS is an approach focused on identifying and changing unsafe behaviors in the workplace. It operates on the premise that a significant number of accidents are due to unsafe behavior rather than unsafe conditions. In India, where rapid industrialization has led to burgeoning workplaces and roads, the importance of BBS cannot be overstated.

As I delve into this topic, it's crucial to understand that BBS is not just about putting rules in place; it's about cultivating a safety culture where every individual is aware of their actions and is committed to safety. The approach has been successful in many Western countries, but its adaptation in India faces numerous challenges. The reasons for the disappointing BBS records in India, particularly regarding road and workplace accidents, are complex and multifaceted.

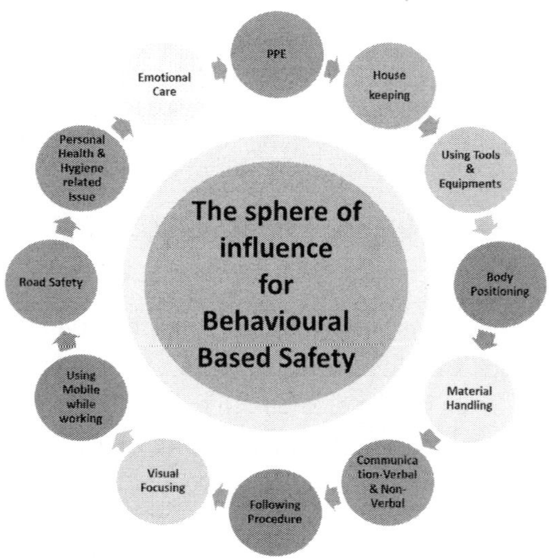

The journey toward appreciating BBS begins with understanding the intricacies of behavior change, the benefits of BBS, the hurdles faced during its implementation in Indian settings, and how it can be effectively applied. Through this comprehensive exploration, we can begin to unravel the factors behind India's safety record and chart a course towards improvement.

UNDERSTANDING THE SCIENCE OF BEHAVIOR CHANGE

Behavior change is a cornerstone of BBS. It's grounded in the science of psychology and hinges on understanding what prompts individuals to act in certain ways, especially when it comes to safety. To comprehend why behavioral-based safety records are not so encouraging in India in terms of road accidents or accidents at the workplace, we must first explore the theories that guide behavior change.

One widely recognized theory is B.F. Skinner's operant conditioning, which suggests that behavior is shaped by consequences. Positive reinforcement can encourage good behavior, while negative reinforcement or punishment can deter bad behavior. However, behavior change is more complex than this simple stimulus-response relationship. It involves a deep understanding of cultural norms, personal attitudes, and the social environment that influences individual behavior.

In the Indian context, behavior change is particularly challenging due to the diversity in cultures, languages, and socioeconomic backgrounds. The traditional mindset often resists change, and there's a tendency to rely on fate or external factors rather than individual responsibility. Overcoming these barriers requires tailored strategies that can speak to the vast array of Indian populations and their unique perspectives.

THE SIGNIFICANCE OF BBS IN PROMOTING WORKPLACE SAFETY

The significance of Behavioral-Based Safety in promoting workplace safety cannot be overstated. BBS doesn't only focus on the physical aspects of safety but emphasizes the human element. In my experience, when employees are engaged in the safety process, they are more likely to commit to safety protocols and take proactive measures to prevent accidents.

Moreover, BBS encourages a shift from a reactive to a proactive safety culture. Rather than responding to accidents after they occur, BBS equips employees with the tools to anticipate and prevent them. This proactive approach is critical in mitigating the risk of accidents, leading to a reduction in injury rates and associated costs.

In India, where the workforce is often seen as a replaceable commodity, the implementation of BBS can signify a shift in how workers are valued. By investing in BBS, companies send a strong message that they prioritize their employees' well-being, which can lead to improved morale, better employee retention, and a more positive brand image.

BENEFITS OF IMPLEMENTING BBS IN INDIA

Implementing BBS in India carries a multitude of benefits. For one, it can lead to a significant reduction in workplace accidents and road traffic incidents. This not only saves lives but also reduces the economic burden caused by accidents, including healthcare costs, lost productivity, and compensation payouts.

Another benefit of BBS is the potential to enhance the overall safety culture within Indian organizations. By focusing on individual behaviors, BBS fosters a sense of personal responsibility and accountability. Employees become more vigilant and conscientious about their actions, which can lead to a more harmonious and safe working environment.

Furthermore, BBS can aid in regulatory compliance. Indian laws and safety standards are becoming increasingly stringent, and companies that proactively adopt BBS are better positioned to meet these regulations. This compliance not only helps avoid legal penalties but can also give companies a competitive edge in an economy where consumers and investors are becoming more attuned to corporate social responsibility.

CHALLENGES IN IMPLEMENTING BBS IN INDIA

Despite its benefits, the implementation of BBS in India is fraught with challenges. One of the primary obstacles is the resistance to change. In many Indian companies, there's a deeply ingrained way of doing things that often prioritizes productivity over safety. Changing this mindset requires sustained effort and a top-down approach from management.

Another challenge is the lack of infrastructure and resources. Implementing a BBS program requires investment in training, monitoring, and feedback systems. In a country where many businesses operate on thin margins, allocating funds for safety initiatives that don't yield immediate financial returns can be a hard sell.

Additionally, the sheer diversity of the Indian workforce, with its multitude of languages, cultural norms, and levels of education, makes standardizing and communicating BBS practices a complicated task. Tailoring programs to be effective across such a diverse population is both resource-intensive and complex.

KEY COMPONENTS OF A SUCCESSFUL BBS PROGRAM

A successful BBS program is built on several key components. Firstly, it requires strong leadership commitment. Leaders must not only endorse BBS but also actively participate in safety practices to set an example for their employees.

Secondly, employee involvement is critical. A BBS program is most effective when employees at all levels are engaged in identifying unsafe behaviors and contributing to the development of solutions. This creates a sense of ownership and accountability among the workforce.

Thirdly, a successful BBS program must include a systematic approach to data collection and analysis. Tracking and reviewing data helps identify trends, measure progress, and adjust strategies as needed. This evidence-based approach ensures that the BBS program is dynamic and responsive to the unique challenges of each workplace.

STEPS TO IMPLEMENT A BBS PROGRAM IN YOUR WORKPLACE

Implementing a BBS program in your workplace involves several strategic steps. First, conduct a thorough assessment of the current safety culture and practices. This assessment will highlight areas for improvement and help tailor the BBS program to the organization's specific needs.

Next, it's essential to develop clear and measurable safety goals. These goals should be aligned with the overall business objectives and should be communicated effectively to all employees. Setting these targets provides direction and purpose for the BBS program.

Following goal setting, the next step is to create a detailed implementation plan. This plan should include timelines, resource allocation, training schedules, and a system for monitoring and feedback. Effective planning ensures that the BBS program is structured and easy to follow.

TRAINING AND EDUCATION RESOURCES FOR BBS IN INDIA

For BBS to be effective, training and education are vital. There are several resources available in India for companies interested in implementing BBS. These include safety training workshops, online courses, and certification programs offered by professional safety organizations.

Additionally, industry conferences and seminars provide platforms for sharing best practices and networking with safety professionals. Access to these resources is critical for keeping abreast of the latest BBS methodologies and technologies.

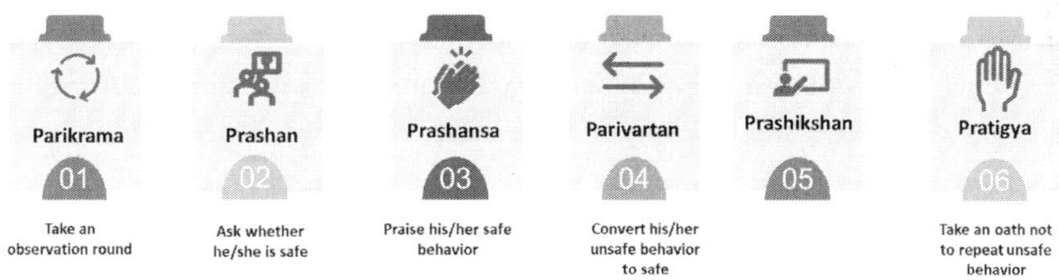

12 STRATEGIES TO IMPLEMENT BBS STRATEGY WITH A HUMAN TOUCH

Many Indian educational institutions have also started to include BBS principles in their curricula, ensuring that the next generation of workers and managers are equipped with the knowledge to promote safety in their future workplaces.

Embracing Behavioral-Based Safety is imperative for India as it continues to expand its economy and modernize its infrastructure. The disappointing safety records in India's roads and workplaces can be improved by understanding and applying the principles of BBS. It requires a cultural shift, a commitment to change, and a willingness to invest in the safety of the workforce.

It's clear that the journey towards safer workplaces and roads is a challenging yet achievable one. By acknowledging the benefits, addressing the challenges, and applying the key components of a successful BBS program, India can foster a safety culture that protects its most valuable asset – its people. A safer workplace is not just a legal or ethical necessity; it's also a smart business strategy that can lead to increased efficiency, improved employee morale, and a better reputation.

For India to realize the full potential of BBS, it will take concerted efforts from all stakeholders - government, businesses, and individuals. It is time to prioritize safety and ensure that India's growth is not marred by preventable accidents. Let's commit to implementing BBS and making safety a core value in every workplace and on every road in India.

As an advocate for workplace safety and a professional in the field, I've witnessed a significant evolution in the way organizations approach the well-being of their employees. One such transformative approach is Behavioral-Based Safety (BBS), a process that has reshaped safety protocols across numerous industries worldwide. In India, a country marked by dynamic industrial growth, the implementation of BBS is not just a strategic move but a necessity for sustainable development.

BBS focuses intensely on what people do, analyzes why they do it, and then applies a research-supported intervention strategy to improve what people do. At its heart, it is a tool for understanding and influencing behavior towards safer outcomes. Given that most accidents are a result of human error, BBS is designed to reduce these errors by changing behaviors.

In my exploration of BBS, I've found that it's not just about following rules; it's about cultivating a culture where safety becomes a core value and is practiced habitually. This proactive approach to safety management is particularly critical in India, where the blend of traditional practices and modern industrialization presents unique challenges in the realm of workplace safety.

BEHAVIOR-BASED SAFETY: THE GAME CHANGER IN THE WORKPLACE

Despite the numerous safety protocols and regulations implemented in workplaces across the globe, occupational accidents still occur. A significant number can be attributed to unsafe behaviors. To address this, many organizations have adopted Behavior-Based Safety (BBS) programs. These proactive strategies are designed to identify and correct unsafe behaviors before they result in accidents.

1. Introduction to Behavior-Based Safety

Behavior-Based Safety (BBS) is a proactive approach to workplace safety that focuses on identifying and eliminating hazardous behaviors. It operates on the principle that at-risk behaviors can be prevented before they lead to injuries or accidents.

1.1 The Philosophy behind BBS

BBS programs emphasize the importance of behavior modification over other safety measures, such as the use of protective equipment or engineering controls. The long-term goal is to create a workplace where employees feel safe, remain productive, and produce quality work.

1.2 The Role of Employees in BBS

BBS places the responsibility of safety on all employees, rather than just management. This approach encourages workers to take ownership of their safety, fostering a culture of prevention and accountability.

2. The Power of Behavior-Based Safety

A successful BBS program can transform a workplace into a safer, more proactive environment. It can lead to improved safety outcomes and increased productivity.

2.1 Impact on Workplace Accidents

BBS programs have been successful in reducing incidents of workplace injuries and illnesses. By focusing on identifying and mitigating at-risk behaviors, employees become more mindful of their actions, leading to fewer accidents.

2.2 Role in Promoting a Safety Culture

BBS programs promote a culture of safety and accountability. They encourage employees to take ownership of their safety and look out for their colleagues. This creates a positive work environment where safety is a top priority.

3. Benefits of Implementing Behavior-Based Safety

Implementing a BBS program can bring numerous benefits to an organization. These include reduced incidents of workplace injuries, lower worker's compensation costs, and increased productivity.

3.1 Financial Benefits

Employers can save on costs associated with workplace injuries, such as lost workdays, medical expenses, and higher insurance premiums.

3.2 Boost to Employee Morale

A successful BBS program can enhance employee morale by promoting a culture of safety and accountability. It motivates employees to actively participate in maintaining a safe workplace.

4. Key Principles of a Behavior-Based Safety Program

A successful BBS program adheres to a set of key principles. These include identifying hazardous behaviors, encouraging employee involvement in safety initiatives, providing regular training, and creating a culture of safety awareness.

4.1 Identifying and Addressing Hazardous Behaviors

The first step in a BBS program is to identify unsafe behaviors. Once these behaviors are identified, the program aims to modify them and make employees aware of potential hazards.

4.2 Encouraging Employee Involvement

Employee involvement is key to the success of a BBS program. Employees must feel comfortable reporting safety concerns and suggestions, and leadership must be willing to listen and act on this feedback.

5. Building a Safety Culture through BBS

Building a culture of prevention through BBS involves creating an environment where employees prioritize safety as a core value. It requires a proactive approach to safety, where employees identify potential hazards and take steps to prevent accidents.

5.1 Importance of Training and Resources

Providing sufficient training and resources is crucial in BBS. Employees need to have the necessary tools and knowledge to work safely.

5.2 Case Study: The Oil and Gas Industry

The oil and gas industry is a good example of a sector that has successfully integrated safety culture into its daily routine. They follow a rigorous set of safety protocols, leading to a significant decline in accidents and fatalities.

6. The Role of Leadership in BBS

Leadership plays a critical role in the success of a BBS program. Leaders need to demonstrate a commitment to safety, follow the same safety rules as their workers, and communicate the program's importance, benefits, and goals to their workforce.

6.1 Importance of Leading by Example

Leaders need to "walk the talk" by following the same safety rules as their employees. This reinforces trust and respect between workers and management and helps establish a safety culture.

6.2 Constant Communication and Coaching

Through consistent coaching and regular conversations, leaders can ensure their team is adapting to new safety standards. This helps in driving continuous improvement in safety.

7. Implementing Behavior-Based Safety

Implementing a BBS program requires commitment and dedication. It involves identifying at-risk behaviors, engaging the workforce in the process, providing regular feedback, and celebrating successes.

7.1 Identifying At-Risk Behaviors

The first step in implementing a BBS program is to identify which behaviors need improvement. This gives a clear starting point for the program.

7.2 Engaging the Workforce

Engaging the workforce in the process is crucial for the success of the program. It ensures that everyone is on board and invested in the program's success.

8. Measuring the Effectiveness of a BBS Program

Measuring the effectiveness of a BBS program is crucial to its success. It involves identifying key performance indicators (KPIs), collecting data regularly, analyzing the data to identify trends, and communicating progress to stakeholders.

8.1 Identifying KPIs

The first step in measuring the effectiveness of a BBS program is to identify the KPIs that will be used to track the program's progress. These KPIs should be aligned with the program's goals.

8.2 Analyzing Data

After collecting data, it needs to be analyzed to identify trends and areas for improvement. This helps in refining the program and making it more effective.

9. Challenges in Implementing BBS

Implementing a BBS program can present several challenges, including resistance from employees, difficulty in maintaining the program, and the possibility of inaccurate reporting.

9.1 Overcoming Resistance

Resistance to change can be a significant challenge in implementing a BBS program. However, this can be overcome by involving employees in the process from the beginning and providing education and training on the benefits of BBS.

9.2 Maintaining the Program

Maintaining a BBS program can be difficult, especially without full support from top management. It requires continuous evaluation and adaptation to changing circumstances.

10. The Future of Behavior-Based Safety

As organizations continue to prioritize safety, it is clear that BBS will remain a crucial part of this effort. Technology and data-driven approaches are expected to play a more significant role in the future of BBS.

10.1 Role of Technology

Technologies such as wearable devices, sensors, artificial intelligence, and predictive analytics can play a significant role in BBS. They offer real-time monitoring and feedback, aiding in the immediate intervention and prevention of accidents.

10.2 Human Behavior Remains Key

Despite the growing role of technology, human behavior remains the most important aspect of BBS. Organizations must continue to prioritize employee engagement to ensure the long-term success of their safety programs.

Behavior-Based Safety is a transformative approach that focuses on modifying behaviors to proactively address workplace hazards. By fostering a culture of safety and continuous improvement, organizations can build a future where workplace injuries and accidents are a thing of the past.

CHAPTER 2

BRINGING PRECISION, CREATIVITY AND ACCURACY IN CORPORATE SAFETY CULTURE TRANSFORMATION

Even the best and big companies (highly-priced in stock markets) have experienced fatalities. This paper is an effort towards understanding precision, creativity and accuracy in safety culture transformation from individual behaviour to organisational behaviour, from safety culture to work culture with honesty and hard-work of employers and employees. Sample included the field visits to 12 site locations and interactions with 160 managers and 150 contractor's workmen. Findings: Myriad aspects of bringing precision, creativity and accuracy in safety culture transformation are described in terms of new challenges (such as critical questions that would haunt business and life perspectives, two things that would make our industry global, 2024 conference on safety culture, leaders express their experiences, tapping root causes of incidents) and new perspectives (such as focus of BBS intervention, beyond BBS culture, problem solving in building safety culture, phased implementation of longterm behavioural safety culture, human factors/errors in safety culture, employees' concerns on safety culture). Practical experiences of industry leaders have added a value to this research findings. Organisations need to widen the focus of safety culture to EHS, make reporting easiest for workers, and make recognition for risk control observers more frequent.

Keywords: Behaviour-based Safety, BBS, Culture, Corporate, Leaders, Workmen.

INTRODUCTION

Almost forty years down since Bhopal and Chernobyl incidents, the industry has moved from the term 'safety' to 'safety culture'. Nevertheless, the clarity and methodology of its implementation varies from the perspectives of an employer, a manager, a researcher, contractor, EHS professional.

This is very critical issue as the fatalities numbers are still unacceptably high when seen through the premise of the OSH Act, which entitles every worker to safe and healthful working conditions and makes all employers and employees responsible for providing a work area free from recognised hazards (Lundell, et al, 2021). Eliminating fatalities and serious injuries is the main challenge for the global industry. Focus is to provide the industry with actionable recommendations and guidance to create safer and healthier workplaces (World Steel Association, 2022).

Almost every third person in workplace or any other place is engaged in an at-risk behaviours, which is why there are fires and fatalities each day, as all incidents are behaviour based. A fire erupted at the All India Institute of Medical Sciences (AIIMS) in Delhi in the morning January 4, 2024. There were no casualties reported from the incident, and the cause of the fire is yet to be determined (Livemint, 2024). Fire broke out at a factory in Delhi's Bawana Industrial Area. 25 fire tenders rushed to the site (Roushan, 2024).

Safety culture is becoming an indispensable forecasting factor in achieving sustainable development (Jasiulewicz-Kaczmarek, 2022). Like a Japanese lecturer says, "there is nothing more important than life". As corporates, our ethics have to be very loud and clear to one and all, which is not. The 'just and fair culture' is on paper, not on ground. The production-safety balancing act needs to be communicated repeatedly by all leaders down the levels every day. The effectiveness of positive safety culture initiatives can sustain for many years (Spigener et al., 2022).

A strong safety culture is predicted by the fact that leadership is clearly committed and involved in safety activities (U.S. Department of Transportation, 2017). "Real safety culture appears when managing director (MD) connects with workers", recalls Mohapatra EHS head of Thermax power business. MD rewards the workers for risk control by their daily observations. The company board meeting's 3/4 time is spent on safety culture actions and only 1/4 time is used to discuss business profits. Workers' fear has gone away and they demand safety actions. They do it only when they know that their safety voices and actions would not be criticised rather appreciated. Once the HR head has intentionally gone to site without safety shoes, the workers noticed it at once and dared to correct him on the spot. The site head, operational head, business head, directors, workers all demand safety. Workers think that safety is their fundamental right. The company focuses on the objective that everyone would report, address root-cause of at-risk behaviours and increase safe behaviours. The leaders conduct safety practically, not by speeches. They present safety progress by site stories and cases, not slides. Empowerment of last worker is the concern. Business heads talk to the workers. Everyone is a BBS mentor.

Rewarding safety actions is the rule, not a monthly ritual. Principles of BBS are followed religiously for incident prevention. Spot-correction of at-risk behaviour is happening and behaviour is changing. Site managements' KPI are linked to BBS. One observes all, all observe one. Corporate leaders find it difficult to connect with workers if they don't visit the site often.

Normally, the managements are not as strict in safety compliance as for business compliance. Hence the incidents make their way. Moreover, it is often the managements' stronger interest for business than for the company's safety culture. Safety culture transformation doesn't get sustained until it is initiated by the safety professionals, adopted by the HODs, monitored by the site/top management, and reviewed by the company Directors. Most top managements give verbal commitments in speeches but don't involve in 'daily safety culture implementation and monitoring' which fails the safety culture progress, and lead to incidents. Management must talk of business as well as risks while they interact with plant managers in terms of planning and implementation (Kaila, 2021).

This paper is an effort towards understanding precision, creativity and accuracy in safety culture transformation from individual behaviour to organisational behaviour, from safety culture to work culture with honesty and hard-work. Bad safety culture suffers in silence, that is why employees are empowered to speak up for safety of each other. Take a moment daily from your life, observe around and save people from incidents to live safer life. If correction of at-risk behaviours is not developed as procedure, unsafe behaviours/ conditions simply go on rising.

We as organisations and individuals together are co-creating a safer society, a safer industry, and a safer nation. You have a moment now to be a part of a bigger universe that can be safer, healthier and happier. We get into problems only when we say something, and do something else, which means there is less clarity and transparency we seek something and we hide something, which is why we don't get results in organisational and societal safety culture. Organisations fail in the balancing act of enforcement and reinforcement for zero-harm and invite bad news of incidents, accidents, fires, fatalities, injuries, disabilities, loss of assets, and so on. The employers, directors, leaders, managers, contractors, workers think differently, and act differently about safety culture as they hail from different cultural backgrounds. Leaders must serve like army commanders who keep in mind only victory for the nation and act only for victory for their nation. However, we can not escape the ground reality that most top management leaders are superficially involved in the company's safety culture initiatives and they are not able to convince the employees for safety involvement and present mass-communications.

OBJECTIVES

To explore precision, creativity and accuracy in safety culture transformation from individual behaviour to organisational behaviour, and from safety culture to work culture, for facilitating organisations towards this process and direction.

METHODOLOGY

Research measures used were the primary data (interviews, and discussions) collected to explore precision, creativity and accuracy in safety culture transformation from individual behaviour to organisational behaviour, and from safety culture to work culture. Interviews based on open-ended questions, focus group interviews, and personal in-depth discussions were conducted during the years 2023-2024. Sample included the field visits to 12 site locations and interactions with 160 managers and 150 contractors workmen comprised a sample of this research. Industry professionals participated in the study as part of an action field survey with the researcher. These research participants had been implementing behavioural safety compliance culture at their work sites. The research participants included the Directors, Managers, Heads of Departments, EHS/HR Professionals and the workmen belonging to the public and private industrial sectors, including chemicals, construction, gas, power and steel, across Indian locations. The sampling method used was random sampling. For statistical analysis, the responses to the relevant questions were collated. Thematic analysis was performed and themes were identified from the qualitative data.

This paper is an extract of a national research program of the Forum of Behavioural Safety under Bharat Bane Surakshit (BBS) mission (Figure 1, 2). The study results and implications are reflected below from a rigorous review of safety culture literature and experiences / case studies shared by industry leaders majorly from the Indian organisations.

Source: Author's own

Figure 1: Sample picture of national research program

Source: Author's own

Figure 2: Sample picture of national research program

RESULTS AND DISCUSSION

The results of this field action research are discussed in terms of the following 5 themes:

A. Critical questions that would haunt business and life perspectives for safety.

B. Two things would make our industry global.
C. 2024 Conference on safety culture.
D. Leaders express their experiences.
E. Tapping root cause of incidents.

A. Critical questions that would haunt business and life perspectives for safety

As 2024 unfolds, it brings with it a renewed focus on workplace safety, challenging safety professionals to adapt and evolve in a rapidly changing environment. This year, the spotlight is on not just implementing new strategies, but also on revisiting and reinforcing the foundational aspects of safety. It's a time for reflection and action, to ensure that the basics of safety are not just assumed but actively maintained and improved. From revisiting the basics to embracing new technologies and methodologies, these priorities represent a holistic approach to workplace safety in the modern era (Harris, 2024).

Some of the real questions that need reflection and consideration are as below.

- Is safety culture on the wish-list of managements in relation to business prospects?
- Are managements ready to take challenges for launching organisation-wide safety culture?
- Do managements play a gamble about safety culture?
- Do managements hold onto strong or weak beliefs about safety culture?
- Are managements too tolerant of unsafe culture due to business operations?
- What is in the mindset of employers, directors, leaders, managers, contractors, workers? They all think differently, and act differently.
- Do managements understand that missed safety culture is to miss business opportunities?
- Understanding what are the managements mental blocks/ conditions for not being able to balance safety and business?
- Reasons as to why the managements do not want to get convinced in order to launch safety culture passionately?
- Do managements understand the safety behaviour and hat its associated factors? also the disparities in safety care of managers and workers. Did employees open up and mirror the issues?

B. Two things would make our industry global

- Best technology in every respect,
- Best care of each and every worker.

We are short only due to these two. Positive work culture sustains only with best technology and best care.

Business trends are largely driven by technology. However, as we develop a better understanding of a technology - Artificial Intelligence (AI) being the obvious example - we also understand what it isn't. In 2024, this will lead to new perspectives on what makes us human (Marr, 2023).

The industry leaders expressed that international business competitions would drive Indian industry to improve safety culture. Like marriage connects us to so many new members of society, similarly, safety culture connects us to everyone for their care from potential incidents. With supportive safety culture, organisations improve the percentage of safe behaviours every day, week and months by spot-correction of at-risk behaviours. Identify barriers to safety concerns to be addressed for spot-correction. Identify and address biggest hazards in safety culture. Review the same over every quarter by the top and site managements.

C. 2024 Conference on safety culture

Conference on safety culture held at IIM Mumbai on 3rd Feb 2024 (Financial Express, 2024) on the theme "*One Nation-One goal, Zero-harm*" discussed the following aspects to achieve freedom from incidents, fires and fatalities. Only single goal is "nobody should get injured".

Major question raised was that is there a change in safety culture from 1st to the 8th BBS national conference being organised every year? Many organisations have still not fully understood the "concept of supportive safety culture" clearly that is why we need to come to the conference - the temple of positive safety culture - again and again to internalise it first. They only understood it as training input. However, there are leaders here who hold unwavering trust in concepts of BBS to achieve zero injuries at work.

Incidents and accidents, fires and fatalities are common and happening almost every day. Yes, change is there, in terms of, increased interest of managements, company Directors and CEOs, and so many ways. Research reports all across India and abroad indicate that still hundred thousands people are killed each year in accidents and incidents at work sites, inspite of the presence of safety systems and professionals. Nevertheless, it is very encouraging to see companies from India take the lead in setting new benchmarks for health safety and well-being (Manufacturing Today, 2022).

The organisations have begun to focus on organisational safety culture, as ISO45001 clearly recommends that organisations must increase internal risk control, as without implementing behavioural aspects of safety, organisations are safe only accidentally.

ISO 45001:2018 mandates that human competence and behavioural elements need to be considered in risk assessment and as an internal issue for managing risks (SEIL, 2023). In this regard, some insights are observed as below:

1. Safety culture is sustainable only with multiple level efforts and actions.
2. Some top management leaders are passively involved, as a result of which they are not able to convince employees at the ground level. Leaders need to be equipped with the knowledge, understanding, and inspiration needed to cultivate a corporate safety culture that transcends borders and safeguards the well-being of all (Gabhane, 2023).
3. Supportive safety culture is essentially long-term planned intervention without which its enthusiasm level drops after some time. Many organisations don't continue implementation of BBS beyond its training.
4. Leaders are committed but sometimes lack engagement with employees down the levels. Leaders deliver change through the safety of cultural intervention and their commitment, passion, and time (Lal, 2022).
5. "Normalisation of Deviance" is biggest hazard that we face", Pavan Rao of Sembcorp Energy says, as because for industry, the small risk is not critical, hence small deviations are considered normal, and it becomes critical.
6. "Employees and companies who care can only bring change in positive safety culture at all levels.

7. Passing the buck is a risky syndrome i.e. following dependent safety culture, shedding ownership down the levels. Hence organisations' zero-harm accountability suffers its results. It is recommended that companies must build safety by stop-passing the buck (CISA, 2023). It never helps to pass the buck. Accept total responsibility for the outcome. (Hyatt, 2023).

8. There are issues with regard to psychological safety in workplace culture due to hierarchy based disconnection between managers and workers, hence people down the levels don't feel psychologically safe to speak up for safety of each other. Hope everyone will take some lessons from here to serve the mission and theme i.e. one Nation-One goal, zero-harm.

9. Safety culture transformation leaders must feel mentally safe, in order to make everyone feel safe. Head of DRB-HICOM's 23 operating companies said, "empowerment of safety culture" program is initiated by the companies Chairman, so we all must support to make it bottom up involvement." Top Managements are now encouraging and are supportive that was lacking earlier.

10. Struggle of companies is too much because of unsafe behaviours of people, may be this conference theme would help for understanding a comprehensive definition of zero-harm. It may take minimum 10 years to achieve this objective since we took 40 years to understand necessity of safety culture since bhopal and Chernobyl incidents. Even the best and big companies (highly priced in stock markets) have experienced fatalities.

11. Zero-harm is not delivered by a speech or slogan, rather it is saving someone's life who feeds a family. It is care, care and actively care. How much employees do feel positive in organisations is important for their psychological safety and health.

12. We follow reactive safety culture for the lowest paid, and practice interdependent safety culture for the well paid. This duality must be replaced with equal concern for low and high income brackets.

Finally, the Institutions may not coordinate with each other over safety culture developments, but definitely, ideas and philosophies of OSHA, ILO, WHO and ISO45003 are in tuning.

D. Leaders express their experiences

"Preventable incident if not prevented is a crime", Dr Radha Krishnan, President of India stated. Industry leaders (Figure 3) expressed as follows. Pavan Rao from SEIL, "Normalisation of Deviance is common, small deviance is not critical. Flirting with Boundary is another common issue, companies flirt with safety in favour of business opportunities, and flirt with safety incidents by paying party funds etc. Importance of positive reinforcement is needed for safety culture journey of organisations".

Source: Author's own

Figure 3: Leaders of safety culture

"Employees safety culture is not going to work if mental health policy is not a part of organisational culture", Dr Harish Shetty, head of psychiatry, Hirananadani hospital emphasised. Distressed mind doesn't listen. We need to bring down the emotional violence and irrelevant practices. To initiate psychological safety, leaders need to inculcate self awareness, understanding their strengths and competence. I listen to understand not to react. Culture of silence is risky, let people speak up. Abundant anonymous appreciation. CEO has to connect and feel like a worker.

KK Sharma, EHS director of DCM Shriram said that safety culture matters how we all behave in all times. What matters is 5 aspects: Vision, skills, incentives, resources, action plan, If you fail to plan, you are planning to fail. If you see something, you say something.

Pavan Rao, EHS head of SEIL opined that everyone has to be a courageous self leader to actively speak up for corrections. Positive reinforcement will take us to next level of positive safety culture."

Vipin Upadhyay, EHS head of Thermax observed that lot of learning started getting implemented with BBS implementation. Every worker has an access to mobile app for reporting observations.

Avinash Harde, who retired as vice-president of HCC found that even in companies after having ISO certification, there is no engagement with workers. Observations are only by safety officers.

Dr Meera Shankar, professor of management at SNDT Women's university empathised that a worker may be an employee in a large company, but he is a world for his family. Save him in every way (Figure 4).

Figure 4: Family aspect of safety culture

Indranil Chakrabarty, corporate EHS head of Thysenkrrup intervened that there's a gap in the involvement of people for building culture as they were not being taken care of. In his company, even the Managing Director will have gemba walk and interact with workers and reward safe behaviours on the spot. Gemba walk is in KPI of employees.

Mohapatra Thermax safety Head put forth that due to safety culture, most important is improvement in incident statistics due to BBS. workers are demanding safety.

Behaviour based zero-harm : BBS culture would behaviouralise zero harm mechanisms involving everyone. Industry must self-regulate safety at their workplaces, stated by DRB-HICOM (Figure 5).

Figure 5: DRB-HICOM participants of Malaysia

Change in care: my colleagues must feel that I as boss care for them for which I need to tone down my behaviours, as expressed by a lady safety professional at DRB-HICOM (Figure 6).

Figure 6: lady safety professionals at DRB-HICOM

Self-regulation is necessary by those who create the risk (management) and those work with the risk (workers) by integrating BBS with zero-harm master plan in a digital way to monitor every month. 'Care-4-life' zero-harm culture project is to be monitored by Apex BBS steering team as well as BBS working committee at each plant.

Safety culture is non-negotiable, its implementation provides many safety mentors in addition to safety professionals. Jitesh Jariwala of EHS Head of Torrent Power (Figure 7) stated that about 60 percent electricity loss is prevented from customers as a result of safety culture. After certification, companies slow down and loosen up on safety implementation. Torrent vendor said, "increase your safety limits and observe everyone, we as vendors must not not hide our unsafe practices, emotionally touch every worker to speak up for safety of each other."

Figure 7: Safety culture at Torrent Power

Earlier, managers practiced reactive safety culture and connected with people down the level but never asked their problem with PPE or otherwise. Now, employees ask what do they get for doing observations. Mindset drives their behaviour and vice versa.

Behavioural safety medicine is powerful to save lives from incidents and fatalities. Employees, contractors, safety, customers safety and public safety are our Torrent company's' responsibility. Sustainable safety culture considers contractual employees as 'own employees' with respect to safety. We strongly believe in it and strive to involve our critical mass, including contractors, in our transformation journey (Tata Steel, 2021). Easy reporting on mobile app helps employees and workmen to report spot-correction daily .

In view of zero-harm, psychological safety and emotional violence are being addressed by companies by way of wellness programs. Also workers must not be allowed to experience loneliness while working alone in the night or otherwise. There must be at least two workers together in any working conditions.

E. Tapping root cause of incidents

A group of 20 managers from IOCL expressed that that we have BBS implementation for long time but its effects are not seen. Dupont is ineffective because it is top down and huge documentation. Workmen don't wear PPE, that is why behavioural safety is needed. How can workmen wear six PPE at a time, which depends upon the criticality of work being done by them. Risk assessment and awareness get updated only after an incident or fatality takes place, not before. Safety is comprised for Production. BBS is emphasised at locations as every incident is mostly due to SOP deviations. Reactive culture needs to be replaced with care, connect and conversation. Monologue needs to be replaced with dialogue between managers and workers.

In Indian industry, we talk about safety excellence, but in practice, we observed that the basic systemic inputs are missing. So when we take up safety culture intervention, we also have to deal with systems required such as PPE, house keeping etc. Hence these aspects emerge as hot spots for systems corrections. Systems are not in place would also mean that the competencies of the safety officers are under question. This means the basics of safety officers also need an updation for improving the systems. The safety culture of an organisation is poor would also trace back to the poor quality of training of safety officers and the poor standards of the training institutions. Hence, the root cause of incidents goes back to the training mentors and the institutions that needs corrections for producing better quality of safety professionals. Thus the root cause of accidents lies not inside the industry but outside in the social culture as well as the educational institutions of the safety professionals. The ministries, government and the heads of institutions must recognise these requirements and the Implications of lack of quality inputs on the economy of the nation that are impacted due to the incidents, disaster, disability, loss of assets and so on. So achieving zero-harm is far from the reality as the real root cause of the incidents is not addressed or. coordinated by agencies and leaders on top. What ever is happening in the name of zero-harm is half way journey of safety excellence. What is most needed is the practical leadership of safety officers and the leaders to roll out behavioural safety culture up and down the levels in plant/site. Also the competencies development charter of safety culture leaders in each plant/site must include interactions skill, mentoring skill, appreciation skill, and results orientation skills.

AFCONS' senior safety officer with 30 years experience said that the project managers are sandwiched between top management and clients for business as well as safety issues. K K Sharma reflected that it's all due to committed management and great team who is committed and their mindset is key for cultural transformation. But the critical question is how do you develop committed management and great team and mindset?. It's like selling a product, how much conviction a professional has in sensitising top management on safety as a corporate value. EHS head, Malghatte from Gharda Chemicals emphasised that it's a really wonderful to hear the campaign for Bharat Bane Surakshit on a consistent basis.

CONCLUSIONS AND RECOMMENDATIONS

Safety culture is an essential aspect of any organisation, shaping its commitment to protecting employees, assets, and the community (The safety master, 2023).

New perspectives are concluded based on this research and recommended as follows.

1. Focus of BBS intervention.
2. Beyond BBS culture.
3. Problem solving in building safety culture.
4. Phased implementation of longterm behavioural safety culture.
5. Human factors/errors in safety culture
6. Employees' concerns on safety culture.

1. Focus of BBS intervention on precision and accuracy in safety culture Transformation

Qualitative as well as quantitative analysis at sites and plants by multiple levels and multiple actions in terms of 12 behaviours being understood by observers, checking BBS score board trends, comparative index of safety statistics before and after BBS intervention, spot-correction of barriers and resources issues identified by observers, participation rate in terms of active observers /total manpower, HODs drive, monthly rewards to observers and departments, understanding BBS tools such as 12-B, 12-P, 6-C, and 4-cultures by observers, safety culture review and monitoring (Figure 8) by Directors/ site managements, constant retraining of observers, practice reverse TBT, Identify hot spots of at-risk behaviours, BBS to be a part of individual KPI as well as company annual HSE index, include BBS in employee families, their children schools and township roads to integrate it as a sustainable care-4-life, release of BBS policy, daily BBS Pledge, evaluation criteria of BBS (listening to employees own experiences in BBS), develop company specific BBS case study and video, include BBS in vendors terms and conditions, identify areas out of view of observers, area coordinator to meet observers for not reporting observation daily, observe safety, health, environment and well-being of employees, share behavioural science aspects such as positive psychology, emotional intelligence, and mindfulness (self-directed-ness), strengthen positive reinforcement by rewards, link corporate values of respect, equality, and care with BBS, thus making behaviour as parampara and personal nature of all worker, employee, director, and families as well as industrial and civil societies. Above aspects would increase depth & intensity in existing safety culture and take it to next levels. India should push for a culture change regarding the way that risks to workers' health, safety, and wellbeing are managed (Kamarajan, 2023).

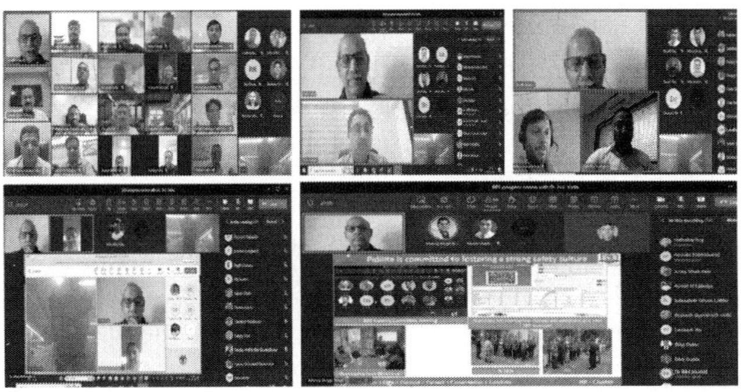

Source: Author's own

Figure 8: Safety culture review and monitoring

2. Beyond BBS culture

A missing or lacking safety culture may lead to concerns such as increased injuries and deaths and more legal issues (RUPERT, 2023). Hence, it is important to focus on a culture more than just safety.

- Focus Safety, health, environment and well-being of employees.

- BBS observers to be trained like mother care attitudes.
- "I worked in a government Electricity company without safety measures, once fell down from a pole, now would follow BBS for self and others", a staff member of Torrent Power.
- Bring behavioural safety in your respective work culture.
- Ask everyone to describe their job, how they do it safely every day.
- Share your health, safety, environment and well-being experience or any incident that occurred to you or your colleagues.
- Power distribution employees can provide safety culture awareness to their customers in large number as do the sugar company's employees for their farmers.

3. Problem solving in building safety culture

Studies and field surveys (Lal and Choueiri, 2023) indicate that there are several critical challenges in transformation of the safety culture for corporates. Several such issues are listed here below.

- It is difficult to convince seniors.
- Employees are not so social, how to talk to people for safety is an issue.
- PPE quality is not sufficient (resources issue).
- "Stop work", is it a safety solution or a problem in business scenario. Raise this issue in the monthly safety review meetings.
- Communication flow of safety culture scenario to all down the levels is required regularly.
- Discuss culture-1 issues for moving to culture-2.
- Role playing on safety culture provides clarity on communication issues, focus on behaviours before and after BBS implementation, emotional touch, patience between observers and observee, respect between junior and senior.
- Rewarding observers provides a sense of pride and responsibility.
- Managers need to talk to people down the levels about certain behavioural science aspects such as positive psychology, emotional intelligence, and mindfulness (self - directedness).
- Digital BBS observation- share daily.
- Discuss body language approach while correction of at-risk behaviours.
- "Emotional housekeeping" of observers is very important as emotional control is risk control.

4. Phased implementation of longterm behavioural safety culture

First awareness of positive safety culture to all at workplaces is necessary, then developing everyone as observer for daily correction of at-risk behaviours, and measuring trends of changes.

"In aspects of safety of life, BBS is an endeavour to promote safety. Aim is to be an observer and to produce more observers. Our life is at our own. Observing with patience and making it our culture is the key. To be an observer, first thing is to be calm and stress-free. BBS cannot be a solution to every problem but a way of life that leads to safety and prosperity of the country and an individual", a mentor of BBS from Oil India, Duliajan (Figure 9).

Source: Author's own

Figure 9: BBS training at Oil India

Safety culture progress in terms of employee reporting depends upon, first the regular training of BBS (Figure 10), second, who at the top level is reviewing the progress, and third, regular recognition of observers.

Source: Author's own

Figure 10: BBS training at Torrent

5. Human factors/errors in safety culture

Organisational relationships and development of positive safety culture are connected to each other. if relationships between employees, departments, unions, contractors and employers are positive, then it is easier to establish proactive safety culture in an organisation. Another human factor is the job satisfaction of employees and associates. If they are not satisfied, they don't pay heed to any safety initiatives of the company. In contrast, the human errors are complex cognitive factors like flirting with boundaries, normalising deviance and so on. Human factors are organisational experiences of employees whereas human error is organisational faulty cognition framework. Both are connected. What employees experience, they tend to think accordingly. If employees are not satisfied, they tend to ignore and normalise deviations with safety.

Importance of life in safety is our BBS perspective for organisations. It is important for everyone to understand and execute this. Everyone is on unsafe side sometimes, says a operations staff member, as he sometimes goes under moving load as my habit, which he would self-correct now as a BBS mentor. Despite self-correction, a residual of our unsafe behaviour remains uncorrected. This requires another observer for correction.

Behavioural safety must include our drivers group importantly, who sometimes drive us to destination if safe behaviours are conducted, and sometimes drive us to even hospital if unsafe behaviour is conducted and not spot-corrected.

Human factors such as mindset differences and communication conflicts increase distance between employees for not coming forward to observe and correct each other. Positive safety culture is care for life, it is beyond your job, company, it is for your life and of others. We need to constantly reinforce and emphasise safety behaviour at multiple level and multiple actions in order to let it become a prampara as it is in worship places with dedication of everyone. Unless one connects his soul and act as a human being to the BBS principles leaving all egos aside, he can't be its true mentor to deliver it. In order to avoid accidents and ill-health, companies need to manage human failure or errors as robustly as the technical and engineering measures they use for that purpose (Health and Safety Executive, 2023).

6. Employees' concerns on safety culture

- Is BBS a psychological analysis or do organisations use it?
- When other systems like 5S and hazards reporting are there, what is the use of BBS?
- What is the relationship between HSE and BBS?
- What is the need for BBS while AI and automation are prevalent?
- How to deal with people who are repeatedly doing at-risk behaviours?
- Is BBS observation /spot-correction applicable to other fields i.e. health, environment, quality?
- What is scientific about BBS?
- BBS means correct on the spot on your own. Spread it to all to make it as parampara.
- Employees take mock drill very casually, they hardly come for it. They say, it is normal, not serious. Employees must check it as part of proactive safety culture.

U Shekhar MD of Galaxy Surfactants said, "organisations must invest on increasing consciousness or mindfulness of safety of workers, as it is dismal on road, start it from homes and schools, how to respect laws. Organisations have covered some distance on safety, but to cover more distances by more safety initiatives due to the context of environment we are in. Employees may have skill and knowledge, but if they don't have mindfulness, organisations can't avoid accidents." We are not safe until our communities are safe. Our reactive leadership would save incidents sometimes, not always.

Dean of IIM Mumbai, said, "maturity of safety intervention is at stake as employees behaved differently for safety actions in different contexts. Human sensitivity approach is needed." For better cultural transformation, safety culture must be linked to career promotions decisions for employees. Self-maturity of mentors in positive safety culture is essential for transformation in safety standards.

The BBS progress review meeting must be very much interactive and fruitful. All clusters must present their BBS progress status in terms of cluster-wise BBS score card, trained number of observers versus actual number employees, behaviours categories and barriers details, number of Reverse Tool box talk (R-TBT), and number of BBS trainings (Figure 11).

Figure 11: Example of BBS Training & awareness

Leaders, at all levels, must understand the range of health and safety risks in their part of the organisation and to give proportionate attention to each of them (Health and Safety Executive, 2022). Joseph Varghese, Director, Pidilite, very aptly said, "Glad to see the momentum and drive from each of the leaders, well done and keep this going". Leadership involvement must be superb in monitoring the progress within short spans of periods. All units under Leadership of Cluster Chiefs had demonstrated their safety excellence journey towards the aim of zero-harm. Positive safety culture is the route for supportive work culture. Top management must work in top gear to succeed in achieving positive safety culture.

Table 1: Precision, creativity and accuracy in safety culture transformation

New Challenges
▸ Critical questions that would haunt business and life perspectives.
▸ Two things would make our industry global.
▸ 2024 Conference on safety culture.
▸ Leaders express their experiences.
▸ Tapping root cause of incidents
New Perspectives
▸ Focus of BBS intervention.
▸ Beyond BBS culture.
▸ Problem solving in building safety culture.
▸ Phased implementation of longterm behavioural safety culture.
▸ Human factors/errors in safety culture
▸ Employees' concerns on safety culture.

Myriad aspects of bringing precision, creativity and accuracy in safety culture transformation are summarised (Table 1) in terms of new challenges (such as critical questions that would haunt business and life perspectives, two things would make our industry global, 2024 conference on safety culture, leaders express their experiences) and new perspectives (such as focus of BBS intervention, beyond BBS culture, problem solving in building safety culture, phased implementation of longterm behavioural safety culture, human factors/ errors in safety culture, employees' concerns on safety culture). Safety culture for schools, roads, worship places must be focused towards building safer societies. We must conduct sessions for CEO's, Site Heads and Directors, with a first session on mental health policy in organisations. CEOs need to write and speak in a way that ensures their company's commitments to a strong safety culture as key strategic elements of their business model (Craig and Amernic, 2023).

Without medical treatment, people lose lives. Without care, people get fatalities. People need health care, safety care, and most important, environmental care to save from pollutions. Companies develop only an organisational structure for positive safety culture in the first few years, however it takes many years to turn it into a passionate care, a humanistic touch, and a sense of satisfaction.

Finally, while it is evident that the cultural shift towards safety consciousness is underway (Financial Express, 2024), several questions are yet to be explored and open to research, such as, how do CEOs who do not bend the safety rules, face challenges of balancing the business achievements and safety excellence to win global scenarios for their organisations. People should not, get injured physically, but also, they should not get injured psychologically by their colleagues. “In my opinion, reprimanding or psychological injury amounts to an offence”, Ex-Director of Factories of Karnataka. According to Pavan Rao, Head HSE, SEIL, “Physical injuries heal after some time whereas psychological injuries takes much longer time and sustained top management interventions.” Regular training workshop on emotional housekeeping is relevant for all levels of employees and associates. It is important that people of all cultures feel safe from the day to day minor or major emotional incidents or accidents at work (Siddiqui and Sangwan, 2022).

Follow simple lessons for practice for employees and everyone: knocking on the door of safety culture again and again. “Excuse me” or ‘ignoring safety culture’ mindset must go. If top man has time for safety culture, everyone else makes time for the same. Behaviour based safety is to be implemented not only as behavioural perspective but also barrier based safety (barriers such as resources, material, manpower) and business based safety (such as business outcomes indicators). All three perspectives make sense to the interests of all stake holders in organisations. Hence corporate safety excellence (in view of precision, creativity and accuracy) has to be matched on organisational behaviours, barriers and business frameworks.

REFERENCES

CISA. (2023, Feb 1). Companies Must Build Safety by Stop Passing the Buck. https://www.cisa.gov/resources-tools/resources/stop-passing-buck-cybersecurity

Craig Russell, Joel Amernic. (2023, May 25). Using “CEO-speak” to prioritise a safety culture. https://www.emerald.com/insight/content/doi/10.1108/SL-03-2023-0033/full/html

Gabhane, L. (2023, Oct 12). Personal communication with DG-NSC of India.

Financial Express. (2024, Feb 22). Transformative Insights Unveiled at the 8th Annual National BBS Conference. https://epaper.financialexpress.com/3832921/Mumbai/February-22-2024#page/18/2

Harris, Christian. (2024, Jan 11). 5 priorities for safety professionals in 2024. https://uk.linkedin.com/in/christian-harris-slip-safety?trk=article-ssr-frontend-pulse_publisher-author-card

Health and Safety Executive. (2022). *Leading and managing for health and safety*. Retrieved from https://www.hse.gov.uk/managing/leading.htm

Health and Safety Executive. (2023). *Human factors: Managing human failures*. https://www.hse.gov.uk/humanfactors/topics/humanfail.htm

Hyatt, Michael. (2023). *Why It Never Helps to Pass the Buck*. https://fullfocus.co/navy-seals/

Jasiulewicz-Kaczmarek, M.; Antosz, K.; Wyczółkowski, R.; Sławi ´nska, M. (2022). *Integrated* Approach for Safety Culture Factor Evaluation from a Sustainability Perspective. *Int. J. Environ. Res. Public Health*, 2022, (19), 11869.

Kaila, Harbans Lal (2021). Behavioural Benchmarking as a Robust Tool of Total Safety Culture in Industries. *The Journal of Insurance Institute of India*, July-Sept 2021, Vol. 9 (1), 82-88.

Kamarajan M. (2023, January 22). Improving construction safety in 2023. https://timesofindia.indiatimes.com/blogs/voices/improving-construction-safety-in-2023/

Lal, Harbans and Choueiri E.M. (2023). The integration of behaviour-based safety (BBS) as a company value is advocated! *World Safety Journal* (WSJ), Vol. 32, No 2, Page 49-55. doi.org/10.5281/zenodo.8105788

Lal, Harbans. (2022). Leadership Attributes for Corporate Safety Culture. *International Journal on Leadership*, 10 (2) 2022, 14-21. http://publishingindia.com/ijl/

Livemint. (2024, Jan 04). A fire erupted at the All India Institute of Medical Sciences. https://www.livemint.com/news/india/fire-breaks-out-at-all-india-institute-of-medical-sciences-delhi-no-casualties-11704349982747.html

Lundell, Mark & Cheri, Cheryl & Marcham,. (2021). *Leadership's Effect on Safety Culture*. https://www.researchgate.net/publication/355364834

Manufacturing Today. (2022, July, 22). 123 Indian companies receive the International Safety Award https://www.manufacturingtodayindia.com/sectors/123-indian-companies-receive-the-international-safety-award

Marr, Bernard. (2023, Sept 25). The 10 Biggest Business Trends For 2024 Everyone Must Be Ready For Now. https://www.forbes.com/sites/bernardmarr/2023/09/25/the-10-biggest-business-trends-for-2024-everyone-must-be-ready-for-now/?sh=5f98708f59ab

Rupert Jones. (2023, April, 17). Understanding The True Cost of a Poor Workplace Safety Culture. https://ohsonline.com/articles/2023/04/17/understanding-the-true-cost-of-a-poor-workplace-safety-culture.aspx

Roushan, Anurag. (2024, January 03). Delhi: Massive fire erupts at factory in Bawana Industrial Area. https://www.indiatvnews.com/delhi/fire-erupts-at-factory-in-bawana-industrial-area-in-delhi-video-casualty-injury-reactions-latest-updates-2024-01-03-910039

SEIL. (2023). *Behaviour Based Safety (BBS) Implemented at SEIL*. https://www.sembcorpenergyindia.com/CSR/BBS

Siddiqui, Shabnam and Sangwan, Ankur. (2022). The Catalytic Role of Perceived Psychological Safety on the Relationship Between 'Support from Supervisor' and 'Workplace Loneliness'. *Journal of Positive School Psychology*, Vol. 6, (6), 8401 – 8412.

Spigener Jim, Gennifer Lyon & Terry McSween. (2022). Behaviour-based safety 2022: today's evidence, *Journal of Organisational Behaviour Management*, 42:(4), 336-359, DOI: 10.1080/01608061.2022.2048943

Tata Steel. (2021, March 15). Risk profiling turns deep shop floor experience into enthusiastic risk-based decision making. https://www.consultdss.com/content-hub/risk-profiling-risk-based-decision-making/

The safety master. (2023, July 28). Enhancing safety culture. https://www.thesafetymaster.com/enhancing-safety-culture-a-comprehensive-guide-by-a-leading-safety-consultant/

U.S. Department of Transportation. (2017, August). Federal Railroad Administration Safety Culture: A Significant Influence on Safety in Transportation. Office of Research Development and Technology Washington, DC 20590.

World Steel Association. (2022). S*afety culture and leadership fundamentals*. https://worldsteel.org/safety-culture-and-leadership-fundamentals/

CHAPTER 3

SUSTAIN LEADERSHIP INSPIRATION IN SUPPORTIVE SAFETY CULTURE FOR GRASS-ROOT CHANGE

Leaders who do not learn new aspects of doing business in terms of positive safety culture shall be automatically rendered out of business by their world competitors, and they would learn in a hard and expensive ways to adapt to a new order of safe work culture. Understanding the core principles of positive safety culture as a behavioural science intervention, the president operations of a group of chemical plants felt and urged all leaders in a meeting that they must relook and review the company HSE policy. While the director operations responded that he would convince his board of directors in this direction, and be very supportive to all plants for the resources required in terms of manpower, finance or infrastructure etc. This paper discusses the challenges and solutions to sustain leadership inspiration in supportive safety culture for grass-root changes. The recommendations are made based on the field visits to 10 site locations and interactions with 257 managers and 250 contractors workmen. Major conclusions are: a) Indian employers have to aim high to be global in safety standards and culture to be global in business. b) Safety culture board team need to be a solution provider at the ground. c) Corporate leadership looks at the larger socio-familial context of their own employees that no one gets injured on any single working day. d) Leadership visible presence on the ground for inspiring positive safety culture. e) the finer role of corporate leadership is to seek inspiration from grassroots leadership and also support for change. f) Human errors often hurdle the safety culture which can be managed by the concept implementation of a totally safe organisation (TSO). In a safety culture, human errors are not punished, as they are seen as opportunities to improve and learn from underlying system problems. A sustained safety culture is not only behaviour-based, but also value-based, a corporate value which is a long-term intervention.

Keywords: Safety, Culture, Corporate, Managers, Workmen.

INTRODUCTION

Culture impacts the grass-root change. Almost forty years down since Bhopal and Chernobyl incidents, the industry has moved from the term 'safety' to 'safety culture.' Nevertheless, the clarity and methodology about its implementation varies from the perspectives of an employer, a manager, a researcher, contractor, EHS professional.

This is very critical issue as the fatalities numbers are still unacceptably high when seen through the promise of the OSH Act, which entitles every worker to safe and healthful working conditions and makes all employers and employees responsible to provide a work area free from recognised hazards (Lundell, et al., 2021). Eliminating fatalities and serious injuries is the main challenge for the global industry. Focus is to provide the industry with actionable recommendations and guidance to create safer and healthier workplaces (World Steel Association, 2022).

Almost every third person in workplace or any other place is engaged in an at-risk behaviours, which is why there are fires and fatalities each day, as all incidents are behaviour based. A fire erupted at the All India Institute of Medical Sciences (AIIMS) in Delhi in the morning January 4, 2024. There were no casualties reported from the incident, and the cause of the fire is yet to be determined (Livemint, 2024). Fire broke out at a factory in Delhi's Bawana Industrial Area. 25 fire tenders rushed to the site (Roushan, 2024).

Like a Japanese lecturer says, "there is nothing more important than life". As corporates, our ethics have to be very loud and clear to one and all, which is not. The 'just and fair culture' is on paper, not on ground. The production-safety balancing act needs to be communicated repeatedly by all leaders down the levels every day. The effectiveness of positive safety culture initiatives can sustain for many years (Spigener et al., 2022).

Safety culture is becoming an indispensable forecasting factor in achieving sustainable development (Jasiulewicz-Kaczmarek, 2022). A strong safety culture is predicted by the fact that leadership is clearly committed and involved in safety (U.S. Department of Transportation, 2017). Leaders deliver change through the safety of cultural intervention and their commitment, passion, and time (Lal, 2022).

Safety culture transformation doesn't get sustained until it is initiated by the safety professionals, adopted by the HODs, monitored by the site/top management, and reviewed by the company Directors. Most top managements give verbal commitments in speeches but don't involve in 'daily safety culture implementation and monitoring' which fails the safety culture progress, and lead to incidents. Management must talk of business as well as risks while they interact with plant managers in terms of planning and implementation (Kaila, 2021).

OBJECTIVES

To explore challenges and solutions to sustain leadership inspiration in supportive safety culture for grass-root changes.

METHODOLOGY

a. Measures

Both primary data (interviews, and discussions) were collected to explore concerns and solutions over corporates' readiness to re-build positive safety culture. Interviews based on open-ended questions, focus group interviews, and personal in-depth discussions were conducted during 2023-2024.

b. Sample and Procedure

Field visits to 10 site locations and interactions with 257 managers and 250 contractors workmen comprised a sample of this research. Industry professionals participated in the study as part of an action field survey with the researcher. These research participants had been implementing behavioural safety compliance culture at their work sites. The research participants included the Directors, Managers, Heads of Departments and EHS/HR Professionals belonging to the public and private industrial sectors, including chemicals, construction, gas, power and steel, across Indian locations. The sampling method used was random sampling.

c. Statistical analysis

The responses to the relevant questions were collated. Thematic analysis was performed and themes were identified from the qualitative data.

This paper is an extract of a national research program of the Forum of Behavioural Safety under Bharat Bane Surakshit (BBS) mission (Figure 1, 2). The study results and implications are reflected below from a rigorous review of safety culture literature and experiences / case studies shared by industry leaders across Indian organisation

Source: Author's own

Figure 1: Sample picture of national research program

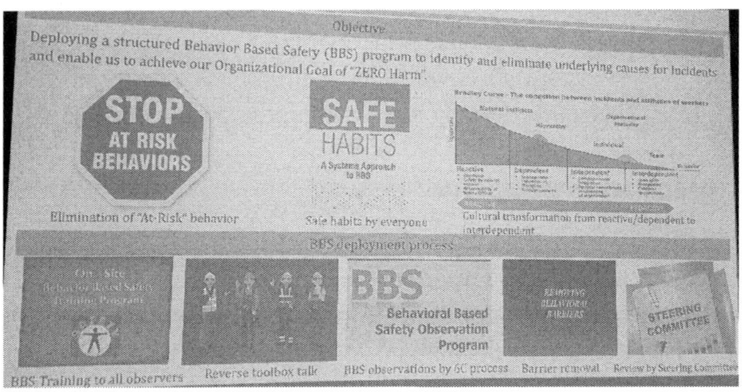

Source: Author's own

Figure 2: Sample picture of national research program

RESULTS AND DISCUSSION

Changing company culture requires a movement, not a mandate. Culture is like the wind. It is invisible, yet its effect can be seen and felt. When it is blowing in your direction, it makes for smooth sailing. When it is blowing against you, everything is more difficult. For organizations seeking to become more adaptive and innovative, culture change is often the most challenging part of the transformation. But culture change can't be achieved through top-down mandate. It lives in the collective hearts and habits of people and their shared perception of "how things are done around here. To create a movement in your organization, start by framing the issue in terms that stir emotion and incite action; then mobilize more supporters by demonstrating quick wins. Broadcast these wins to an even wider audience by leveraging employees' social networks, and using symbolism and pockets of innovation to keep momentum going. It's important to start with actions, not new mission statements or company structures, because culture change only happens when people take action (Walker & Soule, 2017).

Table 1 Highlights below important challenges and solutions to sustain leadership inspiration for grass-root change.

Table 1: Important actions to sustain leadership inspiration for grass-root change

Challenges
▸ Safety culture intervention slows down as some leaders leave and join other organisations.
▸ Contractors workmen are left unsupervised.
▸ Building positive safety culture is a team game.
▸ Positive safety culture is care, care and care.
▸ Understand what can go unsafe at their work areas.
▸ Some seniors come with closed mindset.
▸ New joiners need to be tackled with utmost care for risks.
▸ Top management / site leaders /HODs need to be accountable for supportive safety culture.
▸ Leaders who do not learn new aspects of doing business in terms of positive safety culture.
▸ Leaders must relook and review the company HSE policy.
▸ Human errors in safety culture.

Solutions
▸ Make an organisational case study, a story out of your own BBS successful journey.
▸ Top management reinforces the positive safety culture.
▸ Companies have to have a very strict culture around standard operating procedures.
▸ Leaders visible presence on the grounds.
▸ Safety culture board need to be a solution provider at the ground.
▸ Employers have to aim high to be global in safety culture to be global in business.
▸ Corporate leadership looks at the larger socio-familial context of their own employees.
▸ An unconditional love for your employees and associates just for 5 minutes every day.
▸ Building insights that the positive safety culture is about working towards the greater good.
▸ Leaders must challenge and offer competition to each other in the safety culture board.
▸ Leaders can achieve positive safety culture if he/she does it with a true heart and honesty.
▸ Implementing the concept of Totally Safe Organisation (TSO).

a. Challenges

1. Safety culture **intervention slows down** as some leaders leave the organisation, or it loses excitement what it gains at the time of being rolled out.

2. Most of the major fires and fatalities occurred while **contractors workmen were not supervised**. Even company engineers or contractors supervisor left workers on their own fate, as because these supervisors are also not safety conscious.

3. Remember, **building positive safety culture is a team game** where the entire organisation is gradually brought to a singular dimension of observation and immediate care, correction, and conversation. If that organisational culture doesn't take place (which obviously takes time), organisations remain under threat of incidents.

4. **Positive safety culture is care, care and care.** Everyone cares and no one gets injured. Pleasing people is contrary to positive safety culture. Caring and pleasing are not same. Caring and compulsive caregiving are not be same. Some employees tend to please their managers by being extra by giving gifts or agreeing every time to what they opine.

5. All employees and associates must understand again and again from their seniors and colleagues that **what can go unsafe at their work areas,** and what they must do to immediately control the risk without looking the other way.

6. **Some seniors come with closed mindset**, they are not open to what best others may be saying. Hence these people can be very risky to organisations, as they don't update and sit with fixed ideas.

7. **New joiners need to be tackled with utmost care for risks** around them as they come from different cultures. They take time to understand the norms and values of the workplace.

8. **Top management / site leaders /HODs need to be accountable for supportive safety culture** in terms of their own actions as to what support have they extended down the levels while being on BBS rounds weekly/monthly/daily, more specifically in terms of their safety time, resources, manpower, equipment, approvals, difficulties with customers/ seniors and so on.

9. **Leaders who do not learn new aspects of doing business in terms of positive safety culture** shall be automatically rendered out of business by their world competitors, and they would learn in a hard and expensive ways to adapt to new order of safe work culture.

10. Understanding the core principles of positive safety culture as a behavioural science intervention, the president operations of a group of chemical plants felt and urged all **leaders in a meeting that they must relook and review the company HSE policy.** While the Director operations responded that he would convince his board of directors in this direction, and be very supportive to all plants in terms of resources required in terms of manpower, approvals or infrastructure etc.

b. Solutions

1. You need to **make an organisational case study, a story out of your own BBS successful journey**, for which everyone has to work hard like GAIL, SEIL, Galaxy Surfactants, and others (Lal & Choueiri, 2023).

2. Safety culture board group fails in its duty, if it doesn't work successfully. So the responsibility as group of **top management is to reinforce the positive safety culture**.

3. Companies have to have a very **strict culture around Standard Operating Procedures (SOP).**

4. Corporate speeches and documents are very risky as they don't save people from incidents, they only mean business safety, not human safety. Hence let's ensure that we as **leaders can reinforce safe behaviours by our visible presence on the grounds.**

5. Top leadership team of **safety culture board need to be a solution provider at the ground**, policy reviewer to integrate safety culture, and also importantly internalise BBS actions. More importantly, the personal commitment to communicating down the levels, thinking beyond his/her units, provide support for barriers like infrastructure assurance, getting approvals for resources like safety funds/ manpower, making time to visit plants for behavioural aspects of safety in addition to process safety.

6. India is perceived as not very safety friendly industry. We wait till global scenario changes, then we take safety initiatives in our organisations, which is too late, by then we have already incurred losses to our assets and manpower. **Indian employers have to aim high to be global in safety standards and culture to be global in business.**

7. Let **leadership looks at the larger context**, in which each corporate has an almost ten thousand employees and their families that ought to be part of positive supportive EHS culture. That's excellent really to be a visible leadership on a larger canvass that no one gets injured on any single working day.

8. If I ask you to remember who do remember in your life: you would recall persons who connected and cared for me. That's what is BBS,

which calls for **an unconditional love for your employees and associates just for 5 minutes every day** to ensure that he/she doesn't get injured. Become a family to your employees and associates and ensure like parents do that no one gets hurt or injured. Make it happen daily by connect and care actively.

9. **Building insights that the positive safety culture is about working towards the greater good**, understanding that no one wins alone, it is inclusion of people that brings results that we look for "no one gets injured" around me.
10. Leaders must challenge and offer competition to each other in the safety culture board. Leaders would be an excellent task master of safety culture, yet be very appreciative of safety contributions, like Dr Howard (an Australian clinical psychologist) and U Shekhar (a managing director of a multi-national) who would be very keen and critical observer, yet highly appreciative and friendly for others best performance.
11. "**Leaders can achieve positive safety culture if he/she does it with a true heart and honesty** so that no one gets injured" (Ashok Oza, best BBS poet and observer from Galaxy Surfactants).

CONCLUSIONS AND RECOMMENDATIONS

The leaders must seek clarity to understand that safety culture is sustainable only when it is perceived as an integral reinforcer in other functions like production, health, quality, environment, maintenance, all of which play a key influencer to become emotionally accepted by the workforce in any workplace. That is how safety culture is an organisational behaviour, and not only safety behaviour or safety culture. It must be a work culture. Safety culture is an essential aspect of any organisation, shaping its commitment to protecting employees, assets, and the community (the safety master, 2023).

The managements must consider a few recommendations mentioned here below to sustain leadership inspiration for grass-root change. They advocate a perspective on leadership that gains its inspiration from the grassroots leadership that upholds the traditions and values of an organisation.

Positive safety culture journey gradually expands from individual behaviour to organisational behaviour, from safety culture to work culture, from individual to society and beyond. Positive safety culture is sustainable in positive organisation, not otherwise. In this regard, a research analysis found four factors with a significant impact on safety culture: safety informing by operations managers; safety caring by employers; and safety coordination and safety regulation by safety professionals (Wu, et al., 2010).

The top management must continuously monitor and evaluate their strategies while delivering multifaceted interventions to be more specifically focused and to motivate workers to be enthusiastic in sustaining safety culture (Wong, et al., 2021). Sustainable safety culture considers contractual employees as 'own employees' with respect to safety. We strongly believe in it and strive to involve our critical mass, including contractors, in our transformation journey (Tata Steel, 2021).

Organisations must set up a multidisciplinary steering team coordinated by a safety culture initiative leader (Manufacturing Safety Alliance of BC, 2022).

Leaders, at all levels, must understand the range of health and safety risks in their part of the organisation and to give proportionate attention to each of them (Health and Safety Executive, 2022).

The managements must emphasise the positive relationship between a sustainable corporate safety strategy and stakeholder perceptions that brings advantages to business performance (Hristov, et al., 2022).

It is recommended that companies must build safety by stop-passing the buck (CISA, 2023). It never helps to pass the buck. Accept total responsibility for the outcome. (Hyatt, 2023). The biggest hurdle of safety culture transformation is dumping down the levels by leaders, then asking for a monthly report, not being available for any support or reinforcement. Hence there is a need that the leaders' daily safety time is to be fixed and logged in. Make safety an easy and a supportive culture for all units. Change is a by-product of the leaders' personal commitments which can be sourced and sustained by the inspirations they get from the results that are consistently nurtured by their supportive actions and motivational mechanisms set at the grass-roots levels across plants/sites.

Human errors often hurdle the safety culture. Human errors are cognitive complexities involving unclear perceptions and thinking about workplace dynamics disallowing or disempowering people to take safety initiatives, decisions and actions necessary for creating positive safety cultural transformation towards zero-harm zero-blame perspective. Organisations are often surrounded by some types of human errors as follows. a) Managers not knowing the cost of silence for not correcting at-risk behaviours and barriers. b) Insufficient communication between with senior management and lower levels on developing safety culture. c) Top management being in comfort zones and not perceiving the effect of poor safety culture on company business in terms of incidents. d) Employers and director's mindset to only maximise profits, not safety culture. All these errors can be managed by the concept implementation of a totally safe organisation (TSO) which is like a totally safe family, in which everyone feels connected, safe, and is empowered to talk about all issues with transparency and without any fear. In a safety culture, human errors are not punished, as they are seen as opportunities to improve and learn from underlying system problems (Jay & Jay, 2020).

Defining safety culture is a challenge and must be deeply explored by leaders. The definition of safety culture must include safety perceptions and practices, beliefs and behaviours (Abeje, and Fan, 2023). Positive safety culture is a humanity interaction beyond age, education, designation, nationality and experience. Safety culture is not only in systems, processes and policies, it is in emotional reflection of leaders. Safety culture must be enforced first as rules and regulations, and then reinforced by all people. Safety culture is a correction in culture, and a cultural improvement from a certain percentage of safe behaviour to 100 percent safe behaviours by day-to-day positive conversations among workers. The safety culture can only be nurtured and sustained by common people of an organisation, while the managements inspire and support in every possible way. Leaders inspire workforce while they seek inspiration from the feedback of their stakeholders. The safety culture is sustainable when it is also discussed and reinforced in every boardroom meeting, like profit and production are always first and foremost. Safety culture must also be internalised by board members, as safety incidents do happen even amongst directors own family members. But a deeper query remains unresolved as to why the directorial pitch all across the board is falling short of reinforcing positive safety culture, whether they are company directors or directors of factories, who practically don't connect with workers, is a big challenge in achieving zero-harm culture.

REFERENCES

Abeje, Mesfin & Fan, Luo. (2023). "The Influence of Safety Culture and Climate on Safety Performance: Mediating Role of Employee Engagement in Manufacturing Enterprises in Ethiopia" *Sustainability* 15, 14: 11274. https://doi.org/10.3390/su151411274

CISA (2023, Feb 1). *Companies Must Build Safety by Stop Passing the Buck.* https://www.cisa.gov/resources-tools/resources/stop-passing-buck-cybersecurity

Health and Safety Executive. (2022). *Leading and managing for health and safety.* Retrieved from https://www.hse.gov.uk/managing/leading.htm

Hristov Ivo, Chirico Antonio & Ranalli Francesco. (2022). Corporate strategies oriented towards sustainable governance: advantages, managerial practices and main challenges. *Journal of Management and Governance*, 26. 10.1007/s10997-021-09581-x.

Hyatt, Michael. (2023). *Why It Never Helps to Pass the Buck.* https://fullfocus.co/navy-seals/

Jay, A. Harolds & Jay, A. Harolds. (2020). Quality and Safety in Healthcare, Part LXXXIII: The Culture of Safety in High Reliability Organizations.. *Clinical Nuclear Medicine*, doi: 10.1097/RLU.0000000000003418

Jasiulewicz-Kaczmarek, M.; Antosz, K.; Wyczółkowski, R.; Sławi ´nska, M. (2022). Integrated Approach for Safety Culture Factor Evaluation from a Sustainability Perspective. *Int. J. Environ. Res. Public Health*, 2022 (19), 11869.

Kaila, Harbans Lal. (2021). Behavioural Benchmarking as a Robust Tool of Total Safety Culture in Industries. *The Journal of Insurance Institute of India*, July-Sept 2021, Vol. 9 (1), 82-88.

Lal, Harbans & Choueiri, E.M. (2023). The integration of behavior-based safety (BBS) as a company value is advocated! *World Safety Journal* (WSJ), Vol. 32, No 2, Page 49-55. doi.org/10.5281/zenodo.8105788

Lal, Harbans. (2022). Leadership Attributes for Corporate Safety Culture . International Journal on Leadership, 10 (2) 2022, 14-21. http://publishingindia.com/ijl/

Livemint. (2024, Jan 04). A fire erupted at the All India Institute of Medical Sciences. https://www.livemint.com/news/india/fire-breaks-out-at-all-india-institute-of-medical-sciences-delhi-no-casualties-11704349982747.html

Lundell, Mark & Cheri, Cheryl & Marcham,. (2021). *Leadership's Effect on Safety Culture.* https://www.researchgate.net/publication/355364834

Manufacturing Safety Alliance of BC. (2022). *Safety cul- ture: A guide to effective measurement and improvement.* Retrieved from https://safetyalliancebc.ca/wp-content/ uploads/guidebook/11865/Safety-Culture-Model.pdf

Roushan, Anurag. (2024, January 03). Delhi: Massive fire erupts at factory in Bawana Industrial Area. https://www.indiatvnews.com/delhi/fire-erupts-at-factory-in-bawana-industrial-area-in-delhi-video-casualty-injury-reactions-latest-updates-2024-01-03-910039

Spigener Jim, Gennifer Lyon & Terry McSween. (2022). Behavior-based safety 2022: today's evidence, *Journal of Organisational Behavior Management*, 42:(4), 336-359, DOI: 10.1080/01608061.2022.2048943

Tata Steel. (2021, March 15). Risk profiling turns deep shop floor experience into enthusiastic risk-based decision making. https://www.consultdss.com/content-hub/risk-profiling-risk-based-decision-making/

The safety master. (2023, July 28). Enhancing safety culture. https://www.thesafetymaster.com/enhancing-safety-culture-a-comprehensive-guide-by-a-leading-safety-consultant/

U.S. Department of Transportation. (2017, August). Federal Railroad Administration Safety Culture: A Significant Influence on Safety in Transportation. *Office of Research Development and Technology Washington*, DC 20590.

Walker, Bryan & Soule, Sarah A. (2017, June 20). Changing Company Culture Requires a Movement, Not a Mandate. https://hbr.org/2017/06/changing-company-culture-requires-a-movement-not-a-mandate

Wu Tsung-Chih, Lin Chia-Hung, Shiau Sen-Yu. (2010). Predicting safety culture: The roles of employer, operations manager and safety professional, *Journal of Safety Research*, Volume 41, (5), 423-431, ISSN 0022-4375, https://doi.org/10.1016/j.jsr.2010.06.006.

Wong SY, Fu ACL, Han J, Lin J, Lau MC. (2021). Effectiveness of customised safety intervention programmes to increase the safety culture of hospital staff. BMJ Open Qual. 2021 Oct;10(4):e000962. doi: 10.1136/bmjoq-2020-000962. PMID: 34625426; PMCID: PMC8504354.

World Steel Association. (2022). Safety culture and leadership fundamentals. https://worldsteel.org/safety-culture-and-leadership-fundamentals.

CHAPTER

4

ZERO FATALITIES AMONG CONTRACTORS WORKMEN IS POSSIBLE BY POSITIVE SAFETY CULTURE

Contractors workmen work on heights with least safety equipment and awareness. What do they need from managers are the care and concern, welfare and wellbeing? Emotional care and support are crucial as contractors' workmen lack proper rest place, clean water, dining space and so on. Managers often do not feel concerned about the need of emotional support for workmen. Workmen's personal health and hygiene are critical as they work in oil, water, mud, height, foul smells. In this regard, recommendations are made to overcome fatalities amongst workmen by inculcating supportive safety culture. This study (based on the field visits to almost 54 site locations and interactions with 609 managers and 2500 contractors workmen during two years 2022-2023) highlights contractors workmen's safety culture issues and solutions. Ground reality of safety culture is different from what is reflected in documents. Hence it is vital to visit site areas by each HOD daily as well as incharges of each section/area/shift in organisations for maintaining regular safety conversations with the workers. All serious and non-serious incidents are manageable and stoppable depending upon how many positive safety conversations happen daily between workers and managers at all levels specifically the top management such as business and site heads.

Keywords: Contractors, Safety, Culture, Organisations, Workmen.

INTRODUCTION

It was observed that approximately 48000 workers die every year due of the occupational accidents and one in four workers die in the Indian construction sites. It is a well-known fact that accidents on sites are unavoidable and keeps recurring although the severity and marginally, the number of accidents has been reduced now ((Patel & Jha, 2016).

All serious and non-serious incidents are manageable depending upon how many positive safety conversations happen daily between workers and managers at all levels including specifically the top management such as business and site heads. It helps workmen not only being aware of their safety but also it raises their self-esteem that the managers respect and listen to them. It impacts the business perspective, excellence and sustainability in the long run. Observations and spot-correction build safety culture but conversations build safety mindset and beliefs amongst the workers. The senior-most employees' positive connect with the lowest level workers impact human virtues and business values such as respect and care which go a long way in the life of an organisation (Lal, 2021).

Most of these fatalities across the world happen to the contractors' workmen. Eliminating fatalities and serious injuries is the main challenge for the global industry. The focus is to provide the industry with actionable recommendations and passionate leadership guidance to create safer and healthier workplaces (World Steel Association, 2022).

Industrial accidents kill hundred thousands of people and permanently disable thousands each year. A federal minister told parliament in 2021 that at least 6,500 workers had died while working in factories, ports, mines and construction sites in five years. Labour activists, who worked in the field for years, reported that the figures could be higher as many incidents are not reported or recorded (Shukla, 2022).

It is observed that often contractors and workmen are not included by companies in building safety culture processes which affects workmen's mindset for safe working leading to incidents. Low employability and low job opportunities lead to low EHS compliance amongst the workmen (Lal, 2022). Support them for safety - let them not get injured. Safety culture is about employee's / workmen's observation and spot-correction network of positive safety culture which gradually involves everyone till last person in an organisation. This organisation-wide network turns as safety culture activism (Lal, 2022a).

Companies have given contract workmen a place to work, but not a place in hearts. This disconnect creates a hurdle in safety culture transformation as well as business sustainability. Senior casual workmen should train new casual workers. But nobody sees that these trainers develop workmen as active observers, Nobody cares that after the TBT (tool box talk) whether the workmen are being observed or not. have conversation with workmen after corrections of at-risk behaviours about importance of safe behaviours. Workmen need to observe each other for actual safety culture transformation. Hence primary focus has to be on workers. Managers sit inside their cabins and dump safety culture on the subcontractors and workmen (Lal and Choueiri, 2023).

India reported 1109 deaths and more than 4000 injuries in registered factories, on average, each year between 2017 and 2020. Although about 90% of workers in India are employed in the informal sector, underreporting of incidents from the informal and the formal economy mean these figures are underestimates. India has passed occupational safety and health law reforms in 2020, but experts feel that the new OSH Code is less stringent than the Factories Act, 1948 (Paliath, 2023).

OBJECTIVES OF THIS SURVEY

- To explore the contractors workmen's safety culture mindset and fatalities issues.
- To explore ways to overcome issues about the contractors workmen's safety culture mindset and fatalities.

Figure 1: Site location example of work at height

METHOD

Field visits to almost 54 site locations (Figure 1, 2, 3) and interactions with 609 managers and 2500 contractors workmen comprised sample of this research. Industry professionals participated in the study as part of an action field survey with the researcher. These research participants had been implementing behavioural safety compliance culture at their work sites. The research participants included, the Directors, Managers, Heads of Departments, EHS/HR Professionals belonging to the public and private industrial sectors, including chemicals, construction, gas, power and steel, across Indian locations. The sampling method used was a random sampling.

Both primary data (interviews, discussions) were collected. Interviews based on open-ended questions, focus group interviews and personal in-depth discussions were conducted almost over two year during 2022-2023. The responses to the relevant questions were collated.

The study results and implications are reflected below from a rigorous review of safety culture literature and experiences / case studies shared by the industry leaders across Indian organisations.

Figure 2: Site location example

Training programme on 'Behaviour Based Safety'

Senior officials, along with faculty and participants

Panipat Refinery & Petrochemicals Complex (PRPC) organised a training programme on 'Behaviour Based Safety' on October 30, 2023, at L&D Centre through in-house expert faculty from Mathura Refinery (MR) & PRPC. Mr M K Ray, DGM (MS, L&D), MR, is PhD in BBS and is having vast knowledge on Behaviour Based Safety. The objective of this training programme was to help each participant to understand on the introduction to Behaviour Based Safety; Behavioural Modification, Basic Principles & Techniques; Developing Enterprise Level Behavioral Based Safety Management System; at Risk Behaviour, role of positive feedback and overview of BBS implementation in PRPC through ICC. The training programme started with inaugural address by Mr Utpal Deka, CGM (HSE), wherein he touched upon the importance of Behaviour Based Safety aspects and to implement the same at PRPC. He urged all the participants to interact more & more with the faculty during the training programme to gain maximum learnings. Earlier, Mr Sulochan Sen Kumar, DGM (F&S), PR, delivered the welcome address and gave brief introduction about the programme. Mr Baljeet Singh, GM (MS, L&D) & executives of Fire & Safety were also present during the inaugural session. The programme was compered by Mr Kuldeep Baldia, Mgr (L&D). A total of 32 participants from PRPC attended the programme. The programme received an overwhelming response and appreciation from the participants for its vitality in reinforcing the behavioural safety at PRPC. **(Vivek Sharma, SM (Corp Comm & CSR), PRPC)**

Figure 3: Site location example

RESULTS AND DISCUSSION

This paper dwells on ten aspects of the contractors workmen's fatalities, mindset and safety culture issues as below. Table -1 highlights contractors workmen's safety culture issues and solutions.

1. Long hours of work, no holiday, stinking toilets for contractors workmen affect their health and safety culture. Providing portable toilets help the construction site be a healthy space to work. It also helps the workers to learn that they are respected. In the absence of toilets at construction sites, workers have to defecate in open areas which violate the sanitation guidelines. Workmen often work long hours without a holiday which impacts their personal and family health and wellbeing. Brynn Bourke, executive director of the BTC (Building Trades Council), who lobbied for the change said, "the shift to flush toilets means construction workers will be given the dignity they deserve at work. Nearly every other industry has found a way to bring clean, flushing toilet facilities to mobile sites. Construction workers deserve flush toilets now" (Wilson, 2023). Also allow them holidays as per rule like other employees.

2. Risk blindness or zero perception of risk: some people (about 20 percent) remain exposed to risk with lack of understanding for its effects. Risk exposure is everywhere but its perception and control are important to save oneself. Risk-taking and unsafe behaviors in an organization is partly a result of how the culture is shaped. Culture can contribute to either unsafe or safe behaviors in an organization. Culture is however not behavior per se and should not be confused as such. Culture and behavior are distinguishable, and not to oversimplify by saying that culture is the way we do things around here. It is interesting to discuss how cultural norms and practices are related to behavior since they do specify what kind of behavior is acceptable or wanted. Safety culture is one factor that contributes to behavior, but there are many other factors. Working on routine and being blind-to-flaws results in more risk-taking (Hasse, et al., 2015).

3. Close relationships among managers, immediate next level employees and associates affect safety culture in organisations. What are their expectations from each other, matters in safety assertive behaviours. What are their preferences, matters in delivering these safety responsibilities. Maximum involvement of upper management

in safety activities significantly influence the supervisory practices of a company's line managers (Hsu, 2012).

4. Safety culture improvements: the visualised safety culture can enable group discussions about safety on many organisational levels and can constitute a sizeable input to the continuous improvement processes for safety and safety culture (Ek, et al., 2014). Consider the following ten aspects for safety culture improvements:
    - Is it a compliance or a value?
    - Is it documentation or behaviour?
    - Is it by safety officer or everyone?
    - Is it by workmen or managers or both?
    - Is it by management or Director?
    - Is it daily or rarely?
    - Is it only a slogan, a banner on wall?
    - Is it reviewed and monitored?
    - Is it to please client or customer?
    - Is it only training, or implementation?
5. Authoritarian or reactive organisations are not favourable for business or safety culture either, like authoritarian families are unfavourable for positive growth of children. There is room for both proactive and reactive safety management within all organisations, but the proactive safety management (Safety 2.0) serves the organisation for better results in our understanding of human safety from incidents (Thraen, 2022).

6. Risk perceptions, risk exposure and risk awareness are closely associated. The employees who are not aware of the risk, don't perceive it, and are more exposed to it, and vice versa. Risk perception refers to people's own judgments about the probability of negative occurrences like injury, illness, disease, and fatality. Risk perceptions and risk communications are important because they determine which hazards people care about and how they deal with them. Risk perception has two major dimensions: the cognitive dimension, which relates to how much people know about and understand risks, and the emotional dimension, which relates to how they feel about them (Paek and Hove, 2017).

7. What is lacking at sites are the management visible leadership, corporate tracking, Directors regular communication on safety culture down the levels, HODs presence at site areas. Safety culture implementation doesn't become a daily practice. Project manager attends the safety culture training but leave its implementation to the safety officers. The safety culture transformation team is established but it hardly meets or review the progress regularly. Strong leaders at all organisational levels are critical for prevention of sustained injury and fatality (Quality Safety Edge, 2023).

8. Safety culture vision and its implementation: In most organisations, vision is very strong, but implementation is weak. Positive body language and the presence of top management at the site are essential for sustaining a safety culture. If leaders wish to see the change amongst employees on the shop floor, they must go there amongst employees and workmen (Lal, 2022). The intervention requires management presence, interaction, and openness with workers (Cooper, 2006).

9. Safety performance behaviours are to be assured by the project site head, and to ensure that daily behavioural safety observations/spot-correction have to be linked to individual KPI, appraisal and increments. Then only, every employee/workmen would complete daily BBS expected results. Safety KPIs are performance indicators that serve as metrics for specific company efforts in health and safety. Tracking health, safety and environment KPIs allows a business to determine how safe the work environment is for employees and whether the company is within regulatory compliance. The utilisation of KPIs (key performance indicators) can assist an organisation with achieving significant business goals (Tekmon, 2023).

10. What should be our goal in safety culture - focusing on zero fatalities, zero incident, zero-harm, or attend to zero unsafe behaviours, not the outcomes? If you do believe that no one should get hurt at work, and you believe that all incidents are preventable, leaders should set the expectation that everyone does whatever they must to prevent incidents. Safety isn't the only dimension of performance where zero should be the expectation; it should also be the expectation as a best practice of companies that achieve operational excellence (Wilson Perumal, 2023).

Table 1: Contractors workmen's safety culture issues and solutions

Contractors workmen's safety culture mindset and fatalities issues:	Solutions for Contractors workmen's safety culture mindset and fatalities issues:
1. Long hours of work, no holiday, stinking toilets (92%)	1. Providing portable toilets, and allow holidays like other employees.
2. Risk blindness or zero perception of risk (90%)	2. Strengthen close relationships between managers, supervisor and associates.
3. Relationships between managers, immediate supervisor and associates (88%)	3. Retrain and re-building Safety culture.
4. Lacking effort on safety culture improvements (86%)	4. Consider ten aspects for safety culture improvements.
5. Authoritarian/reactive organisation (85%)	5. Building positive organisation.
6. Risk perceptions, risk exposure and risk awareness (84%)	6. Improve risk perceptions and risk awareness.
7. Lacking management visible leadership, corporate tracking, directors regular communication (82%)	7. Focusing on management visible leadership, corporate tracking, directors regular communication.
8. Lacking Safety culture vision and its implementation (80%)	8. Reinforcing safety culture vision and its implementation.
9. Safety performance behaviours not linked to individual KPI (79%)	9. Safety performance behaviours to be linked to individual KPI.
10. Focus on outcomes, not the zero unsafe behaviours goal (78%)	10. Focus on zero unsafe behaviours goal not the outcomes.

CONCLUSIONS, PRACTICAL IMPLICATIONS AND RECOMMENDATIONS

This study (based on the field visits to almost 54 site locations and interactions with 609 managers and 2500 contractors workmen) highlighted the contractors workmen's safety culture issues and solutions as below.

1. Providing portable toilets, and allow holidays like other employees.

2. Strengthen close relationships between managers, immediate supervisor and associates.
3. Retrain and re-building Safety culture.
4. Consider ten aspects for re-building safety culture.
5. Building positive organisation.
6. Improve risk perceptions and risk awareness.
7. Focusing on management visible leadership, corporate tracking, directors regular communication.
8. Reinforcing safety culture vision and its implementation.
9. Safety performance behaviours to be linked to individual KPI.
10. Focus on zero unsafe behaviours goal not the outcomes.

Based on issues and solutions of the contractors workmen's safety culture, the practical implications and recommendations are framed as below.

Safety Culture and Subcontractors: Engineers, vendors, subcontractors in remote areas normally think that safety means only for vehicles, machines, equipment etc whereas the safety culture is about everything in one's life, and they understand it well when it is clarified to them.

It is never late and always a good wisdom for organisation's leadership choosing a planned longterm positive safety and work culture over fires and fatalities, and save people and plants for achieving better economy (Lal, 2023). This can be fast-tracked as follows, by conducting two hours brief to top management, three hours interaction with site heads, one day practical training with site safety culture steering team, monthly progress tracking on behavioural trends, and quarterly monitoring by company director. Focus is on behaviour not outcomes. Sudhir Kumar, safety head of Jindal Steel said, "positive thought and appropriate direction are needed to keep plant safe" with a BBS time commitment of 5 minutes daily of every person on site.

No reason stands valid for doing Non-compliance. Let's employees create an environment of spot-correction and a culture of big brother safety (BBS) with love not reactive behaviour. BBS is accurate, fast and complete solution for behavioural risk control and leading positive safety culture at sites. There is a positive relationship between safety culture and organisational performance, indicating that a more positive perceptions of safety culture by the workers translates into a greater level of safety performance (Davyda, et al., 2023).

As an observation, it is noticed that even the managing directors' circular for 'safety culture' is avoided for compliance, when it is not reinforced by site Head. Hence it is absolutely necessary that site heads reinforce the 'safety culture' which often gets ignored as a normal practice of sites.

Twelve main fundamentals of positive safety culture for workmen are recommended below:

a. Introduce a culture of spot-correction safety. Follow 6Cs.
b. Understand the psychology of at-risk behaviour.
c. Know twelve behaviour observation categories.
d. Practice twelve observers own approach behaviours.
e. Let workmen know What is BBS and what it is not?
f. BBS steering team must function towards interdependent culture.
g. Analyse monthly BBS score.
h. Track behavioural changes each month.
i. Develop an action plan to review weekly progress.
j. Make plant/site rounds for BBS practice by eveyone.
k. BBS shouldn't replace safety systems.
l. Last person must be an observer.

Fatal incident at site: A dumper at site hit the camphor which had overtaken and parked just in front of it, also the camphor was driven by an unauthorised person accompanied by another two persons at the end of their shift who were in a hurry to go home. Three persons were killed on the spot at a mining site by the dumper that could not apply break all of sudden. This was purely an unsafe behaviours that took life of three employees. Standard Operating Procedures (SOPs) must be developed for all critical activities and be shared with the contractors and their workmen. The companies must target zero at-risk behaviours. HODs daily round is absolutely necessary (OISD, 2023).

Corporate unsafe practices: Unsafe behaviour seeps in all corporate practices, eg. any delays in important decisions about safety culture implementation are considered intentional and business delays which must be replaced with immediate corrections. In a positive safety culture, everyone becomes an active observer. Management makes safety culture a mission, review it every month, and reward best observers, says a HR Head, Mr Setty of Lloyd Metals (Figure 4).

प्रशिक्षण शिविर में सुरक्षा नियमों की दी जानकारी

प्रशिक्षण मे शामिल पदाधिकारी व कर्मी.

प्रतिनिधि, हसनपुर

सुरक्षा नियमों का पालन करने के लिए दो दिवसीय प्रशिक्षण शिविर हसनपुर चीनी मिल सभागार में लगाया गया. मौके पर मुंबई सेफ्टी कल्चर के डायरेक्टर डॉ हरिवंश लाल केला ने अधिकारियों एवं कामगारों को व्यावहारिक सुरक्षा के नियमों का पालन करने की जानकारी दी.

उन्होंने कहा कि खुद की सुरक्षा के साथ-साथ साथी कर्मचारियों की सुरक्षा का ध्यान रखें. इसको आपसी तौर पर व्यावहारिक दृष्टिकोण से अपनाने की जरूरत है. फैक्ट्री में कार्य करते समय हेलमेट पहने, सेफ्टी बेल्ट का उपयोग करने की नसीहत दी.

बाइक चलाते समय हेलमेट व मोबाइल पर बात नहीं करने को प्रेरित किया. पहले दिन प्रशिक्षण शिविर में टीकम सिंह, डॉ रामवीर सिंह, पीके गुप्ता, सहायक महाप्रबंधक गन्ना सुग्रीव पाठक, नवाब सिंह, उदय राज, मोहित अवस्थी आदि थे.

Figure 4: Example of corporate safety culture training

Safety Culture and Human Values go together. Fire and fatalities are regularly common on roads and factories of India due to lack of active safety culture, systems and enforcement. Safety reinforcements by government, public and citizens safety groups are the need of the day. An obligation to work safely and keeping employees safe is a direct result of a fundamental human value of caring for people (Berkley, 2020).

Many questions need answers as follow:

- Why some companies lost International business orders due to fatalities at site?

- Why do managers promise emphatically for implementation of safety culture during the training, but later lack energy to implement? Is it due to lack of monitoring by management? Or because management focus more on production targets than safety culture.
- Why do organisations expect international safety culture from local subcontractors-how to build it?
- Leaders at top management are not even aware that people practice reactive safety culture. One of the Executive Directors asked surprisingly, "is anyone reactive here"?
- How to build 5P for positive safety culture: Passion, Patience, Perseverance, Practice, Perfection.

According to Mr Rajeev Afcons Mokama, "definitely providing knowledge, experience and inputs to sub-contractors would help transforming safety culture of the industry globally." Prof Jitendra Mohan said, "I wish our railway and road transport minister, officials and users could follow safety protocols." Ex-GM IOCL Ramdas Jadhav, "In our country, law should be made applicable for each and every industry to follow positive safety culture procedures.

Build risk perceptions among workers like when they enter confined areas where oxygen is less, how they must care. According to a manager, "risk exposure is like being at gunpoint which can be closed with emotional support and connect with workers." BBS is like changing personal nature how to talk, how to behave, using power of listening. Positive safety culture means all come in unity for increasing internal risk control in organisations as per ISO-45003. It depends largely upon how much ready and committed are the organisations? Understanding risk and how it is perceived is a crucial aspect towards creating programs and campaigns to raise awareness and make communities and workplaces safer (The campbell institute, 2017).

Though, construction industry is one of the biggest sectors of employment in India, it is also the second most riskiest, with an average of around 38 fatal accidents a day. Construction in India is a dangerous business. With fatalities on construction sites a daily occurrence, the central and state governments must increase safety inspections and ensure that the workers can access the social security benefits they are entitled to (Bandyopadhyay, 2022).

For building workmen's mindset for safety culture, it is important to know what goes on inside heart of workmen in order to develop bonding and positive safety culture partnership with a sense of connectedness like a family culture of a company. Know the mind of workmen, talk to them. Help each other burning unsafe behaviours, keeping environment safer and healthier. Let people update their positive psychology software/experiences by increasing safety learnings/conversations at site (Lal, 2021). Primary focus must be on workers. Have conversation with workmen after corrections of at-risk behaviors about importance of safe behaviors. The in-charges need to include 'daily BBS observation per employee /workmen' in KRA/objective target (Lal, 2023).

In the last five years, Pune district reported 119 deaths of construction workers, emphasising the issue of worker safety in the real estate business. According to the authorities, the tragedy occurred due to crane and scaffolding failure, as well as the absence or malfunction of safety belts/nets, etc. According to experts, such occurrences highlighted the negligence of contractors as well as the lack of a strong regulatory framework (Deshpande, 2023). As this data reveal clearly that these fatalities happen every month in each constituency of the respective politician, the political parties and government agencies have done almost nothing to stop these incidents. The construction sites should not only be considered as fund raising sources for political parties. They must be reinforced to stop fatalities amongst the contractors workmen by adopting positive safety cultures by the political parties as well as government agencies for enforcement of safety laws.

The number of industry accidents is rising as the services boom. But the industry has hidden safety records with help from its chief regulator (Seth, 2020). Safety professionals from Industry (Personal Communications, 2023) make it clear that most companies focus only on zero fatality, not zero unsafe behaviour or zero incident. In case, fatal incident happens, they can hide it, they can manage it by paying rupees five hundred thousand and gifts to authorities on festivals. If they employ safety experts, it would cost heavily, hence they explore a middle way to manage business first, safety second. In speech expressions, it is safety first, production next. This is a norm for most private an multi-national organisations. The critical question is how to stop these fatal practices so that workers and employees in plants/sites do not lose lives. This paper has thrown light on developing positive safety culture without much financial implications and employee time. Several companies (such as ITC, SAIL, GAIL, ESSAR, RIL, Colourtex, Everest, Galaxy, Reliance Energy,

Ultratech, CFCL, Sandoz, Tata Motors, M&M, BPCL, ONGC, Suzlon, TUV, DNV, Bajaj Auto, Bayer CropScience, Serum, SMC, NPC, GE, IOCL, BHEL, Oil India, Privi, DRB-HICOM, HPCL, HCC, Kalpatru, Torrent, CTEA, Greentech, ICC, Pidilite, Aarti, Volkswagen, Jindal, Sterlite, Vedanta, L&T, RCF, DCM Shriram, Solaris, Agrocel, Piramal, Dorf Ketal, TRL Krosaki, Sembcorp Energy India Ltd, Uflex, Afcons, Hikal, Sunshield, Gunnebo, Amara-Raja, Hindalco, Ampacet Tata Projects, Toyota, NTPC, Vaaman, Baerlocher, Gharda, CPCL, Godrej, Hirschvogel, Asian Paints, Vasudha, ThyssenKrupp, Grasim, OTPC, Birla Sugar, OPaL, NFIL, Thermax, Everest, Toshiba, Kirloskar) achieved almost zero fatalities/reportable incidents over the years by adopting and practicing widely accepted worldwide important tool like positive/supportive safety culture with collective leadership for interdependent work culture by implementing zero-blame zero-harm practices. Supportive safety culture presupposes that we (everyone at workplace) actively care about our people, places and cultures which is a daily journey and practice not a destination (Manufacturing Today, 2022).

REFERENCES

Bandyopadhyay, Orchie. (2022, October 07). *Construction in India: a dangerous business*. https://www.britsafe.in/safety-management-news/2022/construction-in-india-a-dangerous-business

Berkley. (2020, April 21). *Fundamental Human Value*: Safety. https://www.berkindcomp.com/blog/fundamental-human-value-safety/

Cooper, D. (2006).The impact of management's commitment on employee behaviour: A field study. ASSE- 0307-013. American Society of Safety Engineers Middle East Chapter 7th Professional Development Conference & Exhibition Kingdom of Bahrain, March 18-22, 2006.

Davyda M. Hammond, Adrienne L. King, Margaux Joe, Jeffrey R. Miller. (2023). Understanding the relationship between safety culture and safety performance indicators in U.S. nuclear waste cleanup operations, *Safety Science*, 166,106241, ISSN 0925-7535, https://doi.org/10.1016/j.ssci.2023.106241.

Deshpande, Shrinivas. (2023 Sep 19). 119 construction workers died at construction sites. https://www.hindustantimes.com/cities/pune-news/119-construction-workers-died-at-construction-sites-101695146839777.html

Ek, Åsa & Runefors, Marcus & Borell, Jonas. (2014). Relationships between safety culture aspects – A work process to enable interpretation. Marine Policy. 44. 179–186. 10.1016/j.marpol.2013.08.024.

Hasse Nordlöf, Birgitta Wiitavaara, Ulrika Winblad, Katarina Wijk, Ragnar Westerling. (2015). Safety culture and reasons for risk-taking at a large steel-manufacturing company: Investigating the worker perspective, *Safety Science*, 73, 126-135, ISSN 0925-7535, https://doi.org/10.1016/j.ssci.2014.11.020

Hsu, Shang Hwa. (2012). Safety Management in a Relationship-Oriented Culture. *International Journal of Occupational Safety and Ergonomics* (JOSE) Vol. 18, (1), 35–45.

Lal H. (2021). Behavioural economics of safety culture management in companies. *WSJ*, 30(4).

Lal, Harbans (2022). Leadership Attributes for Corporate Safety Culture. *International Journal on Leadership*, 10 (2), 2022,14-21. http://publishingindia.com/ijl/

Lal H. (2022a). Fast-track industry safety culture and re- duction of incidents/losses. WSJ. 31 (1).

Lal Harbans and Choueiri E.M. (2023). The integration of behavior-based safety (BBS) as a company value is advocated! *World Safety Journal (WSJ)*, 32 (2), Page 49-55. doi.org/10.5281/zenodo.8105788

Lal, H. (2023). Strengthening a positive safety culture despite underlying fear and peer pressure. World Safety Journal, 32(1), 57–64. https://doi.org/10.5281/zenodo.7770080

Manufacturing Today. (2022, July, 22). 123 Indian companies receive the International Safety Award https://www.manufacturingtodayindia.com/sectors/123-indian-companies-receive-the-international-safety-award

OISD. (2023). Fatal incident at Depot construction site. Oil Industry Safety Directorate. https://www.oisd.gov.in

Paek, Hye-Jin and Hove, Thomas. (2017, March 29). Risk Perceptions and Risk Characteristics. https://doi.org/10.1093/acrefore/9780190228613.013.283

Paliath, Shreehari. (2023, Jan, 21). 3 Workers Die Every Day In Indian Factories, Govt Data Show. https://www.indiaspend.com/special-reports/3-workers-die-every-day-in-indian-factories-govt-data-show-850083

Patel, Dilipkumar Arvindkumar and Jha Kumar Neeraj. (2016). AN ESTIMATE OF FATAL ACCIDENTS IN INDIAN CONSTRUCTION. https://www.researchgate.net/figure/State-wise-estimate-of-average-annual-fatal-accidents-in-Indian-construction-sector-from_fig1_308155592

Personal Communications. (2023). Interactions with Dr Anil Jain, Mr Sudhir Kumar.

Quality Safety Edge. (2023). Visible Safety Leadership. https://www.qualitysafetyedge.com/customized-solutions/visible-safety-leadership

Shukla, Archana. (2022, Sept 5). Workplace accidents: Inside India's 'factories of death'. https://www.bbc.com/news/world-asia-india-62631699

Seth, Rosenfeld. (2020, July 1). California Agency Is Hiding Uber and Lyft Accident Reports. https://www.sfpublicpress.org/california-agency-is-hiding-uber-and-lyft-accident-reports/

Thraen, Iona. (2022 Apr. 4). Moving from Reactive to Proactive: Safety 2.0. https://accelerate.uofuhealth.utah.edu/improvement/moving-from-reactive-to-proactive-safety-2-0

The Campbell Institute. (2017, May). Risk Perception: Theories, Strategies, And Next Steps. thecampbellinstitute.org https://www.thecampbellinstitute.org › 2017/05

Tekmon (2023). What are Safety KPIs? https://tekmon.com/top-7-safety-key-performance-indicators-kpis/

Wilson, Carla. (2023, Oct 18). Flush toilets will be required at large construction sites. https://www.timescolonist.com/local-news/flush-toilets-will-be-required-at-large-construction-sites-7699229

Wilson Perumal. (2023). *Zero safety incidents should not be your goal.* https://www.wilsonperumal.com/blog/blog/zero-safety-incidents-should-not-be-your-goal

World Steel Association. (2022). *Safety culture and leadership fundamentals*. Retrieved from https://worldsteel.org/ safety-culture-and-leadership-fundamentals/

CHAPTER 5

EXPLORING GLOBAL STANDARDS OF SAFETY CULTURE FOR WORKFORCE AND BUSINESS PERSPECTIVES

It would be much better, economical, and easier to develop global standards of safety culture for manpower and business perspectives, than having an incident without a resilient strong culture, and get questioned for years on by the courts, media, public, politician and so on. This paper explored global standards of safety culture for manpower and business perspectives. Based on a longitudinal action survey, literature reviews, the field visits to nearly 75 project site locations in India in the year 2022-23 and interactions with a sample of 400 managers brought out the qualitative data categorized into five themes. Action plan to implement global standards of safety culture is suggested as follows: Safety professionals should consider evaluating their individual capacity, and that of the institutions for promoting safety culture, Work on corporate safety mindset as much as safety culture behaviors; Measuring roles of management leadership in sustaining safety culture; Safety culture to be a safety management practice more than as a safety leadership tool; Practice ethics of safety and risk science; Benchmarking in terms of behaviouralization of safety systems; Equality of respect for lowest level workers in terms of cultural safety; Safety culture to be built on safety science as well the risk science; Build positive safety culture as well as positive organization; and Safety culture to be an essential part of business strategic goal. Finally, the global standards are available, what is lacking is "awareness and implementation of the standards" including integrity, ethical values, and actions of all concerned and all involved in the bringing up the safety culture.

Keywords: Business, Global Standards, Manpower, Safety Culture.

INTRODUCTION

What parents demonstrated; their children followed. Similarly what managers demonstrate, their staff and rest of manpower would follow. This makes a beginning of any company standards to practice. Every organization has a deeper side of safety culture which depicts its history of reacting or responding to safety issues of employees and the company business. A corporate HSE head shouted at some colleagues for not demonstrating progress as desired and said, "shut up, it is not accepted". Obviously, this aggressive behaviour is not acceptable to anyone for any work scenario.

The recent research indicates the following highlights on global standards of safety culture:

- Contemplate common challenges, approaches, and mistakes that safety professionals and organizations make when working cross culturally and learn how to identify and avoid these mistakes (Flynn, et al., 2018).
- Boyce (2018) observed that reward behaviors, not outcomes, to Get the Most Value from Safety Incentives. Most organizations would be interested in safety outcomes which are achievable by behavioral science approach implementation.
- Safety culture development depends upon an employee learning from behavioral intervention outcomes, conducive enabling factors, and consistency over time. This framework guides actions to understand and develop safety culture in practice and lends a foundation for advancing the complex cognitive, dynamic processes involved in safety culture development (Bisbey, et al., 2019).
- Significant safety performance improvement cannot be achieved unless human and organizational factors are considered (Sang, 2020).
- Resilience in organizational safety culture is what is needed in today's dynamic work environment. The three sub-systems of resilience safety culture are psychological, behavioral, and managerial capabilities, which in turn are inter-related (Garg & Mohamed, 2020).
- Poor leadership that are prevalent in many organizations prevent employees from speaking up against poor safety practices (Claxton, et al., 2021).
- Proper communication accompanied by appropriate documentation assists the teams working on a common project to achieve the project target on time (Kumbhar, et al., 2021).
- Companies that can convey care, compassion, and a desire for everyone to go home safe at night will have a better response than those that solely deliver a message of restrictions or punishment for missing the target mark (SSOE, 2021).

- The management should continuously monitor and evaluate their strategies while delivering multifaceted interventions to be more specifically focused and to motivate workers to be enthusiastic in sustaining safety culture (Wong, et al., 2021).
- Employees' safety remains one of the priorities. This goes without saying, and it will be one of the leading manufacturing trends in 2023 (Miller, 2022).
- Eliminating fatalities and serious injuries is the main challenge for the global industry. Focus is to provide the industry with actionable recommendations and passionate leadership guidance to create safer and healthier workplaces (World Steel Association, 2022).
- Company leaders that want to be compliant will never get there unless they have a paradigm shift and understand that being compliant is the absolute bare minimum you need to do. If you want to be excellent then it takes enthusiastic commitment from all levels of leadership. (Hatfield, 2023).
- Having a resilient safety culture means continuously improving processes by committed staff who systematically cope with the complexity and unpredictability of today's business environment (MDPI, 2023).
- Progress in positive safety culture is possible over the years of continuity and patience. SEIL completed 6 years of journey and achieved 97% of safety behaviors (SEIL, 2023).
- Policies on employee safety and provision of appropriate equipment that reduce the frequency of accidents, illnesses, and injuries should be the priority of management (Aitaa & Owusu-Antwi, 2023).

OBJECTIVE

To explore global standards of safety culture for manpower and business perspectives and suggest action plan to implement global standards of safety culture in organizations.

METHOD

This article is an interim paper extracted from a longitudinal action survey on nation-wide implementation of safety culture in organizations. The literature reviews, field visits to nearly 75 project site locations in India in the year 2022-23 and interactions with a sample of 400 managers brought out the following results of the qualitative data categorized here below into five themes.

RESULTS AND DISCUSSION

Think of the safety culture of Global Standards for manpower and business perspectives for your organizations: how to achieve it Safety professionals of Tata Projects, Afcons, Sembcorp and many others mentioned the following several ways to achieve the safety culture of global standards:

- First, the senior management must make their mindset and thoughts in line with the Global standards with a concept of "People Matter Most".
- That's an ongoing thought for action always in true safety professional's mind who are passionate bringing a change at workplace.
- Implementation of culture of 4-C: Caring, connecting with manpower, correcting on the spot, and conversations about the risks control.
- HODs to add safety objectives to their departmental and individual goals and give the inputs to Head Safety while setting the SHE goals.
- Safety should always be driven in the organization as core Culture and paramount of business.
- 3P module (Plan, Prevent and Protect) shall be followed by everyone.
- Involvement of top management during safety HIRA preparation, walk downs, MRM, SHE events, audits, safety address, attending TBT, training program, interaction with workmen representatives, rewards, and recognition program.
- Safety leadership walks shall be done on specified topics like collecting observations of behavioral aspects of the workforce, human errors, high risk activity.
- Incident learning, reporting and incident investigation by top management.
- Removing barriers between top management and workers like designation, qualification, casteism, religion, positions so that workers may interact freely during meetings with top management.
- Providing training and skills development programs.
- Health and Safety culture survey to be conducted with implementation of action plan.

- BBS based practices slides to be incorporated in MIS and discuss review meeting.
- Engagement of workers representatives during audits, meetings and other SHE events.
- Implementation of reverse TBT process.
- Initiate awareness campaigns on monthly basis like NMR Campaign, BBS month, mental health and hygiene month etc.
- Integration of EHS in all aspects of business process.
- Connect workforce and potential incident awareness to be addressed by top management.
- Safety perception survey with action plan to be conducted.
- Counseling of workforce by his superior on health, personal, careers, stress management, work life balance matters.
- Training calendar to be developed based on NMR, FAC, HIRA, MS, audit, and inspection outcomes.
- Measuring and monitoring process to be enhanced.
- Safety always should be considered as a ONE Team One Voice.
- Conduct tabletop exercise, developing business resilience, continuity, and recovery plans.
- Strategic assessment, change management, benchmarking process shall be enhanced.
- Safety is not a domain; it is a proactive culture of organization.

The Chief Project manager said, "I used reactive and dependent safety cultures, and didn't know about independent and interdependent safety cultures." Project management consultants said, "Tata management asked me to implement interdependent safety culture so as to prevent any at-risk behaviors that are prevalent at projects sites, so that it doesn't impact their brand value". The senior most people must involve in safety culture so that it becomes a work culture. The safety Head said, "Safety culture observers must give technical explanations also while doing corrections at site". The observers must feel that 'they are somewhat important" in framing the safety culture. The sub-contractor's role in safety culture cannot be underestimated.

Five themes were explored based as below on the qualitative data:

1. What are the global standards of a positive safety culture for an organization?

2. What are the standards of a positive safety culture for an organization that need to be discerned to decide the benchmarking in terms of behaviouralization of safety systems?
3. Are organizations doing their job of evolving positive safety culture?
4. Positive safety culture or Positive Organization.
5. Strategies to stabilizing Safety-Business Culture Relationship in Corporates.

All the above five factors are interconnected and drive the participation and responsiveness of employees into safety culture initiatives of their companies. These aspects would undoubtedly impact the corporates business sustainability in the interest of their stakeholders.

What are the Global Standards of a Positive Safety Culture for an Organization?

Business leaders' involvement is useful for creating a positive safety culture (Dahl, et al., 2022). The research shows that four themes are prevalent in the existing literature: 1) unique challenges entail a need for situated applications, 2) models developed to operationalize safety culture, 3) measuring safety culture, and 4) safety management and leadership as key factors (Berglund, et al., 2023). The safety professionals should consider evaluating their individual capacity, and that of the institutions they represent, to promote safety in cross-cultural settings (Flynn, et al., 2018). Industry should push for a culture change in 2023 regarding the way that risks to workers' health, safety, and wellbeing are managed (Kamarajan, 2023). CEOs need to write and speak in a way that ensures their company's commitment to a strong safety culture as key strategic elements of their business model (Craig & Amernic, 2023).

The Standards of a Positive Safety Culture for an Organization that need to be Discerned to decide the Benchmarking in terms of Behaviouralization of Safety Systems

Unless efforts are made to understand and alter cultural drivers and share these findings within and across industries, the same accidents are likely to continue to occur (Emily, et al., 2021). Leaders, at all levels, need to understand the range of health and safety risks in their part of the organization and to give proportionate attention to each of them (Health and Safety Executive, 2022). The research showed that the more deeply people sense safety leadership, the clearer their risk perception will be and the more helpful it would be in achieving safety performance (Siao-Yun & Kuo Yen-Ku, 2023). Leaders must facilitate behaviouralization of safety systems.

Are Organisations doing their Job of Evolving Positive Safety Culture?

Are organisations doing their job of evolving positive safety culture, is it a matter of real concern? How we can make further sense of the safety culture concept in safety and risk management. Safety culture is here understood as shared beliefs, norms, values, practices, and structures, with respect to safety, in an organization. We argue that risk science (interpreted in its broadest sense to also include safety science) provides important reference points for what these beliefs, norms, values, and practices should be. For example, risk science highlights that complexity needs to be acknowledged and confronted by resilience-based strategies, in addition to the use of risk assessments. A safety culture which is not built on the state of the art of the risk science cannot be considered 'good' (Terje & Marja, 2021). Transparency, honesty, and genuineness are key factors to be followed. Evaluating the just culture, the safety culture of the employees of the organization can be predicted with a high level of certainty, which shows the direct relationship between the just culture and the safety culture. So, increasing the just culture directly contributes to the development of the safety culture (Shabani, *et al.*, 2019).

Positive Safety Culture or Positive Organization

Positive safety culture is a real-time intervention that provides measurable outcomes, transformational work experiences, activated leadership, empowered employees (ILO, 2017). Positive safety culture or Positive organization or both, as because the positive safety culture shall sustain only in a Positive organization. Negative work culture triggers negative safety culture. Ten factors that promote negative safety culture are: lack of leadership buy-in, poor communication between departments, underreporting and misreporting, lack of employee engagement, negative feedback from employees, high accident rates, double standards in place, traditional and conservative mindsets, stubborn employees or managers, cost cutting and profit maximization (Rigid Lifelines, 2023). These negatives serve as signals or a wake-up call, highlighting potential areas of concern that require immediate attention and improvement (Javed, 2023).

When we talk about the positive safety culture or positive organization, it is equally beneficial to know the negatives in the organization or in the company's culture, so that we can fix and focus to remove them, to rebuild a robust culture of the organization. After positive safety intervention, cultural maturity gradually turns towards independent or interdependent over a period (Lal, 2021).

Stabilizing Safety-Business Culture Relationship in Corporates: Mulling Strategies

Companies have given contract workmen a place to work, but not a place in their hearts. This disconnect creates a hurdle in safety culture transformation as well as business sustainability. Moreover, safety celebrations and strong safety culture must go together, merely celebrations do not assure that incidents and accidents are being under control. Mostly celebrations are just a show-off, or to convince the client or customers. If you put good people in bad systems, you get bad results (Safety Culture Team, 2021). At times, employees have felt psychologically unsafe, alienated, helpless, psychological loneliness, and so on (Siddiqui & Sangwan 2022). Remove negative behaviors: don't react, blame, shout, reprimand.

The Campbell Institute believed that EHS is at the core of business vitality and is intrinsic to operational excellence and financial performance for organizations of all sizes and businesses to achieve and sustain excellence (The Campbell Institute, 2022).

Profit oriented organizations grow slower than the safety-oriented organizations, and vice versa. A culture focused on safety directly correlates with business performance. "When workers are getting hurt, it's a sign that things aren't going right," says David Michaels, eight-year OSHA Assistant Secretary of Labor, whose work focuses on helping companies be "safe, productive, and profitable at the same time." In other words, safety isn't a discrete issue for companies: it's actually a key performance indicator of an organization's overall operational effectiveness (Blackline Safety, 2021).

A business that has a poor safety culture won't just sacrifice its profits; it will also put human lives at stake. A missing or lacking safety culture may lead to concerns such as increased injuries and deaths and more legal issues (RUPERT, 2023).

CONCLUSIONS

There is a significant role of employee engagement in promoting a positive safety culture and which has the potential to develop sustainable economies and business success in enterprises, particularly given the high rates of work-related injuries in developing countries (Abeje & Luo, 2023). The following global standards of safety culture (Table 1) for manpower and business perspectives are suggested as an action plan to implement based on literature reviews and industry practices.

Table 1: Action plan to implement global standards of safety culture

1. Safety professionals should consider evaluating their individual capacity, and that of the institutions for promoting safety culture.
2. Measuring roles of management leadership in sustaining safety culture.
3. Safety culture to be a safety management practice more than as a safety leadership tool
4. Practice ethics of safety and risk science.
5. Benchmarking in terms of behaviouralization of safety systems
6. Equality of respect for lowest level workers in terms of cultural safety.
7. Safety culture to be built on safety science as well the risk science.
8. Build positive safety culture as well as positive organization.
9. Work on corporate safety mindset as much as safety culture behaviors.
10. Safety culture is an essential part of business strategic goal.

To initiate this above action plan, we must begin to piece together the positives and negatives of the existing work culture in its realism that drives the corporate mindset for safety culture. The safety professionals of the company must spend a long time in safety culture implementation along with experts or mentors to enhance personal capabilities so that they can help their company in transformation. The safety leadership steering team is required to spend sufficient time every month and work on the weak points of the culture (Williamsen, 2021). Lazar and Chithra (2022) revealed a major benefit of incorporating cultural elements is sustainable behavioral change, so consideration of culture as a dimension helps accomplish sustainable business development. It is recommended that the organization sets up a multidisciplinary steering team, coordinated by a safety culture initiative leader (Manufacturing Safety Alliance of BC, 2022). The responsible leaders can enforce and implement safety standards in the organization through policy making, planning, training, and communication (Saleem & Malik, 2022). The challenge to industry is that the leaders as key players deliver time for driving change (Hackitt, 2022). The board of directors must provide active and visible leadership and direction on occupational health and safety (Health and Safety Executive, 2022a). The global employers' thinktank and networks on OHS scenarios is highly recommended.

Business is difficult when you don't care what you should be caring for in it, that is safety culture. That's what the struggle of organizations is between culture1 and culture2. Culture1 is before transformation to the global standards of safety culture, which keeps hindering while developing the culture2 which is a global standard in terms of safety culture defined or set goals for by the company. The managers need to understand gradually that they need to have tremendous patience in the change processes between these two cultures happening. If they lose faith or patience in the safety culture processes, it would be harder to sustain the safety culture transformation and/ or the business sustainability. Continued planned safety culture interventions are helpful in this direction.

Let's look beyond the borders of organizations which means that all global standards or global HSE institutions essentially assert that all citizens to be safe at work, and that is achievable when all companies, individuals, governments work together to enforce and reinforce all that matters here. Organizations that make families of employees/workers come together to work for a cause must be always safe, at every cost and in all respects. They have a right to be safe which must be protected by one and all, so that no one sheds tears for an injury or fatality that happens at workplace incident. The employers, managers, co-workers, factory inspectors don't take actions required as part of their jobs, as if an injury or fatality is not enough in someone's life that can traumatize family members. What must be reviewed is that global standards are available, what is missing is "awareness and implementation of the standards", including integrity, ethical values, and actions of all concerned and all involved in the bringing up the safety culture (British Standards Institution, 2022). Like a good science does not believe that safety culture is a product, but organizations keep on learning new ways to instill safer environments. The organization must test and validate all hypotheses that would bring up a positive work culture, and not play up with the lives of employees to avoid any of those actions necessary. Avoiding necessary actions or being unaware are intentional and purposeful acts and cannot be justified for any injury to a worker. By employing someone, an organization shouldn't take an employee to guarantee his/her safety. Company Directors must answer this lack of business ethics and integrity. A fatality in an accident kills one person but it does postmortem of so many for not saving life of a person at workplace. It raises several queries. Can we state that some companies are a serial killer in a way that over the years many workers are killed at their work sites, simply because they wanted a job to earn a livelihood for a family? Can we state that companies do not value integrity and ethics so much? Can we state that companies are not truly ready to implement supportive safety cultures? And more such questions. A culture of integrity and accountability for HSE needs to be fostered for all in organizations. Foster a corporate culture that promotes ethical practices, customer focus, service and encourages individual integrity. Integrity in a workplace is not just the responsibility of leaders, it is important that it is everyone's responsibility (OAG, 2018).

ACKNOWLEDGMENT

Contribution of industry professionals is thankfully acknowledged.

REFERENCES

Abeje, M. & Luo, F. (2023). The influence of safety culture and climate on safety performance: mediating role of employee engagement in manufacturing enterprises in Ethiopia, *Sustainability,* 15, 11274. https://doi.org/10.3390/su151411274

Aitaa, S. K. & Owusu-Antwi, J. N. (2023). Imprint of occupational health and safety conditions on employee commitment: a case study of toyota tsusho corporation, *European Journal of Human Resource*, 7(1):1-16. https://doi.org/10.47672/ejh.1338

Berglund, L., Johansson, J., Johansson, M., Nygren, M. & Stenberg, M. (2023). Exploring safety culture research in the construction industry, *Work*, 1-12. 10.3233/WOR-220214.

Bisbey, T., Kilcullen, M., Thomas, E., Ottosen, M., Tsao, K. & Salas, E. (2019). Safety culture: an integration of existing models and a framework for understanding its development. human factors, *The Journal of the Human Factors and Ergonomics Society,* 63, 001872081986887. https://doi.org/10.1177/0018720819868878.

Blackline Safety. (2021). A guide to integrating safety throughout your oil and gas organization. https://www.blacklinesafety.com/blog/integrating-safety-throughout-your-oil-and-gas-organization

Boyce, T. E. (2018). Safety culture and behavioral safety. https://ehsdailyadvisor.blr.com/2016/08/reward-behaviors-not-outcomes-get-value-safety-incentives/

British Standards Institution. (2022). How an organization's values impact food safety culture. https://www.bsigroup.com/en-NZ/blog/food-industry-blog-news/safety-culture-values/

Claxton, G., Hosie, P. & Sharma, P. (2021). Toward an effective occupational health and safety culture: A multiple stakeholder perspective, *Journal of Safety Research,* 82. https://doi.org/10.1016/j.jsr.2022.04.006.

Russell, C. & Amernic, J. (2023). Using "CEO-speak" to prioritize a safety culture. https://www.emerald.com/insight/content/doi/10.1108/SL-03-2023-0033/full/html

Dahl, Ø., Rundmo, T. & Olsen, E. (2022). The impact of business leaders' formal health and safety training on the establishment of robust occupational safety and health management systems: three studies based on data from labor inspections, *Int J Environ Res Public Health,*19(3):1269. https://doi.org/10.3390/ijerph19031269. PMID: 35162292; PMCID: PMC8834684.

Emily, J. T., Katie, A. G., Ann, L. P., Sandra, C. D., Vic, P. & Tammy, R. E. (2021). Safety culture: a retrospective analysis of occupational health and safety mining reports, *Safety and Health at Work,* 12(2):201-208, ISSN 2093-7911, https://doi.org/10.1016/j.shaw.2020.12.001.

Flynn, M., Castellanos, E. & Flores-Andrade, A. (2018). Safety across cultures: understanding the challenges, *Professional Safety,* 63, 28-32.

Garg, A. & Mohamed, S. (2020). Resilient safety culture: A modelling perspective. https://www.researchgate.net/publication/340395615_Resilient_safety_culture_A_modelling_perspective

Hackitt, D. J. (2022). Building safety: the industry safety steering group's third report for the secretary of state and the minister for building safety. https://www.gov.uk/government/publications/industry-safety-steering-group-third-report-on-culture-change-in-the-built-environment-industry/building-safety-the-industry-safety-steering-groups-third-report-for-the-secretary-of-state-and-the-minister-for-building-safety

Hatfield, G. (2023). Faces of EHS: Safety Culture in 2023 - EHS Daily Advisor (blr.com)

Health and Safety Executive. (2022). Leading and managing for health and safety. https://www.hse.gov.uk/managing/leading.htm

Health and Safety Executive. (2022a). RR450 - Case studies that identify and exemplify boards of directors who provide leadership and direction on occupational health and safety. https://www.hse.gov.uk/research/rrhtm/rr450.htm

ILO. (2017). International Occupational Safety and Health Conference 2017. https://www.ilo.org/wcmsp5/groups/public/---ed_protect/---ProTrav/---safework/documents/presentation/wcms_606677.pdf

Javed, B. (2023). 40 Negative indicators of health and safety culture. https://www.hseblog.com/negative-indicators-of-health-and-safety-culture-at-workplace/

Kamarajan, M. (2023). Improving construction safety in 2023. https://timesofindia.indiatimes.com/blogs/voices/improving-construction-safety-in-2023/

Kumbhar, G., Ahuja, B. & Rajhans, N. (2021). Documentation techniques to avoid delays in project. https://www.researchgate.net/publication/352762125_Documentation_Techniques_to_Avoid_Delays_in_Project

Lal, H. (2021). Behavioral economics of safety culture management in companies. *WSJ,* 30(4).

Lazar, N. & Chithra, K. (2022). Role of culture in sustainable development and sustainable built environment: A review, *Environ Dev Sustain,* 24, 5991–6031. https://doi.org/10.1007/s10668-021-01691-8

Manufacturing Safety Alliance of BC. (2022). Safety Culture: A guide to effective measurement and improvement. https://safetyalliancebc.ca/wp-content/uploads/guidebook/11865/Safety-Culture-Model.pdf

MDPI. (2023). Special Issue - Resilient Safety Culture. https://www.mdpi.com/journal/safety/special_issues/resilient_safety_culture

Miller, L. (2022). Big ways the manufacturing industry will change in 2023. (ideasplusbusiness.com)

OAG. (2018). The Integrity Workplace. https://oag.parliament.nz/++theme++oag2018/static/integrity-workplace/link.html

Rigid Lifelines. (2023). https://www.rigidlifelines.com/blog/10-signs-that-your-organization-might-have-a-negative-safety-culture/

Rupert, J. (2023). Understanding the true cost of a poor workplace safety culture. https://ohsonline.com/articles/2023/04/17/understanding-the-true-cost-of-a-poor-workplace-safety-culture.aspx

Safety Culture Team. (2021). Top 20+ safety quotes to improve your safety culture. https://blog.safetyculture.com/industry-trends/top-20-safety-quotes-improve-safety-culture

Saleem, F.; Malik, M.I. (2022). Safety Management and Safety Performance Nexus: Role of Safety Consciousness, Safety Climate, and Responsible Leadership. *Int. J. Environ. Res. Public Health* 2022, 19, 13686. https://doi.org/10.3390/ijerph192013686

Sang, X. (2020). Analysis on the path of safety culture innovation in foshan manufacturing industry. https://doi.org/10.2991/aebmr.k.201111.010.

Shabani Arani, M., Tabatabaei, S. & Mansouri, N. Prediction of safety culture based on of dimensions of just culture in of one of the industrial sections of Tehran, *Iran J Ergon,* 7(1)63-72. http://journal.iehfs.ir/article-1-543-en.html

Siddiqui, S. & Sangwan, A. (2022). The catalytic role of perceived psychological safety on the relationship between 'support from supervisor' and 'workplace loneliness', *Journal of Positive School Psychology,* 6(6)8401-8412.

Terje, A. & Marja, Y. (2021). How risk science can help us establish a good safety culture, *Journal of Risk Research,* 24(11):1349-1367. https://doi.org/10.1080/13669877.2020.1871056

The Campbell Institute. (2022). Defining EHS leadership in world class organizations. https://www.thecampbellinstitute.org/wp-content/uploads/2017/05/Campbell-Institute-Defining-EHS-Leadership-WP.pdf

SEIL. (2023). Behavior Based Safety (BBS) Implemented at SEIL. https://www.sembcorpenergyindia.com/CSR/BBS

Siao-Yun, W. & Yen-Ku, K. (2023). The relationship among safety leadership, risk perception, safety culture, and safety performance: Military volunteer soldiers as a case study, *Frontiers in Psychology,* 14. https://doi.org/10.3389/fpsyg.2023.1000331

SSOE. (2021). Creating a positive safety culture. https://www.ssoe.com/creating-a-positive-safety-culture-2/

Williamsen, M. (2021). Delivering safety excellence: engagement culture at every level, John Wiley & Sons.

Wong, S. Y., Fu, A. C. L., Han, J., Lin, J. & Lau, M. C. (2021). Effectiveness of customized safety intervention programs to increase the safety culture of hospital staff, *BMJ Open Qual,* 10(4):e000962. https://doi.org/10.1136/bmjoq-2020-000962. PMID: 34625426; PMCID: PMC8504354.

World Steel Association. (2022). Safety culture and leadership fundamentals. https://worldsteel.org/safety-culture-and-leadership-fundamentals/

CHAPTER

6

WHY DON'T EMPLOYEES RESPOND TO SAFETY CULTURE INTERVENTION: FINDING SOLUTIONS WITHIN

Safety Culture Intervention (SCI) revolves around 3As: awareness, analysis, and action which are essentially interdependent for its success in achieving increased employee participation in safety culture. However, the question often arises among corporations as to why don't employees respond to SCI? Is it that managers of employees don't reinforce the SCI? In this regard, this study's findings indicate the following seven factors: the managers don't visit the site for the safe care of people, the philosophy of corporate safety culture can be questioned, company is focusing more on production targets than safety implementation, minimum safety culture implementation is carried out, the reactive /dependent safety culture is being practiced, project timelines are delayed and lacking safety reinforcements. These seven factors are inter-connected and drive the non-participation and non-responsiveness of employees in safety culture initiatives of their companies. These observations unquestionably impact the corporates' business sustainability in the interest of their stakeholders. This article is part of a longitudinal national action survey including field visits to nearly 100 project site locations in India and interactions with more than a sample of 600 managers presented the qualitative data categorized here into seven themes. These factors do reflect the corporate mindset of safety culture. Managers need to be aware of and understand the interactive nature of these safety culture drivers. Besides several suggestions, the daily safety conversations, and spot-corrections by employees/ workers in their work areas would make a deeper sense in building a positive and supportive safety culture.

Keywords: Employees, Safety, Culture, Intervention.

INTRODUCTION

Positive safety culture brings up the brand value of corporates, whereas a poor safety culture affects the brand value of corporates negatively due to non-compliance behaviours (Lal and Choueiri, 2023). People grow up with the behaviors as they do. According to Sembcorp (SEIL, 2023), it all

7. Lacking safety reinforcements at 70% locations

Reward and recognition of employees' participation in safety culture is one of the key drivers. Companies that lack safety reinforcements find employees not responding to safety culture interventions. Companies like SEIL that promote safety reinforcements get their employees to participate in safety initiatives (Figures 4, 5). Festival of Rakshya bandhan were observed as surakshya bandhan at PPL plant along with mass safety gathering, inauguration of monthly safety theme banner in presence of senior executives, contract workers, visitors, and stake holders. 30th August every year, is a "Suraksha Rakhi Festival" that the BBS observers promise to each other at sites for actively caring and ensuring zero-harm. Thyssenkrupp says that we do it at our sites since last 5 years.

Figure 4: safety reinforcements through festivals celebrating in plant.

Figure 5: safety reinforcements through festivals celebrating in plant.

CONCLUSION

A poor safety culture affects the brand value of corporates negatively due to non-compliance behaviours, whereas a positive safety culture brings up the brand value of corporates. The company leaders need orientation and re-orientation to remain focused. The question often arises as to why don't some employees respond to the safety culture intervention? The findings indicate the following seven factors: the managers don't visit the site for safety care of people, the philosophy of corporate safety culture does not support, company is focusing more on production targets than safety implementation, minimum safety culture implementation is carried out, the reactive/dependent safety culture is being practiced, project timelines are delayed and lacking safety reinforcements. Daily safety conversations and corrections by employees/ workers make a deeper sense on building positive and supportive safety culture.

HSE professionals suggested the following actions:

- Include BBS in daily TBT with positive care at sites. Have conversation with workmen after corrections of at-risk behaviors about importance of safe behaviors. BBS round to site for all employees is compulsory whether they are from office, operations, quality, maintenance, environment and so on. Project clients should not convey safety compliance by letters but be a partner in daily observation and spot-correction. A client says, "when there is a correction, there is no need for letter of compliance". Safety culture behaviors must be reflected in company's HSE policy and banners displays at plant/ site areas. Workers even don't know how much risk they are exposed to at projects site. "We need safety culture, but we often neglect", an Operations manager opened during the training. Daily safety conversations and corrections by employees/ workers make a deeper sense on building positive and supportive safety culture. Progress in positive safety culture is possible over the years of continuity and patience. SEIL completed 6 years of journey and achieved 97% of safety behaviors (SEIL, 2023).
- A mother can give birth to a few children, but a safety professional can give birth to unlimited safe brothers and sisters. Be polite, patient, and connected with the workforce to bring a revolutionary result. Safety culture means caring for each other with human connection. Corporate review should include one slide on BBS in MIS to reflect on a positive safety

culture. BBS to be integrated with MIS, HSE policy, KPI and Directors' quarterly review. Consider key areas like challenges and solutions to ensure safe working, management response to bad safety outcomes decides psychological safety. focusing on what failed instead of who failed, safety evolution in an organization, and recognizing observers for safety culture transformation, so that the best observers from every plant/site can be rewarded. Boyce (2018) observed that reward behaviors, not outcomes, to Get the Most Value from Safety Incentives. Most organisations would be interested in safety outcomes which are achievable by behavioral science approach implementation. The management should continuously monitor and evaluate their strategies while delivering multifaceted interventions to be more specifically focused and to motivate workers to be enthusiastic in sustaining a safety culture (Wong, et al., 2021).

- The seven findings of this study are inter-connected and boost the non-participation and non-responsiveness of employees in safety culture initiatives of their companies. The corporates must take serious note of these observations as they unquestionably impact the business sustainability in the interest of their stakeholders. This research lays an important tool in the hands of managers to exercise as to why employees don't speak up or care for the safety and health of each other as part of their work culture and save colleagues from injury. These factors do reflect the corporate mindset of safety culture (Table 1) which directly or indirectly governs the safety decisions-making process of organizations. Managers need to be aware of and understand the interactive nature of these safety culture drivers. Quite often, safety behaviors are guided by these corporate mindsets. Hence safety culture is a thought process of an organization that needs a planned intervention for change of employee safety behaviors considering implementation of the results of this research. This corporate mindset or thought process seems to be sort of invisible side of safety culture, but that also gets reflected and discussed during the implementation process of such behavioral intervention. Safety culture development depends upon an employee learning from behavioral intervention outcomes, conducive enabling factors, and consistency over time. This framework guides actions to understand and develop safety culture in practice and lends a foundation for advancing the complex cognitive, dynamic processes involved in safety culture development (Bisbey, et al., 2019).

Table 1: The corporate mindset of safety culture

1. Managers don't visit the site for safety care of people (86%)
2. Philosophy of corporate safety culture does not support (83%)
3. Companies focusing more on production targets than safety implementation (81%)
4. Minimum safety culture implementation is carried out (79%)
5. Reactive/dependent safety culture is being practiced (77%)
6. Delayed project timelines (72%)
7. Lacking safety reinforcements (70%)

REFERENCES

Bisbey, Tiffany, Kilcullen, Molly, Thomas, Eric, Ottosen, Madelene, Tsao, Kuojen & Salas, Eduardo. (2019). Safety Culture: An Integration of Existing Models and a Framework for Understanding Its Development. Human Factors: *The Journal of the Human Factors and Ergonomics Society.* 63. 001872081986887. 10.1177/0018720819868878.

Boyce, T. E. (2018, Apr 13). Safety Culture and Behavioral Safety. https://ehsdailyadvisor.blr.com/2016/08/reward-behaviors-not-outcomes-get-value-safety-incentives/

Catsavis, Lindsay. (2022, April 28). How to Improve Safety Culture in the Workplace and the Company & Employee Benefits of Doing So. https://www.supplychain247.com/article/how_to_improve_safety_culture_in_the_workplace_and_the_benefits_of_doing_so

Claxton, Garry & Hosie, Peter & Sharma, Piyush. (2021). Toward an effective occupational health and safety culture: A multiple stakeholder perspective. *Journal of Safety Research*. 82. 10.1016/j.jsr.2022.04.006.

Flynn, Michael & Castellanos, Elizabeth & Flores-Andrade, Augusto. (2018). Safety across Cultures: Understanding the Challenges. *Professional safety*. 63. 28-32.

Garg, Arun & Mohamed, Sherif. (2020). Resilient safety culture: A modelling perspective. https://www.researchgate.net/publication/340395615_Resilient_safety_culture_A_modelling_perspective

Hatfield Grace. (2023, Apr 6). Faces of EHS: Safety Culture in 2023 - EHS Daily Advisor (blr.com)

Kumbhar, G & Ahuja, B & Rajhans, Neela. (2021). Documentation Techniques to Avoid Delays in Project.https://www.researchgate.net/publication/352762125_Documentation_Techniques_to_Avoid_Delays_in_Project

Lal, H. (2023). Strengthening a positive safety culture despite underlying fear and peer pressure. *World Safety Journal*, 32(1), 57–64. https://doi.org/10.5281/zenodo.7770080

Lal Harbans and Choueiri E.M. (2023). The integration of behavior-based safety (BBS) as a company value is advocated! *World Safety Journal* (WSJ), Vol. 32, No 2, Page 49-55. doi.org/10.5281/zenodo.8105788

MDPI. (2023). Special Issue - Resilient Safety Culture. https://www.mdpi.com/journal/safety/special_issues/resilient_safety_culture

Miller, Lilly. (2022, June 23). Big Ways The Manufacturing Industry Will Change In 2023 (ideasplusbusiness.com)

Sang, Xiaoming. (2020). Analysis on the Path of Safety Culture Innovation in Foshan Manufacturing Industry. 10.2991/aebmr.k.201111.010.

SEIL. (2023). Behaviour Based Safety (BBS) Implemented at SEIL. https://www.sembcorpenergyindia.com/CSR/BBS

SSOE. (2021, November 1). Creating a Positive Safety Culture. https://www.ssoe.com/creating-a-positive-safety-culture-2/

Wong SY, Fu ACL, Han J, Lin J, Lau MC. (2021). Effectiveness of customised safety intervention programmes to increase the safety culture of hospital staff. BMJ Open Qual. 2021 Oct;10(4):e000962. doi: 10.1136/bmjoq-2020-000962. PMID: 34625426; PMCID: PMC8504354.

CHAPTER

7

HOW BEST CAN ORGANISATIONS FORECAST SAFETY CULTURE MORE ACCURATELY FOR ZERO-HARM?

Safety culture could predict the incident rate, but the injury data cannot forecast safety culture. Safety systems believe that safety is the management's responsibility, but safety culture interventions emphasize that safety is an individuals' role to behave safe and also support others. The big question is, are employees safe at workplaces? Most corporates are not willing or able to decide between the safety enforcements and positive safety culture, as because they are not open to learn about the insights of safety cultures' positive effects on business. It is hard for them to think of safety beyond profits, production and business perspective, until a major fire or fatality-like incidents impede their business badly. The corporates cannot take risk of not practicing a positive safety culture strategy and the management action plan. As forecasting mechanisms, it is critical to know also the periodicity aspects of safety culture transformation, and that the behaviour based safety (BBS) 1.0 and 2.0 both together transform the safety culture into a positive work culture. Based on the comprehensive literature reviews and insights from the field practitioners, this paper describes ten stringent measures of forecasting best safety culture more accurately towards achieving vision zero.

Keywords: Forecast, Safety, Culture, Organizations.

INTRODUCTION

Do we want to kill or disable people at work sites, if not then the organizations essentially need to build and sustain a positive safety culture. Safety culture is a empathy in action at personal level applicable at anyplace. Our workplaces are not safe until everyone is active in correcting unsafe behaviours. If our organizational leaders do not choose to make a planned change in their safety culture, any employee is likely to be affected by the incidents. Safety communications by the operations managers was the best predictor of safety culture, as well as developing training programs to help managers to understand safety roles (Tsung, et al. 2010). Positive safety culture is a real-time intervention that provides measurable outcomes, transformational work experiences, activated leadership, and empowered employees (ILO, 2017).

The April 1986 disaster at the Chernobyl nuclear power plant in Ukraine was the product of a flawed Soviet reactor design coupled with serious mistakes made by the plant operators. It was a direct consequence of Cold War isolation and the resulting lack of any safety culture (World Nuclear Association, 2022). Research and experience show that when safety culture is strong, accidents are less frequent and less severe. A strong safety culture is predicted by:

1. Leadership is clearly committed to safety
2. Open and effective communication exists across the organization
3. Employees feel personally responsible for safety
4. The organization practices continuous learning
5. The work environment is safety conscious
6. Reporting systems are clearly defined and not used to punish employees
7. Decisions demonstrate that safety is prioritized over competing demands
8. Employees and the management work to foster mutual trust
9. The organization responds to safety concerns fairly and consistently
10. Safety efforts are supported by training and resources (U.S. Department of Transportation, 2017).

Safety culture remains an undefined and incalculable phenomenon, until and unless there are free and frank discussions on safety issues across the organization. More the safety culture is discussed over a long period of time by most employees, more it gets defined and calculated. Unfortunately, injury data provides no information about safety culture or predictability, but that's what traditional safety does. On the contrary, safety culture can predict the injury data. Forecasting is the foundation of traditional strategic planning and is viewed as something that shapes the future (Long, 2014). We implement solutions aimed at reducing accidents in everyday life, but we are not able to eliminate all accidents from our life (Małysa, 2022).

But there is also a flip side to safety cultures. There is little evidence on the predictive value of safety culture assessment (SCA) in relation to how accident-prone an organisation might be. It is not just demonstrated how a quantitative SCA mis-predicted future safety outcomes, but actually showed an inverse relationship between the assessment and subsequent critical Incidents. Hence, it is to be taken in a very cautious manner, whether a SCA has a predictive capacity for safety outcomes (Boskeljon-Horst, et al., 2022). More than assessments, real time safety would depend upon how each person is active for the workplace surroundings each time.

MEASURES OF FORECASTING SAFETY CULTURE MORE ACCURATELY

The clear picture of safety culture forecasting is possible only when organizations are able to act with regard to each of the series of measures for best safety culture being implemented accurately under the guidance of a team of safety culture experts. The risk that corporates cannot take, is not practicing a positive safety culture strategy and an action plan. You are safe just for now. How can we forecast safety culture more accurately? Table 1 describes 10 stringent measures of forecasting best safety culture more accurately. Whereas each of these measures directly or indirectly impact the success of safety culture, but largely the change is achievable depending upon how long the focus is maintained by the employees. Professional development including systems thinking and safety training are the necessary steps along with the policy changes facilitating organisations to support learning from mistakes which would contribute to reducing human errors (Mahsoon, et al., 2021).

Table 1: Stringent Measures of Forecasting Best Safety Culture More Accurately

1.	Everyone is trained in caring behaviours as safety culture observer.
2.	Everyone is an active observer for spot-correcting at-risk behaviours.
3.	Continuous safety culture retraining for observations.
4.	Daily accounting of at-risk behaviours.
5.	Daily spot-corrections of barriers/hazards in safety.
6.	Achieving a standard of zero at-risk behaviour and vision zero.
7.	How often are the at-risk behaviours out-of-view of the supervisors/ observers?

8.	Are there any work areas that are out-of-view of the observers?
9.	Safety culture is monitored by the corporate board and is linked to HSE index.
10.	Did safe behaviour learned from workplaces transfer to home and other arenas?
To calculate forecasting: each measure carry 10 score multiplied by 10 = 100 total score	

Most industries do not fulfil these measures of forecasting best safety culture more accurately, even after years of safety culture interventions as continued focus gets disappeared. On the contrary, the effectiveness of positive safety culture initiatives can sustain for many years (Spigener et al., 2022).

Let us explain these ten stringent measures of forecasting best safety culture more accurately for better understanding as below.

1. Everyone is trained in caring behaviours as safety culture observer. Many organizations seem to assume that putting a safety culture process in place ensures employees will speak up when observing a co-worker's at-risk behaviour. This is simply not the case. There is certainly value in performing safety observations – safe and at-risk behaviours are recorded, and hazards are sometimes shared for useful education. But what about going a step further and taking the time to provide immediate and caring feedback to ensure employees continue their safe behaviour and correct their at-risk behaviour (Geller, 2018). The observers need to be reinforced for accountability and rewards for their safety observations. Safety culture is increasingly recognised as a basic predictor for the delivery of safe and high-quality care (Ellis, et al., 2022).

2. Everyone is an active observer for spot-correcting at-risk behaviours. Let's understand the difference between caring and acting. No one wants to see an individual get injured on the job. This is caring. Yet, when workers are asked to muster the courage to offer advice to a peer who is working at-risk, many admit they do not act on their caring by providing behavioural feedback. And how many workers act to show sincere appreciation for a co-worker's safe behaviour? Many employees do not actively care for people's safety. They don't go beyond their intrinsic caring and provide proactive injury-prevention action (Geller, 2018).

3. Continuous safety culture retraining for observations. Studies show that an accident and injury at the worksite is the result of workers' behaviour and safety culture. The development of safety culture in the industry through leadership and training roles will provide a safe working environment (Misnan, et al., 2008). Training staff on appropriate safety behaviours and requiring them to complete safety observations helps keep safety a priority and continuously reinforces the facility's commitment to incident prevention (Pritchard, 2022).

4. Daily accounting of at-risk behaviours through creating more and better safety-related interactions improved the safety organizations performance and a changed trend in injury rates and improvement in safety culture was noticed (Nielsen, 2014). Companies should work at several organisational levels at the same time. It is necessary to include levels such as individual, group, workplace and management levels, thus taking a system perspective on at-risk behaviour (Aulin, et al., 2019).

5. Daily spot-corrections of barriers/hazards in safety. it was found that there are the following 4 categories associated with safety barriers: (1) Behaviour Barriers; (2) Management Barriers; (3) Awareness Barriers; and (4) Culture Barriers. At the same time, the most popular barriers are based on appearance in sources: lack of safety training, lack of commitment, work pressure is high when deadlines are approaching, and low-level education, lack of experience, and lack of knowledge. The actual safety of the projects should be focused on to reduce injuries, accidents, and reduce barriers of applying safety, which will enhance the sustainability and development of safe environments within industry (Maliha, et al., 2021). Eliminating fatalities and serious injuries is the main challenge for the global industry. Focus is to provide the industry with actionable recommendations and guidance to create safer and healthier workplaces (World Steel Association, 2022).

6. Achieving a standard of zero at-risk behaviour. The perception of health and safety risks by workers is very different from that of the evaluators. Often, when workers identify a situation as low-risk or even zero-risk, the evaluator assesses the same context as maximum risk (Carpio-de, et al., 2021). Also, there is a need to allow more time for managers and workers to talk about safety issues (Quenon, et al., 2020) in order to achieve zero at-risk behaviour.

7. How often are the at-risk behaviours out-of-view of the supervisors/observers? The supervision/observation of the at-risk behaviours provide challenges for safety culture improvement as it involves adequate time for interactions, discussion and toolbox talks for understanding issues to be rectified (Bayley, et al., 2022). At the same time, daily abusive supervision negatively affects organizational citizenship behaviour for the positive safety environment (Wang and Xiao. 2022).

8. Are there any work areas that are out-of-view of the observers? Research reported that people who perceive it to be normal for site to ignore safety procedures are more likely to report taking safety risks in the future (Mark, et al., 2020). Supervisors shaped implementation climate by carrying out four roles (diffusing, synthesizing, mediating, and selling). The interaction of these roles convey expectations and support which can inform implementation practice (Bunger, et al. 2019).

9. Safety culture is monitored by the corporate board and is linked to the work culture. The psychosocial hazards (such as work culture, relationships, stress, decision making process, work organization) fully mediate the relationship between safety culture and the organizational safety performance (Naji, et al., 2021). Safety cultures endure when they are part of an overall successful organizational culture (Paoletta, 2020). It is difficult, until and unless the company directors want to end and fix the safety culture challenges.

10. Did safe behaviour learned from workplaces transfer to home and other arenas? It requires families interactions on safety about the risks that involves their kins. Also, how actively the employees are able to reduce risks at home environment for their family members and their neighbourhoods in promoting safe behaviours. Employees who adopt safe behaviours at work do not always do the same at home. Yet many people believe that good work practices extend into life at home and are an indicator that safety culture is deeply rooted (Balzer, 2015).

AN EXAMPLE OF A CASE OF STERLITE TECHNOLOGIES LIMITED (STL)

The case below would help understand salient measures of positive safety culture

Due to safety culture implementation and the steering committee meetings being conducted, the workforce feel free to ask questions without fear, and help in correcting rather than criticising at-risk behaviors. Behavioural science approach enhanced the safety culture/ safe behaviours of an organisation and reduced accidents and their resultant costs. The costs can be the human costs (in the form of death or injury) or financial costs (in the form of damage to equipment, raw material, product, etc.

Month-wise data here below indicate that the at-risk behaviours reduced from 24 to 10 percent over a period of six months.

Month Safe Behaviours At-risk Behaviors

October'21. 76% 24%

November'21. 87% 13%

December'21. 88% 12%

January'22 88% 12%

Feb'22. 89% 11%

March'22. 90% 10%

Approach adopted by STL management

- Active participation from all including subcontractor workforce, business head, departmental head, front line managers, engineers, supervisors and workers.
- Empowering and making everyone responsible for their own and team safety.
- Observation and counseling with due respect as a part of organization core value.
- Team leader performance evaluation based on individual performance with respect to process implementation.

- Adherence of transparency in EHS communication.
- Continue observations till reach the safe behavior and learns the concept of self-observation and observing others for safe operations.

Review of safety culture processes checklist for STL sites as below:

Mark each process below out of 10. Check, what's lacking.

1. Safety cultural shift from reactive, dependent culture to independent, interdependent culture - Followed
2. Leadership increased involvement: Followed
3. Monthly BBS meetings - Followed
4. Incidents reduction - Followed
5. Behavioral trends improvement - Followed
6. Sharing of at-risk behaviours during TBT - Followed
7. Motivational reward, recognition for observers/units - Followed
8. Managements regular observation rounds - Followed
9. Regular repeat BBS awareness sessions for spot-correction - Followed
10. Quarterly reviews across units/ sites - Followed

Total score: $10 \times 10 = 100$

STL score: 100%

The change in positive safety culture has happened over the years and its sustainability need to be constantly explored. The management should continuously monitor and evaluate their strategies while delivering multifaceted interventions to be more specifically focused and to motivate workers to be enthusiastic in sustaining safety culture (Wong, et al., 2021). Sembcorp Energy India Limited (SEIL) manages Health, Safety and Environment (HSE) responsibility as its core value (SEIL, 2023a). To further strengthen the safety culture and secure a positive behavioural change within the work place, SEIL has implemented and integrated Behaviour Based Safety into its safety systems across all the assets. ISO 45001:2018 mandates that human competence and behavioural elements need to be considered in risk assessment and as an internal issue for managing risks (SEIL, 2023).

CONCLUSIONS

People are the most important asset in any business and ensuring their health and safety at work is paramount. The time for turning poor health and safety records around is now, and we need your help to make it happen. The benefits of a positive safety culture can include fewer accidents, injuries and lost time (MBIE, 2013). The stringent measures of forecasting best safety culture more accurately as outlined above are critical for implementation and continued follow-ups. Practically, these measures work in combination as they are inter-related to forecast an accuracy of an organizational safety culture. Every organization has a base level of safety culture which needs to be improved further for accurate results and desired outcomes. Safety, health and wellbeing are increasingly becoming an integrated part of the organizational culture as businesses recognize that their success depends more than ever on people, and vision zero is a proactive leading indicator. Think of human factors toward the realization of a safe, secure and well-being society (The Vision Zero Summit Japan, 2022).

Most of the safety culture committees in an organization remain non-functional and as a result of which the benefits to the employees are absent. In fact, such professional teams can do wonders if they are active and focused on the objectives for which they are constituted. Some committee members are active initially, others are mostly passive. Actions of these safety management teams predict the strongest relationship to employees commitment to safety (Cox, et al., 2002). The studies are successful at describing how employees perceive their work environment but are poor at predicting what this means for future (Cole, et al., 2013). Moreover, the safety culture can predict the injury data, but Injury data could not forecast safety culture. Safety culture intervention involves all employees in the organizations for positive changes. Supervisors and training mediate the impact of management on employee commitment. Employee commitment has the biggest impact on safety culture satisfaction. Communication directly supports employee commitment (Tappura, et al., 2022).

Safety culture is becoming an indispensable forecasting factor in achieving sustainable development (Jasiulewicz-Kaczmarek, 2022). There are ups and downs in organizational safety culture. Consultant driven dependent safety culture without adequate leadership and self-driven structure slowed down in several organisations. The steering teams in these companies did not function as adequately as in the beginning of safety culture intervention. Later, they had to rejuvenate and support the interventions so that everyone is alert to observe unsafe behaviour on the spot as a standard operating procedure. As safety reporting is made more descriptive, though the observers do the corrections in the field, they hesitate to report as it is time consuming. The risks of poor safety culture includes not having an easy-to-understand system for managing safety can increase costs significantly (ROSS, 2019). Moreover, it is easy to find fault, but it is easier to provide care, as a basic principle of positive safety perspective. Most companies suffered fatalities, losses of property over the years, much before launching safety culture intervention, as they followed the blaming and fault finding - reactive safety culture loaded with hierarchies. One of the most important causes of industrial incidents, of which 90% is related to human factors, is to refuse to accept errors because of fear of blaming and concealing them. Evaluating the just culture, the safety culture of the employees of the organization can be predicted with a high level of certainty, which shows the direct relationship between the just culture and the safety culture. So, increasing the just culture directly contributes to the development of the safety culture (Shabani, et al., 2019).

Safety systems could give safety climate, but not the safety culture. Safety culture enhances safety behaviours. Some organizations customise their safety culture intervention bypassing its core principles, which can prove to be risky in terms of real time safety performance. Managements' sincere sympathy for employees safety is a precondition for safety culture implementation. The first few months of implementation initiate safety climate, but it takes continued efforts for building safety culture resulting in an expected levels of increased compliances and significantly reduced incidents towards achieving vision zero. Companies who implement Zero Accident Vision has an ambition that all accidents are preventable, and they achieve it by their commitment, safety communication, safety culture and safety learning (Zwetsloot, et al., 2017). A Vision Zero city with approximately 680,000 residents, Oslo, Norway, had zero pedestrian fatalities, zero bicycle fatalities, and only one traffic death in 2019 (Short 2020). Vision Zero action plan implementation consider the ethics and value of human life (Safarpour, et al., 2022), and how quick the organizations are in decision making and utilise their safety resources. Most organizations move slow in deciding matters on safety culture goals due to lack of accurate guidance and mentoring. Safety culture areas of improvement should be prioritised and immediately tackled, and strengths of safety culture should be maintained (Mrayyan, 2022). Interventions designed to improve safety culture foster organisational environments that prevent safety events and support organisational learning when events do occur. A safety culture supports the required workforce behaviours and norms that enable safe care and well-being (Finn, et al., 2022).

Every moment is a safety moment and an observation time, or it can be a moment of an incident, as risk is live anytime anywhere. It requires managements' will, motivation of employees, and meaningfulness of safe work to everyone to personalize safety culture. Forecasting best safety culture accurately is an integral and persistent to any work culture.

As forecasting mechanisms, it is critical to know the periodicity aspects of safety culture transformation, and that the behaviour based safety (BBS) 1.0 and 2.0 both together transform the safety culture into a positive work culture. The periodicity of safety cultural change would vary and depend upon size of the organisation, existing culture, leadership and so on.

Table 2: Periodicity of Positive safety culture features and transformation

1st six months	2nd six months	3rd six months	4th six months
1. Conceptual Awareness	Training/re-training/Tool Box Talk (TBT)	Mass-communications	Reverse TBT
2. Reactive safety culture	Dependent safety culture	Independent safety culture	Interdependent safety culture
3. HSE drive	Steering teams drive	HODs drive	Sites drive
4. Employees involvement	Contractors workmen	Office staff	Families
5. Correction based	Conversations	Care	Connect
6. Formal Reviews	Critical Reviews	Directors Reviews	Site Reviews
7. Quantitative analysis	Qualitative analysis	Barriers rectifications	Resources Provision
8. Observations driven	Data driven	Performance driven	Core Value

1st six months	2nd six months	3rd six months	4th six months
9. Safety systems activation	Behavioural safety	Psychological safety	Human factors/ human error/ cultural safety
10. Reporting Participation 20%	Reporting Participation 50%	Reporting Participation 70%	Reporting Participation 90-100%

The periodicity of the positive safety culture transformation is an important forecasting mechanism at sites which reveals (Table 2) that during the first six months, there is about 20 percent change in the company's safety culture in terms of reporting and participation, though the awareness and training is most likely 80 percent completed. Dependent safety culture prevails as mostly HSE officers take ownership. The steering teams at head office and regional offices are not taking ownership as they don't demand or enquire safety reporting from the sites. Thus, despite, safety culture trainings, there is only 20 percent reporting by employees. Moreover, behavioural corrections by observers at sites don't necessarily entail conversations for imbibing safe behaviours. The disconnect between managers and observers remain. The employees need to talk everyday about safety observations which can happen only when safety is performance-based, and managers stress it daily during their site rounds (Kaila, 2022).

It is good to note that behaviour based safety (BBS) 1.0 and 2.0 both together transform the safety culture into a positive work culture. BBS 2.0 focuses more on organisational culture factors, rather individual behaviour. BBS 1.0 is observational in nature, whereas BBS 2.0 is more conversational for developing response mechanisms to combat multi-faceted organisational barriers while evaluating accountability of leaders for leading the positive safety culture intervention as a long-term roadmap for businesses. Table 3 describes how BBS 2.0 is implemented qualitatively and conversationally at organisational levels for establishing safety dialogues across the board from topmost level to down-most/ last person. It is important to fix accountability of each of the BBS steering teams leaders. It is important to understand that BBS 2.0 does not replace BBS 1.0 but both are complementary to each other (Lal, 2023).

Table 3: Basic difference between BBS 1.0 & 2.0

Culture building - Broad Focus of BBS 1.0 is on:	Perspective building - Focus of BBS 2.0 is on:
1. Observations and corrections	Increased open and empathic conversations across levels, critical reviews, mass-communications
2. Employees as observers at all levels/areas	Integrating contractors, customers, stakeholders
3. Individual Behaviours	Organisational barriers/antecedents, resources provision
4. Corporate Steering teams	MD level, Board of Directors reporting, Challenge management's passionate involvement
5. Behavioural safety culture	Total safety culture:Psychological safety, human factors, human error, cultural safety, digitalising, integration
6. Steering teams commitment for months/years	Accountability evaluation of leaders/ managers, performance & policy based commitment for long-term
7. Actively caring with empathy	HSE as core value and zero-harm, corporate rewards and reinforcements (digital and non-digital)
8. Quantitative score-board/ measurement	Qualitative Site steering team/HODs monitoring
9. Safety and business perspective	Health, Safety, Environment, Well-being, Sustainability
10. Monthly monitoring and recognitions	Weekly monitoring and spot-rewards at sites

REFERENCES

Aulin, R., Ek, Asa and Edling, C. (2019), "Underlying Causes for Risk Taking Behaviour Among Construction Workers", Lill, I. and Witt, E. (Ed.) 10th Nordic Conference on Construction Economics and Organization *(Emerald Reach Proceedings Series*, Vol. 2), Emerald Publishing Limited, Bingley, pp. 419-426. https://doi.org/10.1108/S2516-285320190000002012

Balzer, Philippe. (2015). Safety at work must be consistent with safety at home. https://www.icsi-eu.org/en/publication/thought-safety-work-home

Bayley, K., Trembath, D. & Leif, E. (2022). Supervision for Aspiring Behaviour Analysts in Australia: An Exploration of Current Practices, Challenges, and Opportunities. *Behav Analysis Practice*. https://doi.org/10.1007/s40617-022-00739-z

Boskeljon-Horst Leonie, Simone Sillem, Sydney W. A. Dekker. (2022, December 27). 'Ladder'-based safety culture assessments inversely predict safety outcomes. https://doi.org/10.1111/1468-5973.12445

Bunger, A.C., Birken, S.A., Hoffman, J.A. et al., Elucidating the influence of supervisors' roles on implementation climate. Implementation Sci 14, 93. (2019). https://doi.org/10.1186/s13012-019-0939-6

Carpio-de Los Pinos AJ, González-García MLN, Pentelhão LC, Baptista JS. 2021 Zero-Risk Interpretation in the Level of Preventive Action Method Implementation for Health and Safety in Construction Sites. *Int J Environ Res Public Health*. Mar 29;18(7):3534. doi: 10.3390/ijerph18073534. PMID: 33805434; PMCID: PMC8038139.

Cole Kerstan S., Susan M. Stevens-Adams, & Caren A. Wenner. (2013, March). A Literature Review of Safety Culture Human Factors & Statistics. Sandia National Laboratories Albuquerque, New Mexico 87185 and Livermore, California 94550.

Cox, Sue & Tomás, José & Cheyne, Alistair & Oliver, Amparo. (2002). Safety Culture: The Prediction of Commitment to Safety in the Manufacturing Industry. *British Journal of Management*. 9. 3 - 11. 10.1111/1467-8551.9.s1.2.

Ellis LA, Pomare C, Churruca K, et al. (2022). Predictors of response rates of safety culture questionnaires in healthcare: a systematic review and analysis. *BMJ Open* 2022;12:e065320. doi: 10.1136/bmjopen-2022-065320

Finn M, Mellon L, Walsh A et al. (2022). What effect do safety culture interventions have on health care workers in hospital settings? A *systematic review of the international literature*. HRB Open Res 2022, 5:48 (https://doi.org/10.12688/hrbopenres.13576.2)

Geller, Krista S. (2018, December 4). Actively caring for people's safety - The crucial difference between "caring" & "acting". https://www.ishn.com/articles/109877-actively-caring-for-peoples-safety

ILO. (2017, Oct 18). International Occupational Safety and Health Conference 2017. https://www.ilo.org/wcmsp5/groups/public/---ed_protect/---protrav/---safework/documents/presentation/wcms_606677.pdf

Jasiulewicz-Kaczmarek, M.; Antosz, K.; Wyczółkowski, R.; Sławi ́nska, M. (2022). Integrated Approach for Safety Culture Factor Evaluation from a Sustainability

Perspective. Int. J. Environ. Res. Public Health 2022, 19, 11869. https://doi.org/10.3390/ ijerph191911869

Kaila, Harbans Lal (2022). Long Term Safety Culture Implementation. Prints Publications, New Delhi. ISBN-13: 9788192769462, https://www.printspublications.com/book/long-term-safety

Lal, H. (2023). Strengthening a positive safety culture despite underlying fear and peer pressure. *World Safety Journal*, 32(1), 57–64. https://doi.org/10.5281/zenodo.7770080

Long, Rob. (2014, Aug 23). Forecasting Safety. https://safetyrisk.net/forecasting-safety/

Mahsoon AN, Dolansky M. (2021). Safety culture and systems thinking for predicting safety competence and safety performance among registered nurses in Saudi Arabia: a cross-sectional study. *Journal of Research in Nursing*. 26(1-2):19-32. doi:10.1177/1744987120976171

Maliha, Mohammed N., Yazan I. Abu Aisheh, Bassam A. Tayeh, and Ali Almalki. 2021. "Safety Barriers Identification, Classification, and Ways to Improve Safety Performance in the Architecture, Engineering, and Construction (AEC) Industry: Review Study" Sustainability 13, no. 6: 3316. https://doi.org/10.3390/su13063316

Małysa, T. (2022). Application of Forecasting as an Element of Effective Management in the Field of Improving Occupational Health and Safety in the Steel Industry in Poland. *Sustainability* 2022, 14, 1351. https:// doi.org/10.3390/su14031351

Mark Rubin, Anna Giacomini, Rebecca Allen, Richard Turner, Brian Kelly. (2020). Identifying safety culture and safety climate variables that predict reported risk-taking among Australian coal miners: An exploratory longitudinal study. *Safety Science*, 123, 104564.

MBIE (2013, September). People Come First. https://www.mbie.govt.nz/assets/4e336f62d8/people-come-first.pdf

Mrayyan M. T. (2022). Predictors and outcomes of patient safety culture: a cross-sectional comparative study. BMJ Open Quality 2022;11:e001889. doi:10.1136/bmjoq-2022-001889

Naji GMA, Isha ASN, Mohyaldinn ME, Leka S, Saleem MS, Rahman SMNBSA, Alzoraiki M. (2021). Impact of Safety Culture on Safety Performance; Mediating Role of Psychosocial Hazard: An Integrated Modelling Approach. *Int J Environ Res Public Health*. Aug 13;18(16):8568. doi: 10.3390/ijerph18168568. PMID: 34444314; PMCID: PMC8394037.

Misnan, Mohd Saidin & Mohammed, Miswan abdul hakim & Mohammed, & Wan Zahari, Wan Yusoff & Wan Mahmood, Wan Yusoff & Hendra, Syamsul & Mat, & Abdullah Mohd Asmoni, Mat. (2008). Development of safety culture in the construction industry: The leadership and training roles. Proceedings of

2nd International Conference on Built Environment in Developing Countries (ICBEDC 2008).

Nielsen, Kent J. (2014). Improving safety culture through the health and safety organization: A case study. *Journal of Safety Research*, 48, 7-17, ISSN 0022-4375, https://doi.org/10.1016/j.jsr.2013.10.003.

Paoletta, David. (2020, July 1). Core Attributes of a World-Class Safety Culture. https://safesitehq.com/safety-culture/

Pritchard, Andy. (2022 June 23). A Digital Do-Over: Transforming a Failing BBSO Program. https://weeverapps.com/safety-management/bbso-digital-do-over/

ROSS. (2019). The Risks of Poor Safety Culture. https://www.rosstechnology.com/news/poor-safety-culture-risks/

Safarpour Hamid, Khorasani-Zavareh Davoud, Soori Hamid, Ghomian Zohreh, Bagheri-Lankarani Kamran, Mohammadi Reza. (2022, Jul 5). The Challenges of Vision Zero Implementation in Iran: A Qualitative Study. *Frontiers in Future Transportation*, Vol. 3, DOI=10.3389/ffutr.2022.884930

SEIL. (2023). Behaviour Based Safety (BBS) Implemented at SEIL. https://www.sembcorpenergyindia.com/CSR/BBS

SEIL. (2023a). Safety at the Core. https://www.sembcorpenergyindia.com/AnnualReport2020/safety-at-the-core.php

Shabani Arani M, Tabatabaei S, Mansouri N. Prediction of safety culture based on of dimensions of just culture in of one of the industrial sections of Tehran. *Iran J Ergon* 2019; 7 (1) :63-72 URL: http://journal.iehfs.ir/article-1-543-en.html

Short, A. (2020). Vision Zero! Norwegian Capital Completely Quashes Road Deaths. Streetsblog USA. Streetsblog USA.

Spigener Jim, Gennifer Lyon & Terry McSween. (2022). Behavior-based safety 2022: today's evidence, Journal of Organizational Behavior Management, 42:4, 336-359, DOI: 10.1080/01608061.2022.2048943

Tappura Sari, Aki Jääskeläinen, Julius Pirhonen (2022). Creation of satisfactory safety culture by developing its key dimensions, *Safety Science*, 154, 105849, ISSN 0925-7535, https://doi.org/10.1016/j.ssci.2022.105849.

The Vision Zero Summit Japan. (2022). https://japan.visionzerosummits.com/japan-2022/

Tsung-Chih Wu, Chia-Hung Lin, Sen-Yu Shiau. (2010). Predicting safety culture: The roles of employer, operations manager and safety professional, *Journal of Safety Research*, 41(5), 423-431, ISSN 0022-4375, https://doi.org/10.1016/j.jsr.2010.06.006.

Quenon, JL., Vacher, A., Faget, M. et al. (2020). Exploring the role of managers in the development of a safety culture in seven French healthcare facilities: a qualitative study. *BMC Health Serv Res*, 20, 517 https://doi.org/10.1186/s12913-020-05331-1

U.S. Department of Transportation. (2017, August). Federal Railroad Administration Safety Culture: A Significant Influence on Safety in Transportation. Office of Research Development and Technology Washington, DC 20590.

Wang H and Xiao J. (2022). How and When Daily Abusive Supervision Affects Daily Organizational Citizenship Behavior for the Environment. Front. *Psychol.* 13:791803. doi: 10.3389/fpsyg.2022.791803

Wong SY, Fu ACL, Han J, Lin J, Lau MC. (2021). Effectiveness of customised safety intervention programmes to increase the safety culture of hospital staff. *BMJ Open Qual*. 2021 Oct;10(4):e000962. doi: 10.1136/bmjoq-2020-000962. PMID: 34625426; PMCID: PMC8504354.

World Steel Association. (2022). Safety culture and leadership fundamentals. https://worldsteel.org/safety-culture-and-leadership-fundamentals/

World Nuclear Association. (2022, April). Chernobyl Accident 1986. https://world-nuclear.org/information-library/safety-and-security/safety-of-plants/chernobyl-accident.aspx

Zwetsloot, Gerard & Kines, Pete & Ruotsala, Riikka & Drupsteen, Linda & Merivirta, Maija-Leena. (2017). The importance of commitment, communication, culture and learning for the implementation of the Zero Accident Vision in 27 companies in Europe. *Safety Science*. 96. 10.1016/j.ssci.2017.03.001.

ACKNOWLEDGMENT

The contribution of industry professionals is thankfully acknowledged.

CHAPTER

8 QUALITY OF CORPORATE DEFINITION OF POSITIVE SAFETY CULTURE IS CRITICAL FOR BUSINESS SURVIVAL

Organisational safety culture can not be over-defined or under-defined, rather it becomes practically a company-specific definition for operational purposes. Global definitions or case studies are good points of learning for self-assessment and improvements. The quality of safety culture depends upon as per its existing steps and stages for a particular company for continuous improvements, which also varies from a company to company. Corporate definitions of the organisational safety culture suffer between the dichotomies of production and profits. Good safety culture is the struggle rather than the outcome, for making safety culture a personal and society value and practice it daily. This paper discusses the problems and solutions of defining safety culture in terms of moving from old culture 1 to new culture 2. Important recommendations are made to overcome the challenges in reaching and deciding the implementable corporate definitions of company-specific safety culture based on the field visits to almost 50 site locations and interactions with 400 managers. Major conclusions are: a) Dichotomies of production and profits need focus and clarity to all. b) Make safety culture a personal and society value and practice it daily. c) Good safety culture is the struggle rather than the outcome. d) Safety culture is for inspiring people to adopt safer practices and e) visible leadership for inspiring positive safety culture.

Keywords: Business, Definitions, Safety, Culture, Corporate.

INTRODUCTION

An efficient safety management system ought to be based on safety awareness that should then become a culture in the industry. Efficient safety culture should be demonstrated as a good value business (Misnan, et al, 2007). Safety culture is a very important factor in a successful business endeavour. Employees who feel safe find meaning in their work and are motivated for changes in the company. safety culture, as a sub-culture of the organizational culture controls the business success factors of the company. It is well recognized how human, technical and organizational factors are influenced by safety culture, and a successful company competitive strategy is built on the quality of the safety culture in the company, and that the meaning of work and the motivational potential of the working task are influenced by and the result of different organizational cultures. Managers should carefully consider the quality of the safety culture and its impact on the motives of the employees when they implement organizational changes in the company (Milan, 2015).

Safety culture is a nebulous concept related to the links between organizational culture, prevention practices and safety performance (Risk Engineering, 2020). No other concept in safety science is as studied, yet poorly understood (or measured) as safety culture, in terms of conceptual and methodological clarity with an argument to encourage industry to adopt closer definitional-methodological alignment (Casey, et al., 2022).

In a positive safety culture, all employees are accountable for maintaining standards and procedures. Safety culture refers to the enduring value, priority and commitment placed on safety by every individual and every group at every level of the organisation (Canso, 2023).

The definition of safety culture has been broadened since the onset of this concept in the year 1984, now including safety perceptions and practices, beliefs and behaviours and so on (Abeje, and Fan, 2023). The concept of safety culture in industry that enables staff and patients to be free from harm, is characterised by complexity, multifaceted-ness, and indefinability. Over the years, unclear definitions have resulted in a proliferation of measurement tools, with lack of consensus on how safety culture can be best measured and improved. There are challenges and complexities in safety culture assessment relating to definition, tools, dimensionality and response rates. The aim is to prompt critical reflection on these issues and point to possible solutions (Ellis, et al, 2023).

Fire and fatalities are a daily affair in India which reflects upon the lack of training, re-training, enforcement and reinforcement of safety culture by management and workers in organisations.

Safety professionals from industry make it clear that most companies in India focus on zero fatality, not on zero unsafe behaviour or zero incident. In case, fatal incident happens, they can hide it, they can manage it by paying rupees five hundred thousand and gifts to authorities on festivals. If they employ a safety expert, it would cost heavily, hence they explore a middle way to manage business first, safety second. In speech expressions, it is safety first, production next. This is a norm for most private an multi-national organisations.

The critical question is how to stop these fatal practices so that workers and employees in plants/sites do not lose lives. Practically, the business definitions of safety implementation are customised and based the prevailing calculations of managers about the production targets and manipulations of safety practices that are possibly hand-in-glove with authorities, local politicians, factory inspectors and so on. Though some organisations and corporate try maximum to be ethical in safety care of workers. But mostly, due to lack of awareness of safety methodologies and usefulness, the companies and top managements prefer and prioritise to bypass safety norms considering safety budgets, and find out loopholes to do so. In this process, they lose their businesses, in the long run, as they adopt unsafe short-cuts to achieve business heights. However, there is no short-cut for better business and/or safety culture, but the same can be fast-tracked with easy and scientific ways with professional mentors involved.

Safety culture is a mindset issue of top managements, and a set of behavioural interventions are the solutions for change in the positive culture mindsets of the organisations. This requires an undeterred determination of company leaders which can do wonders for saving human lives and businesses towards achieving better economies.

Practically, the safety culture is to develop an organisational support network to enable all those factors responsible for keeping safety practices/values as low, poor, reactive, uncaring and so on.

OBJECTIVES OF THIS SURVEY

- To explore problems in the quality of corporate definition of safety culture terms of moving from old culture -1 to new culture-2.
- To explore challenges and solutions in reaching and deciding the implementable corporate definitions of company-specific safety culture.

METHOD

Field visits to almost 50 site locations and interactions with 400 managers comprised sample of this research. Industry professionals participated in the study as part of an action field survey with the researcher. These research participants had been implementing behavioural safety compliance culture at their work sites. The research participants included, the Directors, Managers, Heads of Departments, EHS/HR Professionals belonging to the public and private industrial sectors, including chemicals, construction, gas, power and steel, across Indian locations. The sampling method used was a random sampling.

Both primary data (interviews, discussions) were collected. Interviews based on open-ended questions, focus group interviews and personal in-depth discussions were conducted over the year 2023. The responses to the relevant questions were collated.

The study results and implications are reflected below from a rigorous review of safety culture literature and experiences / case studies shared by the industry leaders across Indian organisations.

RESULTS AND DISCUSSION

This paper dwells on four themes of exploring problems in the quality of corporate definition of safety culture terms of moving from old culture (1) to new culture (2). Table -1 highlights the problems of safety culture-1 and solutions for moving to culture-2.

Problems in the quality of business definition of an existing old safety culture-1 and Solutions for the implementable corporate definitions of company specific new safety culture-2

There are five aspects or problems in the quality of business definition of an existing old safety culture-1 of companies that need attention and focus as highlighted below. These factors (mindset of top leadership; more focus on profits, less on safety culture; lack of awareness about safety culture; internal politics for not adopting safety culture; and visible leadership for inspiring positive safety culture are interconnected and push each other for poor safety culture affecting financial performance and sustainability of the organisations.

1. **Mindset of top leadership about safety culture**: 92% of managers believed that the mindset of top leadership is a problem in the quality of business definition of an organisational safety culture. Solution

for this issue involves providing orientation to top leadership for a new culture-2. Successful safety leaders encourage robust and open communication among team members. Good safety leaders actively energize the employees. This is very critical issue as the fatalities numbers are still unacceptably high when seen through the promise of the OSH Act, which entitles every worker to safe and healthful working conditions and makes all employers and employees responsible to provide a work area free from recognized hazards (Lundell, et al, 2021).

2. **More Focus on profits, less on safety culture (90%):** Nearly 90% of managers expressed that companies focused more on profits rather safety culture for employees, being an issue for low quality of an existing safety culture. Solution strategy for this aspect is in balancing perceptions about profits and safety culture. More recent studies have found the superior stock performance by organizations that achieve a culture of health, safety, and well-being. Nearly three decades of research suggest the importance of corporate culture and financial performance of companies that demonstrated that they valued employees (Fabius and Phares, 2021).

3. **Lack of awareness about safety culture (80%):** Almost 80% of managers observed that the lack of awareness about safety culture is a reason for poor quality of business definition of an existing safety culture of companies. Solution for this aspects lies in increasing awareness about safety culture to all at site. Poor awareness about safety culture has contributed to many major incidents and personal injuries. An organisation's culture can have as big an influence on safety outcomes as the safety management system (HSE, 2023).

4. **Internal politics for not adopting safety culture (75%):** Managers (75%) perceived that the internal organisational politics for not adopting transformation in safety culture is a factor for low quality definition of an existing safety culture of companies. Solution involves in recreating positive mindset into internal politics which is a difficult challenge but not impossible. A study draws particular attention to the influence of political factors and the impact of organizational factors on the successful transfer of training, areas not consistently considered in safety training design and delivery. It provides a useful tool for discriminating between different contextual factors and the level at which they operate. This could enable more effective

management of these factors to improve the potential for transfer of safety training from the classroom to the workplace (Pilbeam and Karanikas, 2023).

Table 1: Problems of safety culture-1 and solutions for moving to culture-2

Problems of old safety culture-1	Solutions for shifting to new safety culture-2
▸ Mindset of top leadership (92%) ▸ More Focus on profits, less on safety culture (90%) ▸ Visible leadership for inspiring positive safety culture (87%) ▸ Lack of awareness about safety culture (80%) ▸ Internal politics for not adopting safety culture (75%)	▸ Orientation to top leadership for culture 2 ▸ Balancing perceptions about profits and safety ▸ Leaderships' daily safety time at shop-floors ▸ Awareness about safety culture to all at site ▸ Recreating positive mindset into Internal politics

As the results of this study point out that what is most problematic in promoting safety culture in organisations is the business-profits orientations over and above the lack of awareness about the value of safety culture, which impact the mindset of top leadership leading to group dynamics turning into internal politics for being comfortable with the poorest definitions of organisational safety culture leading to incidents to manpower and a big threat to business sustainability.

CONCLUSIONS AND IMPLICATIONS

a. **Balanced dichotomies of safe production and profits need focus and clarity to all:** business definitions of the organisational safety culture suffer between the dichotomies of production and profits. The purpose of safety culture is not clear to organisations due to unserious and essentially a fluffy thinking. Safety culture becomes like a pickle that everyone tastes but it remains a side dish, not a part of main menu or major focus thrust area of the company.

   Dichotomy is due to the fact that one is the background to which the new safety culture is to be registered and established (culture 1), and second is the manner and clarification by which the concepts in training by the mentor for new safety culture is imparted and grasped by the employees (culture 2). There are two issues, one is that the organisations are not aware of the right definition and approach of safety culture, and second, they don't intend to adopt the same due to internal safety politics. The managements need to understand and emphasise the positive relationship between a sustainable corporate safety strategy and stakeholder perceptions that bring advantages to business performance (Hristov, 2022).

b. **Make corporate safety culture a personal and societal value for employees:** Unless safety culture is a personal persuasion, it becomes very difficult to sustain the same at workplace or in personal life. The thrust of safety culture at sites impacts the learning transfer to personal lifestyle. Every day, there are road accidents killing young adults who are national human capital of any country. They must be saved. Companies organise safety learning programs on road safety for employees to see that safety behaviours are personalised (Figure 1-2).

   Develop a win-win situation for creating psychological safety, clarify the rationale for speaking up, stamp out the fear of punishments, and amplify rewards. Make it safe for employees to speak up, to spot-correct at-risk behaviours and safety barriers (Hadley, et al, 2023).

c. **Good safety culture is the struggle rather than the outcome**:

   Good safety culture demands continued struggle and persistence. If you are convinced that your organisation has a good safety culture, you are almost certainly mistaken, a safety culture is something that is striven for but rarely attained. The virtue and the reward lies in the struggle rather than the outcome (Canso, 2023). Safety culture transformation and preventing fatalities is a big hurdle for companies to reach and achieve global businesses. That's because, nobody at top levels takes complete responsibility for zero-harm or vision zero, as safety culture outcomes are not immediately visible but in long term very useful in business sustainability.

   Make it safe for employees to speak up to spot-correct at-risk behaviors and safety barriers. Clarify the rationale, stamp out the fear of punishments, and amplify rewards. Ex-Chief general manager of ONGC says, "It's absolutely true, for nurturing a safety culture in any industry.

ONGC general manager says, "we should instil the openness for speaking out". Ex-General manager of IOCL says,"offer some awards/rewards for successful spreader/ transponder of positive safety culture."

d. **Safety culture is for inspiring people:** All employees and associates who don't find time to participate very actively daily in the "positive safety culture initiative of the company" are the ones actually who are to be made aware that they are (directly or indirectly) responsible for any incidents at sites, and they need to be regularly encouraged and cared by their HODs as well as steering teams. Those who involve more actively are to be credited more actively. Follow at-risk behaviour (for spot-correction) not the outcomes. When safety culture is under direct radar of the managing directors' office, its implementation is faster and more accurate and vice versa. When safety becomes ingrained in the organizational values and practices, it becomes everyone's responsibility. Building a safety culture requires the active participation and commitment of all employees, from top management to frontline workers (Kelly, 2023).

This study identified a set of four factors (mindset of top leadership; more focus on profits, less on safety culture; lack of awareness about safety culture; and internal politics for not adopting safety culture) that push each other in combination as constraints for for better safety culture affecting the mindset of stakeholders and investors adversely impacting the financial performance and sustainability of an organisation. The next set of four factors (balanced dichotomies of safe production and profits need focus and clarity to all, making corporate safety culture a personal and society value for employees, understanding that good safety culture is the struggle rather than the outcome, and safety culture is for inspiring people) helps to restore the safety culture transformation for the interests of business and manpower safety. The synthesised conceptualisation of these safety culture aspects can be used to provide greater depth and practical applicability of safety culture, by increasing our understanding of the interactions between cultural and contextual variables in a given workplace and the effect they have on safety (Edwards, et al., 2013). However, safety culture development depends on employee learning from behavioral outcomes, conducive enabling factors, and consistency over time (Bisbey, et al., 2019). This requires a culture of safety that allows people to say what they really think (McKinsey & Company, 2023). Thus, the development of quality of definition of safety culture in any organisation goes through an indigenous process and journey of the factors discussed above, which is necessarily a company based definition for corporates as they are always in a particular stage or phase of the quality of safety culture.

e. **Clarity on Visible leadership for inspiring positive safety culture:** When you wish to drive BBS in plants, it would first depend upon how well do you understand it as a behavioural science application? Mostly in general, top managements are less committed for visible safety culture participation, more so true in case of government companies in comparison to private multinationals. Government organizations demonstrate active participation due to enforcement by ministers. There's a need to amplify top leaders visible presence as a value addition in positive safety culture activism in shop shopfloor. Visible leadership of top management team in safety culture Transformation must be part of their KRA. Like a business Head of SEIL comes fortnightly to site and conducts BBS mass-communication as well as takes account of weekly report on BBS implementation progress, which impacts participation of all HODs visibility and accountability in safety culture at sites. During the weekly round at site of each top management members, the barriers to safety culture must be spot-closed, such as providing material, resources, engineering controls, unsafe conditions, process hazards, systemic and administrative issues to demonstrate visible leadership. The Directors must define the concepts of visible leadership in positive and supportive safety cultural roles and values emphasis at sites. Management members are aware of production numbers at any point of time, why they are not aware of the behavioural trends of safety each month, as behavior is the base of all incidents, and organizations that are not aware of behavioural aspects of safety are safe only accidentally. Management team is the core team of safety culture transformation and if the team members don't act to their role, safety culture doesn't take place, whatever else companies do. Visible leadership is about inspiring, energising and mobilizing employees and associates into their safety culture's active involvement. Management speeches and frequent field presence must come together for charismatic results in safety, culture and business. There are examples of leaders in industry who are demonstrating these behaviors but not each one of them, which slows down the spirit of positive work culture.

For enhancing visible leadership in positive safety culture transformation, the following ten aspects need to reflect in the management KRA (Lal and Choueiri, 2023).

1. How many spot-corrections did you engage in every day for at-risk behaviors and barriers-in-safety?
2. How many BBS Gemba walks did you complete today and rewarded observers?
3. Did you enter your daily contribution of spot-correction on the BBS conpany folder?
4. How many safety budgets did you approve of today?
5. How many BBS Mass-communication in a week did you have on shop floor?
6. Do you know the weekly behavioural trends of at-risk behaviors and Barriers of your plants?
7. Did you participate in participate in weekly and monthly BBS meetings?
8. Did you consult and respect the EHS department before taking safety decisions?
9. Do you know an overall increase of BBS mentors and observers of your plants each month?
10. Have you personally stopped your own at-risk behaviors?

RECOMMENDATIONS

The industry practitioners recommended several ways of defining positive safety culture as below while moving from old culture-1 to new culture-2. ONGC Karaikal, executive director, Uday Paswan says, "People should not only be saved from physical injury but also from psychological harm at workplaces. I was recognised at ONGC more as safety person and trained in safety systems as I demonstrated interest in safety culture." Safety head of Nagpur Mumbai tunnel project, Subhrakanta Khuntia, said, "the entire project is completed without any reportable incidents, due to top management support. In my 22 years experience (HSE), it is very clear that if Project Manager will lead, support and believe in HSE person (without any duplicity) then I am sure not a single incident will happen, and we will successfully achieve safety culture." U Shekhar, MD, Galaxy Surfactants stated, "Quarterly review of all sites related to Legal, Safety, process safety along with Factory Managers and seniors can be started. Only high risk points can be discussed and progress can be reviewed. Some of the aspects of leading / lagging indicators monitoring and display related to their own safety performance to be displayed as first slide in each meeting by individual Process head. Safety pause is one which have to be made mandatory and in some of meetings where top management present should also share safety pause .This will create positive impact. Being concerned on total environmental, we need to improve and evaluate all off site incident thoroughly. Internal incident we have intense review. Let all managers variable pay have Safety as one of the component. External support partner strengthening like our transporter. Many of onsite vehicle incident are because of either misbehaving of driver, poor vehicle conditions. Stressing safety approach even in personal life is the support when seniors visit the site is the support I seek." Arun Deore, HOD, Afcons, says, "The Construction Project Manager and Project HSE Heads expect proactive commitment from top management and directors. They rely on Top Management and Directors to actively support safety initiatives. This involves dedicating sufficient budget and resources for regular safety training programs, ensuring the availability of modern safety equipment, and promoting a safety-first culture throughout the organization. They expect leaders to conduct periodic site visits to demonstrate a personal commitment to safety, actively participate in safety meetings, and promptly address any safety-related concerns raised by on-site teams. Additionally, clear communication of safety goals, the enforcement of safety policies, and regular safety audits are crucial aspects of the support they seek to foster a positive safety culture across all construction sites." KK SHARMA, Director EHS DCM Shriram emphasised, "As part of top management, I feel supporting plant heads and EHS heads in terms of execution of their plans by allocating adequate resources and budgets. Above all highest level of trust in them will go in long way for building a positive safety culture empowering them for various decisions at plant level." Pavan Rao, EHS Head, SEIL, said, "Support in actions instead of words. Act on advice of HSE Head. Clear verbal and non-verbal communications to all. Clear safety KPI for HODs and Line Managers". Arvind Roy, EHS Head of Agra metro Project observed, "Top management and directors should give authority to plant heads and HSE Heads in screening deployment of workforce in view of employees competency and safety orientation to develop safe work culture - no work with safety should be allowed - safety is never expensive- incident is always expensive and causes loss of moral of employees and organisation." MK Rao, ex Executive director of IGL, "Visibility in the top managements' support by promptly approving proposals to improve working conditions, automation and quality of PPEs, and ensuring that related implementations are on course". These practical inputs would help to draw a broader view of defining positive safety culture for corporates (Personal Communications, 2023).

REFERENCES

Abeje, Mesfin, and Fan, Luo. (2023). "The Influence of Safety Culture and Climate on Safety Performance: Mediating Role of Employee Engagement in Manufacturing Enterprises in Ethiopia" *Sustainability* 15(14): 11274. https://doi.org/10.3390/su151411274

Bisbey, Tiffany & Kilcullen, Molly & Thomas, Eric & Ottosen, Madelene & Tsao, Kuojen & Salas, Eduardo. (2019). Safety Culture: An Integration of Existing Models and a Framework for Understanding Its Development. *Human Factors: The Journal of the Human Factors and Ergonomics Society*. 63. 001872081986887. 10.1177/0018720819868878.

Canso. (2023). Safety Culture: Definition and Enhancement Process. civil air navigation services organisation. https://www.icao.int/NACC/Documents/Meetings/2018/ASBU18/OD-10-Safety%20Culture%20Definition%20and%20Enhancement%20Process.pdf

Casey, TW, Hu, X, Reid, C, Tran, PA, Guldenmund, FW. (2022). Rolling up our sleeves and pulling up our socks: A critical review of safety culture definitions and measures, and innovative ways to move the field forward. DOI: https://doi.org/10.4337/9781788976268.00027

Edwards, Jason & Davey, Jeremy & Armstrong, Kerry. (2013). Returning to the roots of culture: A review and re-conceptualisation of safety culture. *Safety Science*. 55. 70-80. 10.1016/j.ssci.2013.01.004.

Ellis Louise A., Falkland Emma, Hibbert Peter, Wiig Siri, Ree Eline, Schultz Timothy J., Pirone Christy, Braithwaite Jeffrey. (2023). Issues and complexities in safety culture assessment in healthcare. *Frontiers in Public Health*, 11, DOI: 10.3389/fpubh.2023.1217542

Fabius, Raymond and Phares, Sharon. (2021, June). Companies That Promote a Culture of Health, Safety, and Wellbeing Outperform in the Marketplace. *Journal of Occupational and Environmental Medicine* 63(6):p 456-461, DOI: 10.1097/JOM.0000000000002153

Hadley, Constance Noonan, Mortensen, Mark and Edmondson Amy C. (2023, April 25). Make it safe for employees to speak up, especially in risky times. https://hbr.

org/2023/04/make-it-safe-for-employees-to-speak-up-especially-in-risky-times

Hristov, I. (2022). Advantages, managerial practices and main challenges. Springer. https://link.springer.com

HSE. (2023). Why is organisational culture important? https://www.hse.gov.uk/humanfactors/topics/culture.htm

Kelly, Michael. (2023, June 30). Building a Safety Culture: Everyone's Responsibility. https://www.linkedin.com/pulse/building-safety-culture-everyones-responsibility-michael-kelly

Lal Harbans and Choueiri E.M. (2023). The integration of behavior-based safety (BBS) as a company value is advocated! *World Safety Journal (WSJ)*, Vol. 32(2), 49-55. doi.org/10.5281/zenodo.8105788

Lundell, Mark & Cheri, Cheryl & Marcham,. (2021). Leadership's Effect on Safety Culture. https://www.researchgate.net/publication/355364834

McKinsey & Company. (2023, Apr 13). The State of Organizations 2023. https://www.mckinsey.com/~/media/mckinsey/business%20functions/people%20and%20organizational%20performance/our%20insights/the%20state%20of%20organizations%202023/the-state-of-organizations-2023.pdf

Milan, Ambroz. (2015). Safety culture in organization. DOI:10.13140/RG.2.1.2611.3121.

Misnan, Mohd Saidin & Mohammed, Miswan abdul hakim & Mohammad, Izran Sarrazin & Nesan, L. (2007). Problem and Issues in Developing Safety Culture in Construction Industry. *Malaysian Journal of Real Estate*. 2. 61-69.

Pilbeam, Colin and Karanikas, Nektarios. (2023). Safety training in context: technical, cultural and political factors affecting its design, delivery and transfer, *Journal of Safety Research,* 85, 308-320. https://doi.org/10.1016/j.jsr.2023.03.004.

Personal Communications. (2023, December). Interaction with industry practitioners.

Risk Engineering (2020, March 30). Safety culture: A contentious and confused notion. https://risk-engineering.org › concept› safety-culture

ACKNOWLEDGMENT

The contributions of industry professionals is thankfully acknowledged.

CHAPTER 9

BIG CONCERNS AND SOLUTIONS ABOUT LEADERS' READINESS TO RE-BUILD POSITIVE SAFETY CULTURE

Empowered and enabled positive safety culture methodology works is possibly a best option to deliver zero-harm objective. This paper dwells on a theme of exploring concerns and solutions over corporates' readiness to re-build positive safety culture. Important recommendations are made to help organisations overcome the challenges for corporates' readiness to re-build positive safety culture, based on the field visits to almost 45 site locations and interactions with 330 managers. Biggest concern is dumping safety culture transformation down the levels by leaders, then asking for a monthly report, not being available for resources support or culture reinforcement. Make behavioural safety positive culture a boardroom agenda, a zero-blame SOP in our organisation as long-term perspective towards our mission of "one nation one goal - zero harm." Fix safety culture accountability of each department (IT, CSR, HR, CC, Operations). Let everyone be on-board for safety culture intervention, make it organisation-wide and purpose-driven at a scale, and all leaders take it as personal responsibility for safety of all employees, associates and stake holders.

Keywords: Safety, Culture, Corporate, Leadership, Concerns, Readiness, Solutions.

INTRODUCTION

Companies and employees are participating in safety culture programs but are they ready for change and implementation, is a question, which is why they don't take it beyond training programs? Some say, we have a shortage of manpower, how to implement safety culture? They need to understand that safety culture is for saving existing manpower, less or more. They say, our company's main focus is production, they need to understand that they must go for safe production, otherwise, unsafe behaviours would bring down even the existing production targets. Employees would implement safety culture only when managements would constantly reinforce safety culture through their visible presence in shop-floors. Positive safety culture with behavioural safety as a tool would reduce distance and disconnect between executives and employees, and create brotherhood. What is important is to make this safety cultural change as purpose-driven and making it a scale (McKinsey & Company (2023)[1].

Good safety culture demands continued struggle and persistence. If you are convinced that your organisation has a good safety culture, you are almost certainly mistaken, a safety culture is something that is striven for but rarely attained. The virtue and the reward lies in the struggle rather than the outcome (Canso, 2023)[2]. In the process of developing safe behaviour culture, companies have already injured and killed so many. Positive safety culture ensures that no one gets injured physically, emotionally or culturally. This is to safeguard right to safety of each individual at work place in a more democratic and holistic manner. With Behaviour Based Safety (BBS) initiative, every aspect of safety comes under spot-correction for behaviours, barriers, resources, any matters pending for approval etc. Safety culture is becoming an indispensable forecasting factor in achieving sustainable development (Jasiulewicz-Kaczmarek, 2022).

Safety culture trainings to the staff don't help much unless the location leaders are ready to be supportive in launching the same to next levels. ONGC Karaikal ED Uday Paswan, said, "People should not only be saved from physical injury but also from psychological harm at workplaces. I was recognised at ONGC more as safety person and trained in safety systems as I demonstrated interest in safety culture." Proactive safety management serves the organisation for better results in our understanding of human safety from incidents (Thraen, 2022)[3].

Unsafe is essential sometimes. Some people from Oil India were of the opinion that employees have to conduct some at-risk behaviours due to night time, rainy season, at height due to compulsion, otherwise work would stop. Whereas the management is of the view that BBS is mandatory at oil India. BBS is a teamwork and brotherhood approach which is possible to achieve in the long run when safe behaviour becomes a mindset (parampara) and nature

1 McKinsey & Company (2023, April 13). The State of Organisations 2023. https://www.mckinsey.com/

2 Canso (2023). Safety Culture: Definition and Enhancement Process. civil air navigation services organisation. https://www.icao.int/

3 Thraen, Iona (2022 Apr. 4). Moving from Reactive to Proactive: Safety 2.0. https://accelerate.uofuhealth.utah.edu/

of people. Says BBS coordinator of Oil India, "we have to inculcate safety in behaviour, it is mandatory program for us." Spot-correction may not be easy for many people, it may begin with safety conversations first. Each SOP needs to be behaviouralised, it should be ensured that it is behaviour based SOP (Lal and Choueiri, 2023).

The major hurdles in organisational readiness for safety culture transformation encompasses the power of position being used by executives to justify production over safety. Insulting words are used to suppress safety officers. Language control is necessary for managers for not being reactive while suppressing juniors for non-compliance safety behaviours. Most of the times, the safety heads are not consulted for safety issues and decisions as they hold low positions in Organisational hierarchy, they remain vulnerable. Most top managements give verbal commitments in speeches but don't involve in 'daily safety culture implementation and monitoring' which fails the safety culture progress, and lead to incidents. Management should talk both of business and risks while they interact with plant managers in terms of planning and implementation. Is safety budget a really issue for plants? Why safety budgets are delayed by corporates top management for approval whereas safety culture planning is done well in advance perfectly? Building a safety culture requires the active participation and commitment of all employees, from top management to frontline workers (Kelly, 2023).[4]

OBJECTIVES

- To explore concerns over corporates' readiness to re-build positive safety culture.
- To find solutions for corporates' readiness to re-build positive safety culture.

METHODOLOGY

a. Measures

Both primary data (interviews, and discussions) were collected to explore concerns and solutions over corporates' readiness to re-build positive safety culture. Interviews based on open-ended questions, focus group interviews,

4 Kelly, Michael (2023, June 30). Building a Safety Culture: Everyone's Responsibility. https://www.linkedin.com/

and personal in-depth discussions were conducted almost over two years during 2022-2023.

b. Sample and Procedure

Field visits to almost 45 site locations and interactions with 303 managers and 590 contractors workmen comprised a sample of this research. Industry professionals participated in the study as part of an action field survey with the researcher. These research participants had been implementing behavioural safety compliance culture at their work sites. The research participants included the Directors, Managers, Heads of Departments, and EHS/HR Professionals belonging to the public and private industrial sectors, including chemicals, construction, gas, power and steel, across Indian locations. The sampling method used was random sampling.

c. Statistical analysis

The responses to the relevant questions were collated. Thematic analysis was performed and themes were identified from the quantitative data.

This paper is an extract of a national research program of the Forum of Behavioural Safety under Bharat Bane Surakshit (BBS) mission. The study results and implications are reflected below from a rigorous review of safety culture literature and experiences / case studies shared by industry leaders across Indian organisations.

RESULTS AND DISCUSSION

This paper dwells on the major theme on exploring concerns and solutions over corporates' readiness to re-build positive safety culture (Table-1).

Concerns over corporates readiness to re-build positive safety culture

Re-building positive safety culture is very critical issue as the fatalities numbers are still unacceptably high when seen through the promise of the OSH Act, which entitles every worker to safe and healthful working conditions and makes all employers and employees responsible to provide a work area free from recognized hazards (Lundell, et al, 2021)[5].

5 Lundell, Mark & Cheri, Cheryl Marcham (2021). Leadership's Effect on Safety Culture. https://www.researchgate.net/publication/355364834

There are 10 big concerns over readiness to re-build positive safety culture in plants.

1. **In favour and not in favour of safety culture implementation:** there are groups of employees divided over some concern that they are not in favour and some who are in favour of safety culture implementation due to certain cultural reasons unexplained.

2. **Balancing safety versus business targets:** for some employees, there are hurdles to balance it, and for others it is possible to balance.

3. **Managements readiness for safety culture transformation:** some leaders have reasons for not being ready for change versus others who are for this change in culture. There are two issues, one is that the organisations are not aware of the right definition and approach of safety culture, and second, they don't intend to adopt the same due to internal safety politics. The managements need to understand and emphasise the positive relationship between a sustainable corporate safety strategy and stakeholder perceptions that brings advantages to business performance (Hristov, et al., 2022).

4. **Safety cultural frame of reference:** those who follow reactive and dependent safety culture find it very difficult to change versus those who follow independent and interdependent safety culture, find it possible to change.

5. **Safety decisions are hard in the organisation:** people find that there are procedural struggles to process safety decisions. Do plants have to struggle for lot of procedure for safety budget approvals, and they get demotivated? Therefore plant and EHS heads tend to avoid the procedure hassles and decide not in favour of safety culture transformation actions. However, they receive immense pleasure when top management walk the talk and extend immediate support for safety reasons that builds culture.

6. **Safety culture - personal versus business goal:** if it is not a personal goal for employees, it is a weak business goal for them.

7. **Top management expectations:** plants expect support from top management for understanding their practical hurdles in business goals, whereas top management think that plants are the custodian of safety culture. The discrepancy or distance between meeting both's expectations make it impractical to achieve business or safety goals.

8. **Safety mindsets:** Management precisely remember production targets by heart, but they don't know how much is the behavioural safety risks, as it is not part of their culture.
9. **Perception about behavioural risks:** People didn't recognise behavioural risks and their impact on business or safety of manpower. Now they think that its important to understand this issue of human behaviour and necessary to fix the same.
10. **Safety budget:** Is safety budget a really issue for plants? Why safety budgets are delayed by corporates for approval whereas safety culture planning is done almost in advance perfectly?

Industrial accidents kill hundreds of thousands of people and permanently disable thousands each year. A federal minister told parliament in 2021 that at least 6,500 workers had died while working in factories, ports, mines and construction sites in five years. Labour activists, who worked in the field for years, reported that the figures could be higher as many incidents are not reported or recorded (Shukla, 2022)[6]. The corporates must consider above concerns for safety culture readiness.

Table 1: Concerns and solutions over corporates readiness to positive safety culture

Concerns	Solutions
▸ Employees divide in favour of safety culture (92%) ▸ Poor balance: safety versus business target (90%) ▸ Managements divisiveness for safety culture transformation (87%) ▸ Negative Safety cultural frame of reference (80%) ▸ Safety decisions are hard in the organisation(75%) ▸ Safety culture - personal versus business goal	▸ Find the differences between companies who implemented positive safety culture and those have not. ▸ Managements need to know BBS as a behavioural science application and a long term planned intervention. ▸ Implement action plan for global standards of safety culture. ▸ Focus on measures of forecasting best safety culture more accurately.

6 Shukla, Archana (2022, Sept 5). Workplace accidents: Inside India's 'factories of death'. https://www.bbc.com/

Concerns	Solutions
▸ Top management vs plants expectations (73%) ▸ Low Safety mindsets (71%) ▸ Low perception about behavioural risks (70%) ▸ Safety budget issues (70%)	▸ Qualitative Review of safety culture processes.

ASSESSING CORPORATES READINESS TO POSITIVE SAFETY CULTURE ON 20 ASPECTS

Poor awareness about safety culture has contributed to many major incidents and personal injuries. An organisation's culture can have as big an influence on safety outcomes as the safety management system (HSE, 2023).[7] Therefore, it is crucial to assess corporates readiness to positive safety culture through many aspects in terms of 20 critical queries (See Appendix) into the organisation's work culture. There are challenges and complexities in safety culture assessment relating to definition, tools, dimensionality and response rates. The aim is to prompt critical reflection on these issues and point to possible solutions (Ellis, et al, 2023).

FINDINGS AND ANALYSIS

India reported 1109 deaths and more than 4000 injuries in registered factories, on average, each year between 2017 and 2020. Although about 90% of workers in India are employed in the informal sector, underreporting of incidents from the informal and the formal economy mean these figures are underestimates. India has passed occupational safety and health law reforms in 2020, but experts feel that the new OSH Code is less stringent than the Factories Act, of 1948 (Paliath, 2023)[8].

Leadership safety time for safety culture implementation is to be fixed and logged in. Make safety an easy and a supportive culture for all units. Safety Leadership means getting everyone on-board (QHSE, 2022)[9]. If any

7 HSE (2023). Why is organisational culture important? https://www.hse.gov.uk/

8 Paliath, Shreehari (2023, Jan, 21). 3 Workers Die Every Day In Indian Factories, Govt Data Show. https://www.indiaspend.com/

9 QHSE (2022, Dec 28). Safety Leadership: Getting Everyone On-Board! https://www.blog-qhse.com/en/

leader is not involved in safety culture, the incidents potential is high in his/her work areas. It normally happens that all leaders are not focused with equal intensity for safety culture. This is a concern which needs to be communicated to corporate leaders. It is crucial that everyone in the company gives safety time each day to look around for risk and its spot-control. This is a continuous and big challenge for every plant or project site.

The concerns and solutions over corporates' readiness to re-build positive safety culture are categorised in the following ways.

a. Make safety culture eventful and digital to achieve its milestones by employees Empowerment - Ten Milestones:

1. Develop BBS Awareness till last person
2. Develop Active observers till last person
3. Monitor month-wise behavioural trends for each area and section
4. Track responsibility/ accountability of each manager for BBS reinforcement
5. Monthly progress review by top management
6. Quarterly Directors review
7. Include/monitor BBS as KRA
8. Enable BBS policy framework
9. Celebrate BBS Annual progress
10. Include BBS in Annual HSE Index

Positive culture of visible leadership and a culture of spot-correction of any at-risk behaviours and barriers, takes company's safety culture towards fulfilling zero-harm objective.

b. Model of safety culture: difference management

Organisational safety mindset triggers employees behaviours (safe or unsafe) which lead to consequences (zero-harm or incidents). BBS is to move from mindset-1 to mindset-2 for creating positive safety culture transformation.

Employees need to understand and experience the following in terms of:

1. Are you ready to mentor for BBS culture?
2. Have you corrected your own at-risk behaviours?
3. Who are in favour and not in favour of positive safety culture?
4. Is BBS a behavioural correction, observations, mindset, leadership visible presence in field, Organisational behaviour such as overemphasising production, pressures to work in unsafe conditions, only speeches not behaviours, reactive safety culture, zero fatalities, and so on?
5. What is your company's defined vision of positive safety culture?

c. Difference between critical and non-critical at-risk behaviours is to be understood

When company asks managers to aim for zero fatalities, they focus only on critical behaviours, whereas when employees don't care about less critical behaviours, they also pay less attention to critical behaviours, and when less critical at-risk behaviours are ignored, they gradually turn into serious or non-serious incidents.

d. Suraksha Aadhar

Research findings provide strong support for the premise that companies with policies aimed at improving employee health and safety, employee training, or having safety management systems positively influence safety performance, which in turn has a positive impact on financial performance (Bautista-Bernal, et al, 2024). Hence it is critical to link safety culture actions to individual performance, appraisal, promotion, variable pay, entire career that it gets intensified so much so that everyone makes one observation and spot-correction daily for minimum 5 minutes. Top management needs to structure it passionately to act-ionise it for top to bottom. If required, incentivise this positive and supportive safety culture for all.

e. Self observations

Live safer life, login your BBS observation score every day on company portal. Employees who were trained in positive safety culture, observed that they had their own critical at-risk behaviours that they corrected such as speeding vehicles above 150 kph, not able to focus on their job due to multitasking, not wearing PPE, and so on. They found it difficult to show commitment to implement safety culture even after being trained due to many Organisational factors such as main focus of management on production, pressures to work even during night, rainy season, etc. However, employees were in favour of positive safety culture transformation. The definition of safety culture has been accepted and broadened since the onset of this concept in the year 1984, now including safety perceptions and practices, beliefs and behaviours and so on (Abeje, and Fan, 2023).

f. Clarity on Visible leadership for inspiring positive safety culture

When you wish to drive BBS in plants, it would first depend upon how well do you understand it as a behavioural science application?

Mostly, top managements are less committed for visible safety culture participation, more so true in case of government companies in comparison to private multinationals. Government Organisations demonstrate active participation due to enforcement by ministers. There's a need to amplify top leaders visible presence as a value addition in positive safety culture activism in shop-floor. Visible leadership of top management team in safety culture Transformation must be part of their KRA. Like business Head of SEIL comes fortnightly to site and conducts BBS mass-communication as well as takes account of weekly report on BBS implementation progress, which impacts participation of all HODs visibility and accountability in safety culture at sites. During the weekly round at site of each top management members, the barriers to safety culture must be spot-closed such resources, engineering controls, unsafe conditions, process hazards, systemic and administrative issues to demonstrate visible leadership.

The Directors must define the concepts of visible leadership in positive and supportive safety cultural roles and values emphasis at sites. Management members are aware of production numbers at any point of time, why they are not aware of the behavioural trends of safety each month, as behaviour is the base of all incidents, and Organisations that are not aware of behavioural aspects of safety are safe only accidentally. Management team is the core team of safety culture transformation and if the team members don't act to their role, safety culture doesn't take place, whatever else companies do. Visible leadership is about inspiring, energising and mobilising employees and associates into their safety culture's active involvement. Management speeches and frequent field presence must come together for charismatic results in safety, culture and business. There are examples of leaders in industry who are demonstrating these behaviours but not each one of them, which slows down the spirit of positive work culture. Strong leaders at all organisational levels are critical for the prevention of sustained injury and fatality (Quality Safety Edge, 2023)[10].

Arun Deore, HOD, Afcons, says, "The project manager and HSE heads expect proactive commitment from top management and directors. They rely on Top Management and Directors to actively support safety initiatives. This involves dedicating sufficient budget and resources for regular safety training programs, ensuring the availability of modern safety equipment, and promoting a safety-first culture throughout the Organisation. They expect leaders to conduct periodic site visits to demonstrate a personal commitment to safety, actively participate in safety meetings, and promptly address any safety-related concerns raised by on-site teams. Additionally, clear communication of safety goals, the enforcement of safety policies, and regular safety audits are crucial aspects of the support they seek to foster a positive safety culture across all sites". What should be our goal in safety culture - focusing on zero fatalities, zero incidents, zero harm, or attending to zero unsafe behaviours, not the outcomes? If you do believe that no one should get hurt at work, and you believe that all incidents are preventable, leaders should set the expectation that everyone does whatever they must to prevent incidents (Wilson, 2023)[11].

CONCLUSION

This paper explored concerns and solutions over corporates' readiness to re-build positive safety culture. Most organisations move slow in deciding matters on safety culture goals due to lack of accurate guidance and mentoring. Safety culture areas of improvement should be prioritised and immediately tackled, and strengths of safety culture should be maintained (Mrayyan, 2022). Important recommendations are made to help organisations overcome the challenges for corporates' readiness to re-build positive safety culture,

10 Quality Safety Edge (2023). Visible Safety Leadership. https://www.qualitysafetyedge.com/

11 Wilson Perumal (2023). Zero safety incidents should not be your goal. https://www.wilsonperumal.com/

based on the field visits to almost 45 site locations and interactions with 330 managers. Biggest concern is dumping safety culture transformation down the levels by leaders, and not being available for resources support or cultural reinforcement. Corporates need to make positive safety culture a boardroom agenda, a zero-blame SOP in the organisation as long term perspective towards mission of "one nation one goal - zero harm." Fix safety culture accountability of each departments such as IT, CSR, HR, CC, Operations. Let everyone be on-board for safety culture intervention, make it organisation-wide purpose-driven at a scale, and all leaders internalise it and take it as personal responsibility for safety of their employees, associates and stake holders. It is utmost important to raise position of safety professionals within company. There are only few companies where safety heads are holding positions such as GM, ED, Director that render equation to justify their roles for safety culture transformation in the company.

RECOMMENDATIONS

Whereas each of the measures discussed above, directly or indirectly, impact the success of safety culture, largely the change is achievable depending upon how long the focus is maintained by the employees. Professional development including systems thinking and safety training are the necessary steps along with the policy changes facilitating organisations to support learning from mistakes which would contribute to reducing human errors (Mahsoon, et al., 2021). Managements need to know the positive safety culture as a behavioural science application and a long term planned intervention in terms of its concepts and measurable units such as behavioural trends, rate of participation of manpower, comparison of safety statistics before and after its implementation.

For positive safety culture implementation, identify and fix the role of each member of top management each month as well as director's quarterly review. Follow Global standards of safety culture. Release BBS Policy signed by the managing director and display at each site. Know the Success Stories of BBS Culture of GAIL, SAIL, VEDANTA, DCM SHRIRAM, GALAXY SURFACTANTS, TOYOTA, SEMBCORP, Thermax, Thysenkrupp, Torrent, Hikal and so on (Kaila, 2023).

Most important, when company announces a safety culture intervention, first communication has to go to down the levels by the corporate communications department in a very succinct manner to build a favourable perception of employees toward safe behaviour practices. Moreover, each leader has to reinforce the same down the levels in their respective areas and departments. There is a positive relationship between safety culture and organisational performance, indicating that a more positive perceptions of safety culture by the workers translates into a greater level of safety performance (Davyda, et al, 2023).

a. Find the Differences between companies who implemented supportive and positive safety culture and those have not, in terms of:

A. They don't walk the talk, only speeches.

B. They are not clear about safety and safety culture Transformation.

C. They dumped safety culture on plants down the levels.

D. They need to know the difference between C1 and C2 in terms of ABC

E. Directors /Top management have not reviewed safety culture transformation regularly in a structured manner. F. Effect on last workmen involvement is visible.

G. Site management is actively engaged in mobilising manpower in safety culture reviews.

H. Active Involvement of IT, CSR, CC, HR, Finance, Security departments.

I. Driving positive safety culture in a more structured/ innovative way.

J. Positive safety culture or positive workplace / positive Organisation.

Supportive safety culture presupposes that we (everyone at workplace) actively care about our people, places and cultures which is a daily journey and practice not a destination (Manufacturing Today, 2022)[12].

12 Manufacturing Today (2022, July, 22). 123 Indian companies receive the International Safety Award. https://www.manufacturingtodayindia.com/

b. Check the directors and top management's role in strengthening the safety culture ecosystem: way forward in terms of:

- Are top management leaders a part of the behavioural safety culture steering team?
- Are they actively participating in monthly safety culture meetings?
- Are they conducting weekly observations round for reinforcing spot-corrections?
- Are they rewarding observations of active observers every month at sites/plants?
- Are they appreciating HODs for their role in developing and increasing observers at sites/plants?
- Do they conduct mass-communication each month for employees/associates?
- Do they discuss the monthly improvement in behavioural safety culture score dashboard?
- Are Directors focused on the overall performance of safety culture intervention?
- Are they concerned about which behaviours are frequently causing incidents?
- Are they reinforcing support such as resources, spot-correction of safety barriers, reward and recognising best practices across businesses?

Empowered and enabled positive safety culture methodology works better and faster, is an only option to deliver zero-harm objective for industry. Biggest concern of safety culture transformation is dumping down the levels by leaders, then asking for a monthly report, not being available for any support or reinforcement. Let's all make behavioural safety culture a boardroom agenda, and BBS a SOP (Standard Operating Procedure) in our organisation as long term perspective for zero-harm, zero-blame implementation with a big brother safety approach and Bharat Bane Surkshit mission. SOPs must be developed for all critical activities and be shared with the contractors and their workmen. The companies must target zero at-risk behaviours. HODs daily round is absolutely necessary (OISD, 2023)[13].

---

13 OISD (2023). Fatal incident at Depot construction site. Oil Industry Safety Directorate. https://www.oisd.gov.in

Make safety an emotional experience for each employee, let it be publicised like a product by the corporate communication (CC) department people, as Fevicol is the best selling product of Pidilite company and that has made a place in every home, similarly, positive safety culture is to be a belief, and CC leaders have an active role in it. Make safety culture your product line - "All our products are made in positive safety culture." It is a safety culture - vision implementation by one and all. Internal communication mechanisms are critical to engage staff in safety culture activities. Corporate communications create a favourable viewpoint of employees about safety culture. Communication directly supports employee commitment (Tappura, et al., 2022).

Position power of a corporate leader is to be used to ensure that no one gets injured in organisations. It is crucial to realise that towards this objective, how do you get yourself accountable with your daily actions and more importantly, how do you get everyone in the organisation accountable for this goal every day in order to achieve zero-harm? This is what is a big concern for organisations. Ultimately, safety leadership is about taking personal responsibility for the safety of others, which involves creating a workplace where individuals at every level from the C-suite to frontline employees are actively engaged in supporting and advocating for safe practices (Evotix, 2023)[14].

REFERENCES

Abeje, Mesfin & Fan, Luo. (2023). "The Influence of Safety Culture and Climate on Safety Performance: Mediating Role of Employee Engagement in Manufacturing Enterprises in Ethiopia" *Sustainability* 15, 14: 11274. https://doi.org/10.3390/su151411274

Bautista-Bernal Irene, Quintana-García Cristina, and Marchante-Lara Macarena. (2024). Safety culture, safety performance and financial performance. A longitudinal study, *Safety Science*, 172, 106409, ISSN 0925-7535. https://doi.org/10.1016/j.ssci.2023.106409.

Davyda M. Hammond, Adrienne L. King, Margaux Joe, & Jeffrey R. Miller. (2023). Understanding the relationship between safety culture and safety performance indicators in U.S. nuclear waste cleanup operations, *Safety Science*, 166, 106241. https://doi.org/10.1016/j.ssci.2023.106241.

14 Evotix (2023, Sept. 29). What Is Safety Leadership and Why Is It Important? https://www.linkedin.com/

Ellis Louise A., Falkland Emma, Hibbert Peter, Wiig Siri, Ree Eline, Schultz Timothy J., Pirone Christy, Braithwaite Jeffrey. (2023). Issues and complexities in safety culture assessment in healthcare, *Frontiers in Public Health*, 11, 2023.

Hristov Ivo, Chirico Antonio & Ranalli Francesco. (2022). Corporate strategies oriented towards sustainable governance: advantages, managerial practices and main challenges. *Journal of Management and Governance*, 26. 10.1007/s10997-021-09581-x.

Jasiulewicz-Kaczmarek, M.; Antosz, K.; Wyczółkowski, R.; Sławi ́nska, M. (2022). Integrated Approach for Safety Culture Factor Evaluation from a Sustainability Perspective. *Int. J. Environ. Res. Public Health*, 2022, 19, 11869.

Kaila, H L. (2023). Exploring Global Standards of Safety Culture for Manpower and Business Perspectives'. *Industrial Safety Chronicle*, July-Sept. 2023, 67-73.

Lal, Harbans & Choueiri, E.M. (2023). The integration of behaviour based safety (BBS) as a company value is advocated! *World Safety Journal* (WSJ), 32(2), 49-55. doi.org/10.5281/zenodo.8105788

Mahsoon AN, Dolansky M. (2021). Safety culture and systems thinking for predicting safety competence and safety performance among registered nurses in Saudi Arabia: a cross-sectional study. *Journal of Research in Nursing*, 26(1-2):19-32. doi:10.1177/1744987120976171

Mrayyan M. T. (2022). Predictors and outcomes of patient safety culture: a cross-sectional comparative study. *BMJ Open Quarterly*, 2022;11:e001889. doi:10.1136/bmjoq-2022-00188

Tappura Sari, Aki Jääskeläinen & Julius Pirhonen. (2022). Creation of satisfactory safety culture by developing its key dimensions, Safety Science, Volume 154, 105849, ISSN 0925-7535, https://doi.org/10.1016/j.ssci.2022.105849.

APPENDIX: ASSESSING CORPORATES READINESS TO POSITIVE SAFETY CULTURE ON 20 ASPECTS

1. Do you think, your managers are ready to achieve positive safety culture?
2. Are you aware of your plants' process risks, behavioural risks and so on?
3. Is your commitment and support for positive safety culture visible to employees?
4. Are you aware what the plant/ EHS heads expect from you in terms of safety culture support for their plants?

5. Are you able to fulfil their expectations of qualified resources provision for achieving safety culture?
6. Do you address mass-communications of employees and associates on plant's safety culture?
7. Do you participate in BBS meetings/ BBS celebrations/ appreciation of BBS team/ involvement in BBS planned activities/ personally discuss on BBS with all you meet?
8. Are you realistically and practically involved in safety culture Transformation along with finance approvals /allocation?
9. Do you think, your commitment is reflected in achieving the safety behaviour at floor, and in culture, which includes clear communication of safety expectations, adequate resource allocation for safety programs, regular safety audits, and a commitment to continuous improvement in safety practices?
10. Do you give message to those who don't support BBS or hinder BBS progress?
11. Do you: Support in actions instead of words. Act on advice of HSE Head. Clear verbal and non-verbal communications to all. Clear safety KPI for HODs and Line Managers?
12. Do you ensure HSE as top driven approach, and walk the talk as well without duplicity?
13. Do you give authority to plant heads & HSE Heads in screening deployment of workforce in view of employees competency?
14. Do you demonstrate concern, timely support and actions on safety by heart?
15. Do you assure visibility of your support by promptly approving proposals to improve working conditions, automation and quality of PPEs, and also ensuring that related implementations are on course?
16. Do you often communicate company's vision and mission statements towards Safety?
17. Do you think that while implementing safety culture, top management environment is very much required and ultimately plant head supports expectations from the top management for the safety culture implementation?

18. Do you think you need to know BBS as a long-term planned intervention?
19. Do you think yourself passionate to drive BBS in plants under your areas of influence?
20. Do you empower and enable your plant / EHS heads for various decisions at plant level for building a positive safety culture?

ACKNOWLEDGMENT

Contributions of all industry professionals is thankfully acknowledged.

CHAPTER

10

TOP LEADERS' ROLE AND APPROACH IN TRANSFORMING CORPORATES' SAFETY CULTURE

Power of position is used by executives to justify production over safety. Insulting words are used to suppress safety officers. Language control is necessary for managers to not be reactive while suppressing juniors for non-compliance safety behaviors. Most of the time, the safety heads are not consulted for safety issues and decisions as they hold low positions in the organisational hierarchy, and they remain vulnerable. What kind of support do the plant heads and EHS heads expect from the top management and the directors, in order to successfully achieve positive safety cultures at plants/sites? This paper unfolds the top management's role and approaches in transforming the safety culture of plants based on field visits to almost 30 site locations and interactions with 243 managers which comprised a sample of this research. It is of utmost importance to raise positions as well as respect the opinions of safety professionals within the company. There are only a few companies where safety heads are holding positions such as GM, ED, and Director that render equation to justify their roles for safety culture transformation in the company. Based on the comprehensive literature reviews and insights from the field practitioners, this paper describes insights and recommendations on the top managements' role and approach in transforming the safety culture of plants which shall be useful for corporates.

Keywords: Top management, Safety, Culture, Plants, Behaviour.

INTRODUCTION

Research findings provide strong support for the premise that companies with policies aimed at improving employee health and safety, employee training, or having safety management systems positively influence safety performance, which in turn has a positive impact on financial performance (Bautista-Bernal, et al, 2024).

Safety culture transformation doesn't get sustained until it is initiated by the safety professionals, adopted by the HODs, monitored by the site/top management, and reviewed by the company Directors. Any long-term safety culture corporate intervention requires management presence, interaction, and openness with workers (Cooper, 2006). Managers' sincere sympathy for employees' safety is a precondition for safety culture implementation. The first few months of implementation initiate a safety climate, but it takes continued efforts to build a safety culture resulting in an expected level of increased compliances and significantly reduced incidents towards achieving vision zero. Companies that implement Zero Accident Vision have an ambition that all accidents are preventable, and they achieve it through their commitment, safety communication, safety culture, and safety learning (Zwetsloot, et al., 2017). Most top management give verbal commitments in speeches but aren't involved in 'daily safety culture implementation and monitoring' which fails the safety culture progress and leads to incidents. Management should talk both about business and risks while they interact with plant managers in terms of planning and implementation (Kaila, 2021).

Is safety budget a real issue for plants? Why safety budgets are delayed by corporate top management for approval whereas safety culture planning is done well in advance perfectly? How have leaders behaved to achieve a positive safety culture successfully? When leaders say to the plant heads, you are trained to be the custodian of safety culture, shouldn't they ask them, what support do you expect from the top management to achieve positive outcomes? In this regard, the business Head of Thyssenkrupp asked the safety Head of the site, if you have any problem with the client, you may put me on call, I am available to support. On another hand, the business head of Sembcorp Energy offered to regularly address mass communications of employees and associates on the plant's safety culture. Safety Head of the Nagpur Mumbai tunnel project, Subhrakanta Khuntia, said, "The entire project is completed without any reportable incidents, due to top management support. In my 22 years of experience (HSE), it is very clear that if a Project Manager leads, supports, and believes in an HSE person (without any duplicity) then I am sure not a single incident will happen, and we will successfully achieve safety culture" (Personal Communication, 2024).

The HSE Heads of companies such as Sembcorp Energy, ONGC, Torrent, and Thermax emphasised that the leaders need to mentor a positive safety culture. If leaders do it, nobody can stop this best practice from being integrated with the work culture. Most organisations move slowly in deciding matters on safety culture goals due to a lack of accurate guidance and mentoring. Safety culture areas of improvement should be prioritised and immediately tackled, and the strengths of safety culture should be maintained (Mrayyan, 2022).

What is lacking at sites are the management's visible leadership, corporate tracking, Directors' regular communication on safety culture down the levels, and HODs' presence at site areas. Safety culture implementation doesn't become a daily practice. The project manager attends the safety culture training but leaves its implementation to the safety officers. The safety culture transformation team is established but it hardly meets or reviews the progress regularly. Strong leaders at all organisational levels are critical for the prevention of sustained injury and fatality (Quality Safety Edge, 2023).

OBJECTIVES OF THIS SURVEY

- To explore challenges and problems in the top management's role and approach in transforming the safety culture of plants.
- To explore implications and recommendations on the top management's role and approach in transforming the safety culture of plants.

METHOD

This paper is an extract of a national research program of the Forum of Behavioural Safety under the Bharat Bane Surakshit (BBS) mission (Figure 1, 2). Field visits to almost 30 site locations and interactions with 243 managers comprised a sample of this research. Industry professionals participated in the study as part of an action field survey with the researcher. These research participants had been implementing behavioural safety compliance culture at their work sites. The research participants included the Directors, Managers, Heads of Departments, EHS/HR Professionals, and contractors belonging to the public and private industrial sectors, including chemicals, construction, oil, gas, power, and steel across Indian locations. The sampling method used was random sampling.

Both primary data (interviews, and discussions) were collected. Interviews based on open-ended questions, focus group interviews, and personal in-depth discussions were conducted over the year 2023. The responses to the relevant questions were collated. The themes from the qualitative data were identified for thematic analysis.

The study results and implications are reflected below from a rigorous review of safety culture literature and experiences / case studies shared by industry leaders across Indian organisations.

Figure 1: Participants of this research study at Pidilite Industries

Figure 2: Participants of this research study at Oil India

RESEARCH QUESTION

What kind of support do the plant heads and EHS heads expect from the top management and the directors, to successfully achieve positive safety cultures at sites?

RESULTS AND DISCUSSION

Responses of Industry leaders

What kind of support do the plant heads and EHS heads expect from the top management and the directors, to successfully achieve positive safety cultures at sites? Responses of Industry leaders are revealed as follows. Participation by Top Management & Directors in BBS meetings/ BBS celebrations/ appreciation of the BBS team/ involvement in BBS planned activities/

personally discussing BBS with all they meet (Karjule from Thermax). Their realistic and practical involvement along with finance - Manager of Privi Organics. "Their vision and mission statements towards Safety. One of the objectives must clearly outline their commitment towards HSE. Excellence beyond compliance. In PSUs , There is a separate committee by the name "HSE committee" which is headed by either a government nominee or an Independent director. Regular PSU directors in CMD are the members of that committee (Atul Garg, ex-general manager of ONGC).

Plant heads and EHS heads expect the communication that shows and reflect the commitment of management in achieving safety behaviour at the floor, and in culture. Typically, they expect strong support from top management and directors to successfully cultivate positive safety cultures at sites. This support includes clear communication of safety expectations, adequate resource allocation for safety programs, regular safety audits, and a commitment to continuous improvement in safety practices. Additionally, visible leadership involvement in safety initiatives and fostering a proactive safety mindset throughout the organisation are crucial elements of support (Aakash Thakur, Director Omya).

Sunil Acharya, GM, retired from the Chemical plant, says, the plant heads and EHS Heads expect support for - 1. Financial Approvals, 2. Motivational words 3. Ask in between about BBS progress and encourage 4 Link BBS with Performance Rating and Career Advancements 5. Message to those who don't support BBS or hinder BBS progress etc. Awareness and assessment of risks at higher levels, Budgets, and Qualified resources (Anmol Singh, HR Head, Ashok Leyland). Support in actions instead of words. Act on the advice of the HSE Head. Clear verbal and non- verbal communication to all. Clear safety KPI for HODs and Line Managers (Pavan Rao, EHS Head, SEIL). HSE to be top driven approach, and walk the talk by top management as well (Srinivas, Project Lead of Thyssenkrupp)."Concern, timely support and actions on safety by heart" (KK Gupta, ex-executive Director of IOCL).

According to Arvind Roy, EHS Head of Agra Metro Project, "Top management and directors should give authority to plant heads & HSE Heads in screening deployment of the workforce given employees competency and safety orientation to develop safe work culture - no work with safety should be allowed - safety is never expensive- the incident is always expensive and causes loss of moral of employees and organisation." "Visibility in their support by a) promptly approving proposals to improve working conditions, automation and quality of PPEs and b) Ensuring that related implementations are on course" (MK Rao, ex Executive director of IGL). "100 percent free hand / freedom" (Guru Pratap, EHS professional of Vasudha Pharma). Ramdas Jadhav, ex-general manager of IOCL, says, "While implementing safety culture in any industry, top management environment is very much required and ultimately plant head supports expectations from the top management for the safety culture implementation. To get an environment in the activities and support to all employees for their good behaviour and safe practice/plans implementation" (Personal Communication, 2024).

KK Sharma, Director EHS DCM Shriram, "As part of top management, I feel supporting plant heads and EHS heads in terms of execution of their plans by allocating adequate resources and budgets. Above all highest level of trust in them will go in long way for building a positive safety culture empowering them for various decisions at the plant level" (Personal Communication, 2024).

Subodh, EHS professional, Navin Flourine, plants need top management support not only their word, but they need support from heart. Some of the top management says only dialog in big forums when they need support, then saying different dialog. Any error or mistake in managing at-risk behaviours can increase the company's struggle to save the business and the interests of its stakeholders and may put the company two years back. Therefore companies who delay the safety culture decisions, or make wrong decisions for their qualified resources, are increasing problems for their management. Organisations need to identify and strengthen positives and be open to converting their negatives to move fast on safety culture transformation. Appreciate people for they control the risk, and remind them when they forget to do so, hence reward and reinforcement bring a positive safety culture to organisations.

According to U Shekhar, MD, Galaxy Surfactants, "Quarterly review of all sites related to Legal, Safety, process safety along with Factory Managers and seniors can be started. Only high risk points can be discussed and progress can be reviewed. Some of the aspects of Leading / Lagging indicators monitoring and display related to their own safety performance are to be displayed as the first slide in each meeting by the individual Process head. Safety pause has to be made mandatory and in some of the meetings where top management is present should also share safety pause. This will create a positive impact. Being concerned about the total environment, we need to improve and evaluate all off-site incidents thoroughly. For internal incidents, we have an intense review. Let all Managers' variable pay have Safety as one of the components. External support partner strengthening like our transporter. Many onsite vehicle incidents are because of either misbehaving of the driver, or poor vehicle conditions. Stressing safety approach even in personal life is the support when seniors visit the site is the support I seek" (Personal Communication, 2024).

Arun Deore, HOD, of Afcons, says, "The Construction Project Manager and Project HSE Heads expect proactive commitment from top management and directors. They rely on Top Management and Directors to actively support safety initiatives. This involves dedicating sufficient budget and resources for regular safety training programs, ensuring the availability of modern safety equipment, and promoting a safety-first culture throughout the organisation. They expect leaders to conduct periodic site visits to demonstrate a personal commitment to safety, actively participate in safety meetings, and promptly address any safety-related concerns raised by on-site teams. Additionally, clear communication of safety goals, the enforcement of safety policies, and regular safety audits are crucial aspects of the support they seek to foster a positive safety culture across all construction sites" (Personal Communication, 2024).

There are myriad elements that remain indispensable for assessing the safety culture, such as leadership commitment, open communication, and learning from mistakes, and also family engagement, psychological safety, and employees' engagement in decision-making and innovation (Carvalho, et al, 2023).

How did other leaders behave to learn how we need to behave?

First, deal with profit-safety ethical sync following 'respect empathy care ownership' value culture. Then there is a need for enquiry on serious introspections towards zero-harm goals. Thirdly, understand, the view of top management on safety culture for clarification on the difference management from culture-1 to culture-2. Regarding above, the following questions would help.

1. Do you think, your managers are ready to achieve a positive safety culture?
2. Are you aware of your plants' process risks, behavioural risks, and so on?
3. Is your commitment and support for a positive safety culture visible to employees?
4. Are you aware of what the plant/ EHS heads expect from you in terms of safety culture support for their plants?
5. Are you able to fulfil their expectations of qualified resources provision for achieving a safety culture?
6. Do you address the mass-communications of employees and associates on the plant's safety culture?
7. Do you participate in BBS meetings/ BBS celebrations/ appreciation of the BBS team/ involvement in BBS planned activities/ personally discuss BBS with all you meet?
8. Are you realistically and practically involved in safety culture Transformation alongwith finance approvals /allocation?
9. Do you think, your commitment is reflected in achieving safety behaviour on floor, and in culture, which includes clear communication of safety expectations, adequate resource allocation for safety programs, regular safety audits, and a commitment to continuous improvement in safety practices?
10. Do you give a message to those who don't support BBS or hinder BBS progress?
11. Do you: Support in actions instead of words? Act on the advice of the HSE Head. Clear verbal and non-verbal communications to all. Clear safety KPI for HODs and Line Managers?
12. Do you ensure HSE is top driven approach, and walks the talk as well without duplicity?
13. Do you give authority to plant heads & HSE Heads in screening deployment of the workforce given employees competency?
14. Do you demonstrate concern, timely support, and actions on safety by heart?

15. Do you ensure visibility of your support by promptly approving proposals to improve working conditions, automation, and quality of PPEs, and also ensuring that related implementations are on course?
16. Do you often communicate the company's vision and mission statements towards Safety?
17. Do you think that while implementing a safety culture, a top management environment is very much required and ultimately plant head supports expectations from the top management for the safety culture implementation?
18. Do you think you need to know BBS as a long-term planned intervention?
19. Do you think yourself passionate about driving BBS in plants under your areas of influence?
20. Do you empower and enable your plant / EHS heads for various decisions at the plant level for building a positive safety culture?

One rule of positive safety culture is followed: no hierarchy, zero-harm, zero-blame, zero-hurt. A positive safety culture is sustainable in the positive organisation, not otherwise. BBS is big brother safety, not a big boss safety approach, validated across companies and countries for vision zero. BBS is behavioural science to bridge the gap between safety documentation and safe behaviour. In this regard, a research analysis found four factors with a significant impact on safety culture: safety information by operations managers; safety caring by employers; and safety coordination and safety regulation by safety professionals (Wu, et al, 2010).

Ten Insights on Top managements' Role and Approach in Transforming Safety Culture

1. **Leadership daily safety time:** The heads of organisations need to be made aware of these four levels of culture, the lack of daily culture monitoring by them, and its implications in terms of business effects and sustainability. Leaders' effectiveness depends on how much they own what's on their plate. They usually reject responsibility out of self-protection from blame. It is recommended that companies must build safety by stop-passing the buck (CISA, 2023). It never helps to pass the buck. Accept total responsibility for the outcome.

(Hyatt, 2023). The biggest hurdle of safety culture Transformation is dumping down the levels by leaders, then asking for a monthly report, not being available for any support or reinforcement. Hence there is a need for Leaders' daily safety time to be fixed and logged in. Make safety an easy and supportive culture for all units.

The concept of safety culture that enables workers to be free from harm, is characterised by complexity, multifaceted-ness, and indefinability. Over the years, disparate and unclear definitions have resulted in a proliferation of measurement tools, with a lack of consensus on how safety culture can be best measured and improved. This section described key challenges and complexities in safety culture assessment relating to the definition, tools, dimensionality, and response rates. The aim is to prompt critical reflection on these issues and point to possible solutions and measures for future directions as below (Ellis, et al., 2023).

2. **Stringent Measures of Forecasting Best Safety Culture More Accurately:** Safety culture is an essential aspect of any organisation, shaping its commitment to protecting employees, assets, and the community (the safety master, 2023). However, there are 10 following measures to forecast how well the organisations can manage it.

    - Everyone is trained in caring behaviours as safety culture observers.
    - Everyone is an active observer for spot-correcting at-risk behaviours. Continuous safety culture retraining for observations.
    - Daily accounting of at-risk behaviours.
    - Daily spot-corrections of barriers/hazards in safety.
    - Achieving a standard of zero at-risk behaviour and vision zero.
    - How often are the at-risk behaviours out of view of the supervisors/observers?
    - Are there any work areas that are out of view of the observers?
    - Safety culture is monitored by the corporate board and is linked to the HSE index.
    - Did safe behaviour learn from workplaces transfer to home and other arenas?
    - To calculate forecasting: each measure carries 10 score multiplied by 10 = 100 total score

3. **Example of Qualitative Review of safety culture processes** checklist for sites as below: Mark each process below out of 10. Check, what's lacking.
   - Safety cultural shift from reactive, dependent culture to independent, interdependent culture - Followed
   - Leadership increased involvement: Followed
   - Monthly BBS meetings - Followed
   - Incidents reduction - Followed
   - Behavioural trends improvement - Followed
   - Sharing of at-risk behaviors during TBT - Followed
   - Motivational reward, and recognition for observers/units - Followed
   - Managements regular observation rounds - Followed
   - Regular repeat BBS awareness sessions for spot-correction - Followed
   - Quarterly reviews across units/ sites - Followed

   Total score: $10 \times 10 = 100$.
4. **Measure long-term supportive safety culture** as a planned intervention of applied behavioural science to sustain as personal way of life (Kaila, 2022). Kindly ensure that the BBS Implementation is progressing as discussed in 20 points below:
   - Formation of site BBS steering teams;
   - Developing observers for each area;
   - Creating BBS awareness to all at the site;
   - Displaying BBS banners at site areas;
   - Daily BBS Mass-communication at sites;
   - Reverse BBS TBT daily at the site for sharing observations from employees/associates;
   - Monthly follow-up, hand-holding, support, and review along with expert guidance;
   - Maintaining site BBS scoreboard; BBS policy display, Dashboard for Inter-observers sharing of at-risk behaviours across departments weekly;

- Monthly circular of Corporate/Site Head;
- BBS Month/Annual celebration;
- Daily 5-minute observation round as per 12-point BBS checklist by everyone till the last person to be linked to employees performance (KRA), and reward best observers each month;
- BBS linked to EHS Annual index/policy;
- Linking BBS to Vendors T&C;
- Linking BBS to families and Schools; Observations of self, colleagues, and seniors;
- Measure BBS on monthly safety statistics;
- Regular Involvement of top management;
- Safety Cultural change from 1 to 4;
- BBS Project is named for its identity;
- Develop Lead trainers and Site BBS active coordinator for weekly reviews at locations;
- Develop IT enabled BBS observation checklist for data analysis each month.

Measure $20 \times 5 = 100$ percent BBS performance

Continuous focus and daily review of planned activities by HODs. We need to review the onsite quarterly BBS Implementation progress and find out gaps in actions.

5. **BBS Monthly Progress review template for each plant / project site (Kaila, 2023):**
   - Names of all plant BBS steering team members
   - Total number of observers trained out of total manpower
   - Feedback from BBS area coordinators,
   - Feedback Sharing by any two Observers
   - Display of BBS Banners across plant/office areas
   - Sharing any site photos, site video
   - Circular of BBS Steering team Chairperson down the levels
   - HSE statistics before/after the BBS launch
   - List of BBS trainings conducted during the month
   - Video of BBS implementation at the site

- Plant head Review of implementation
- Monthly / weekly BBS scoreboard of the plant
- Way forward by steering team Chairman
- Experts' comments and appreciation. Q & A - Doubts, clarifications
- Group photo, and Closing, Thanks, and next review date.

6. **Ten aspects of BBS - Converting Safety Compliance to Safety Culture (Lal, 2021).**
   - BBS is an un-complicating safety implementation.
   - BBS is de-hierarchying safety implementation.
   - BBS is involving top to bottom.
   - BBS is involving top to bottom.
   - BBS is spot correction of at-risk behaviour.
   - BBS is creating an interdependent safety culture.
   - BBS is achieving zero unsafe behaviour.
   - BBS is the personalising correction of at-risk behaviour.
   - BBS is accounting for safe and unsafe behaviour each month.
   - BBS is a continuous journey.
   - Finally, BBS is saving human lives and businesses both.
7. **Top management's role in strengthening the safety culture ecosystem: way forward**
   - Are top management leaders a part of the behavioural safety culture steering team?
   - Are they actively participating in monthly safety culture meetings?
   - Are they conducting weekly observation round for reinforcing spot-corrections?
   - Are they rewarding observations of active observers every month at sites/plants?
   - Are they appreciating HODs for their role in developing and increasing observers at sites/plants?
   - Do they conduct mass communication each month for employees/ associates?

- Do they discuss the monthly improvement in the behavioural safety culture score dashboard?
- Are Directors focused on the overall performance of safety culture intervention?
- Are they concerned about which behaviours are frequently causing incidents?
- Are they reinforcing support such as resources, spot-correction of safety barriers, reward, and recognizing best practices across businesses?

Let's all make behavioural safety culture a boardroom agenda, and BBS an SOP in our organisation as a long-term perspective for zero-harm, zero-blame implementation with a big brother safety approach and Bharat Bane Surkshit mission! (Lal, 2021a).

By reintroducing BBS at PIL, the management is empowering and enabling every employee as well as workmen to care and speak up for the safety of each other, and make time daily to observe and spot-correct at-risk behaviours of colleagues and also rectify safety barriers, and thus come together to recreate an interdependent safety culture. Focus on Behaviours, not Outcomes

8. **Unsafe is essential sometimes**

   Some people from Oil India thought that employees have to conduct some at-risk behaviours due to night time, rainy season, at height due to compulsion, otherwise, work would stop. Whereas the management is of the view that BBS is mandatory in Oil India. BBS is a teamwork and brotherhood approach that is possible to achieve in the long run when safe behaviour becomes a mindset (parampara) and the nature of people. Says the BBS coordinator of Oil India, "we have to inculcate safety in behaviour, it is a mandatory program for us". Spot correction may not be easy for many people, it may begin with safety conversations first. Each SOP needs to be behaviouralised, it should be ensured that it is behaviour based SOP.

9. **Companies and employees are participating in safety culture programs but are they ready for change and implementation, this is a question,** which is why they don't take it beyond training programs. Some say, we have a shortage of manpower, how to

implement a safety culture? They need to understand that safety culture is for saving existing manpower, less or more. They say, our company's main focus is production, and they need to understand that they must go for safe production, otherwise, unsafe behaviours would bring down even the existing production targets. Employees would implement a safety culture only when management would constantly reinforce safety culture through their visible presence on shop-floors. A positive safety culture with BBS as a tool would reduce the distance and disconnect between executives and employees, and create a brotherhood (Lal, 2023).

10. **Safety Culture Foundation - Suraksha Aadhar:** How do you link BBS to individual learning, performance, appraisal, promotion, variable pay, and entire career that it gets intensified so much so that everyone makes one observation and spot-correction daily for 5 minutes? Top management needs to structure it passionately to actionize it from top to bottom. If required, incentivize this positive and supportive safety culture for all.

    Live a safer life, and login your BBS observation score every day. Employees who were trained in positive safety culture observed that they had the critical at-risk behaviours that they corrected such as speeding vehicles above 150-kmh, not being able to focus on their job due to multitasking, not wearing PPE, and so on. They found it difficult to show commitment to implementing a safety culture even after being trained due to many organisational factors such as the main focus of management on production, pressures to work even during the night, rainy season, etc. However, employees were in favour of positive safety culture transformation.

CONCLUSIONS AND IMPLICATIONS

The difference between critical and non-critical at-risk behaviours is to be understood. When a company asks managers to aim for zero fatalities, they focus only on critical behaviours, whereas when employees don't care about less critical behaviours, they also pay less attention to critical behaviours, and when less critical at-risk behaviours are ignored, they gradually turn into serious or non-serious incidents. Maximum involvement of upper management in safety activities significantly influences the supervisory practices of a company's line managers (Hsu, 2012).

Clarity on Visible leadership for inspiring positive safety culture: when you wish to drive BBS in plants, it would first depend upon how well do you understand it as a behavioural science application. Mostly in general, top management is less committed to visible safety culture participation, more so true in the case of government companies in comparison to private multinationals. Government organisations demonstrate active participation due to enforcement by ministers. There's a need to amplify top leaders' visible presence as a value addition to positive safety culture activism on the shop floor. Visible leadership of the top management team in safety culture Transformation must be part of their KRA. Like business Head of SEIL comes fortnightly to the site and conducts BBS mass communication as well as takes account of weekly reports on BBS implementation progress, which impacts participation of all HOD's visibility and accountability in safety culture at sites. During the weekly round at the site of each top management member, the barriers to safety culture must be spot-closed such as resources, engineering controls, unsafe conditions, process hazards, and systemic and administrative issues to demonstrate visible leadership.

The Directors must define the concepts of visible leadership in positive and supportive safety cultural roles and values emphasis at sites. Management members are aware of production numbers at any point in time, why they are not aware of the behavioural trends of safety each month, behaviour is the base of all incidents, and organisations that are not aware of behavioural aspects of safety are safe only accidentally. Management team is the core team of safety culture transformation and if the team members don't act to their role, safety culture doesn't take place, whatever else companies do. Visible leadership is about inspiring, energising, and mobilizing employees and associates into their safety culture's active involvement. Management speeches and frequent field presence must come together for charismatic results in safety, culture, and business. There are examples of leaders in the industry who are demonstrating these behaviours but not each one of them, which slows down the spirit of positive work culture (Lal and Choueiri, 2023).

The safety culture transitions never happen randomly or by accident. It follows a process of change and growth. As a company expands its safety consciousness, it is important to assess managements' KRA for visible leadership in this cultural transformation in terms of the following:

1. How many spot-correction did you engage in every day for at-risk behaviours and barriers in safety?

2. How many BBS Gemba walks did you complete today and rewarded observers?
3. Did you enter your daily contribution of spot-correction on the BBS company folder?
4. How many safety budgets did you approve of today?
5. How many BBS Mass-communicatio in a week did you have on the shop floor?
6. Do you know the weekly behavioural trends of at-risk behaviours and Barriers of your plants?
7. Did you participate in participate in weekly and monthly BBS meetings?
8. Did you consult and respect the EHS department before making safety decisions?
9. Do you know an overall increase of BBS mentors and observers of your plants each month?
10. Have you personally stopped your at-risk behaviours?

Physical safety matters just as much as psychological safety (EHS Daily Advisor, 2023). ONGC Karaikal ED Uday Paswan says, "People should not only be saved from physical injury but also from psychological harm at workplaces. Safety culture training to the staff don't help much unless the location leaders are supportive of launching the same to the next level. I was recognised at ONGC more as a safety person and trained in safety systems as I demonstrated interest in safety culture." It is natural for people to hold back and avoid taking risks at work. This can mean a reluctance to report mistakes, ask questions, offer new ideas, or challenge a plan. People, whether they're aware of it or not, try to protect their reputations and jobs. Unfortunately, the same behaviours that feel risky to individual employees are precisely what their companies need to thrive in this uncertain economic climate. To solve this dilemma, we encourage leaders to adopt a winning formula for achieving a more psychologically safe workplace and the benefits it provides (HBR, 2023).

In the process of developing safe behaviour culture, companies have already injured and killed so many. A positive safety culture ensures that no one gets injured physically, emotionally, or culturally. This is to safeguard the right to safety of each individual at wor place in a more democratic and holistic manner. With an initiative of a positive safety culture, every aspect of safety comes under spot-correction for behaviours, barriers, resources, and any matters pending.

RECOMMENDATIONS

The model of safety culture for difference management describes that the organisational safety mindset triggers employees' behaviours (safe or unsafe) which leads to consequences (zero harm or incidents). BBS is to move from mindset-1 to mindset-2 to create positive safety culture transformation with introspections in terms of the following issues (Lal, 2022a).

1. Are you ready to mentor for BBS culture?
2. Have you corrected your at-risk behaviours?
3. Who are in favour and not in favour of positive safety culture?
4. Is BBS a behavioural correction, observations, mindset, leadership visible presence in the field, organisational behaviour such as overemphasising production, pressures to work in unsafe conditions, only speeches not behaviours, reactive safety culture, zero fatalities, and so on?
5. What is your company's defined vision of positive safety culture?

By coming on the safety culture board as BBS steering team, each member can write a new chapter in company's growth. Robyn Denholm said, "I'm delighted to join the Safety Culture board as the company looks towards its next phase of growth. What Luke and the team have already accomplished is remarkable, and I look forward to contributing to the next chapter of this incredible story" (Safety Culture Team, 2023). However, each member on-board has to consider following concerns for cultural transformation that would take company business to new levels.

There are ten big concerns over readiness to re-build positive safety culture as follows.

1. **In favour and not in favour of safety culture implementation:** There are groups of employees divided over some concern that they are not in favour and some who are in favour of safety culture implementation due to certain cultural reasons unexplained.

2. **Balancing safety versus business targets:** For some employees, there are hurdles to balance it, and for others, it is possible to balance.
3. **Managements readiness for safety culture transformation:** Some leaders have reasons for not being ready for change versus others who are for this change in culture.
4. **Safety cultural frame of reference:** Those who follow reactive and dependent safety culture find it very difficult to change versus those who follow independent and interdependent safety culture, find it possible to change.
5. **Safety decisions are hard in the organisation:** People find that there are procedural struggles to process safety decisions. Do plants have to struggle with lot of procedures for safety budget approvals, and they get demotivated? Therefore plant and EHS heads tend to avoid the procedure hassles and decide not in favour of safety culture transformation actions. However, they receive immense pleasure when top management walks the talk and extends immediate support for safety reasons that build culture.
6. **Safety culture - personal versus business goal:** If it is not a personal goal for employees, it is a weak business goal for them.
7. **Top management expectations:** Plants expect support from top management for understanding their practical hurdles in business goals, whereas top management thinks that plants are the custodians of safety culture. The discrepancy or distance between meeting both's expectations makes it impractical to achieve business or safety goals.
8. **Safety mindsets:** Management precisely remember production targets by heart, but they don't know how much is the behavioural safety risks, as it is not part of their culture.
9. **Perception about behavioural risks:** People didn't recognise behavioural risks and their impact on business or safety of manpower. Now they think that it's important to understand this issue of human behaviour and necessary to fix the same.
10. **Safety budget:** Is safety budget a real issue for plants? Why safety budgets are delayed by corporates for approval whereas safety culture planning is done almost in advance perfectly?

In the integrated culture, safety is everyone's responsibility, it's not just for managers. All staff, from employees to managers and directors are involved. It is necessary to make safety culture eventful and digital to achieve employee empowerment in terms of 10 milestones as follows:

1. BBS Awareness till the last person
2. Active observers till the last person
3. Monitor month-wise behavioural trends for each area and section
4. Tracking responsibility of each manager for BBS reinforcement
5. Monthly top management progress review
6. Quarterly Directors review
7. Include/monitor BBS as KRA
8. Enable BBS policy framework
9. Celebrate BBS Annual progress
10. Include BBS in the Annual HSE Index

Leaders at top management are not even aware that people practice reactive safety culture. One of the Executive Directors asked surprisingly, "Is anyone reactive here?" Managements need to know BBS as a behavioural science application and a long-term planned intervention in terms of its concepts and measurable such as behavioural trends, rate of participation of manpower, and comparison of safety statistics before and after its implementation.

For BBS implementation, identify, fix and account for the role of each member of top management as well as Director's quarterly review each month. Follow Global standards of safety culture. Release BBS Policy signed by the Director and displayed at each site. Know the Success Stories of BBS - Culture drives behaviour (GAIL, SAIL, VEDANTA, DCM SHRIRAM, GALAXY SURFACTANTS, TOYOTA, SEMBCORP, Thermax, Thysenkrupp, Torrent, Hikal). Positive culture of visible leadership and a culture of spot-correction of any at-risk behaviours and barriers, take company's safety culture towards fulfilling the zero-harm objective (Lal, 2022).

Find the Differences between companies who implemented positive safety culture and those have not, in terms of:

A. They don't walk the talk, only speeches.

B. They are not clear about safety and safety culture Transformation.

C. They dumped safety culture on plants down the levels.

D. They need to know the difference between C1 and C2 in terms of ABC

E. Directors /Top management have not reviewed safety culture Transformation regularly in a structured manner. F. Effect on last workmen involvement is visible.

G. Site management is actively engaged in mobilizing manpower in safety culture reviews.

H. Active Involvement in IT, CSR, CC, HR, Finance, Security departments.

I. Driving a positive safety culture in a more structured/ innovative way.

J. Positive safety culture or positive workplace / positive organisation.

Companies need to follow an action plan to implement global standards of safety culture as described below.

- Safety professionals should consider evaluating their individual capacity, and that of the institutions for promoting safety culture. Measuring roles of management leadership in sustaining safety culture.
- Safety culture to be a safety management practice more than a safety leadership tool
- Practice ethics of safety and risk science.
- Benchmarking in terms of behaviouralization of safety systems
- Equality of respect for lowest level workers in terms of cultural safety.
- Safety culture to be built on safety science as well the risk science.
- Build a positive safety culture as well as a positive organisation.
- Work on corporate safety mindset as much as safety culture behaviours. Safety culture is an essential part of a business strategic goal.
- The top management must continuously monitor and evaluate their strategies while delivering multifaceted interventions to be more specifically focused and to motivate workers to be enthusiastic in sustaining safety culture (Wong, et al., 2021).

REFERENCES

Bautista-Bernal Irene, Quintana-García Cristina, and Marchante-Lara Macarena. (2024). Safety culture, safety performance and financial performance. A longitudinal study, *Safety Science*, Volume 172, 106409, ISSN 0925-7535, https://doi.org/10.1016/j.ssci.2023.106409.

Carvalho REFL, Bates DW, Syrowatka A, Almeida I, Sousa L, Goncalves J, Oliveira N, Gama M, Alencar AP. (2023). Factors determining safety culture in hospitals: a scoping review. *BMJ Open Qual*. Oct;12 (4): e002310. doi: 10.1136/bmjoq-2023-002310. PMID: 37816540; PMCID: PMC10565149.

CISA. (2023, Feb 1). Companies Must Build Safety by Stop Passing the Buck. https://www.cisa.gov/resources-tools/resources/stop-passing-buck-cybersecurity

Cooper, D. (2006).The impact of management's commitment on employee behaviour: A field study. ASSE- 0307-013. American Society of Safety Engineers Middle East Chapter 7th Professional Development Conference & Exhibition Kingdom of Bahrain, March 18-22, 2006.

EHS Daily Advisor. (2023, Oct 20). What We Learned From Safety Culture Week 2023. https://ehsdailyadvisor.blr.com/2023/10/what-we-learned-fromsafety-culture-week-2023/

Ellis Louise A., Falkland Emma, Hibbert Peter, Wiig Siri, Ree Eline, Schultz Timothy J., Pirone Christy, Braithwaite Jeffrey. (2023). Issues and complexities in safety culture assessment in healthcare, *Frontiers in Public Health*, 11, 2023. https://www.frontiersin.org/articles/10.3389/fpubh.2023.1217542. DOI=10.3389/fpubh.2023.1217542. ISSN=2296-2565

HBR. (2023). Make It Safe for Employees to Speak Up - Especially in Risky Times. https://hbr.org/2023/04/make-it-safe-for-employees-to-speak-up-especially-in-risky-times

Hsu, Shang Hwa. (2012). Safety Management in a Relationship-Oriented Culture. *International Journal of Occupational Safety and Ergonomics* (JOSE) 18(1), 35–45.

Hyatt, Michael. (2023). Why It Never Helps to Pass the Buck. https://fullfocus.co/navy-seals/

Kaila, Harbans Lal. (2021). Behavioural Benchmarking as a Robust Tool of Total Safety Culture in Industries. The Journal of Insurance Institute of India, July-Sept 2021, Vol. 9 (1), 82-88.

Kaila, Harbans Lal. (2022). Long Term Safety Culture Implementation. Print ISBN-13: 9788192769462, https://www.printspublications.com/book/long-term-safety

Kaila, H L. (2023). Exploring Global Standards of Safety Culture for Manpower and Business Perspetives.' *Industrial Safety Chronicle*, July-Sept. 2023, 67-73. https://nsc.org.in/wp-content/uploads/2023/11/July-September-2023-CHR.pdf

Kaila, Harbans Lal. (2022). Long Term Safety Culture Implementation. Prints Publications, New Delhi. ISBN-13: 9788192769462, https:// www.printspublications.com/book/long-term-safety

Lal, H. (2021). Behavioural economics of safety culture management in companies. WSJ, 30(4).

Lal, H. (2021a). Why Industry is Losing Faith in HSE Awards?: Professionals Rethink. IJTD, 51(1), 82- 90.

Lal, H. (2022). Revitalise and Fast-track Safety Culture in Industry or Face Incidents/ Losses. *International Journal of Applied Marketing and Management*, 7 (1) 2022, 01-16. http://publishingindia.com/ijamm/

Lal H. (2022a). Fast-track industry safety culture and reduction of incidents/losses. WSJ Vol. 31, No.

Lal, H. (2023). Strengthening a positive safety culture despite underlying fear and peer pressure. *World Safety Journal,* 32(1), 57–64. https://doi.org/ 10.5281/ zenodo.7770080

Lal H. and Choueiri E.M. (2023). The integration of behaviour-based safety (BBS) as a company value is advocated! *World Safety Journal* (WSJ), Vol. 32, No 2, Page 49-55. doi.org/10.5281/zenodo.8105788

Mrayyan M. T. (2022). Predictors and outcomes of patient safety culture: a cross-sectional comparative study. *BMJ Open Quality* 2022;11:e001889. doi:10.1136/ bmjoq-2022-001889

Safety Culture Team. (2023, Mar 27). Robyn Denholm to join the SafetyCulture board as the company eyes next phase of growth. https://blog.safetyculture.com/media-release/robyn-denholm

The safety master. (2023, July 28). Enhancing safety culture. https://www.thesafetymaster.com/enhancing-safety-culture-a-comprehensive-guide-by-a-leading-safety-consultant/

Personal Communication. (2024). *Personal Communication with Industry Leaders.*

Quality Safety Edge. (2023). Visible Safety Leadership. https://www.qualitysafetyedge.com/customized-solutions/visible-safety-leadership

Wu Tsung-Chih, Lin Chia-Hung, Shiau Sen-Yu. (2010). Predicting safety culture: The roles of employer, operations manager and safety professional, *Journal of Safety Research*, 41, (5), 423-431, ISSN 0022-4375, https://doi.org/10.1016/j.jsr.2010.06.006.

Zwetsloot, Gerard & Kines, Pete & Ruotsala, Riikka & Drupsteen, Linda & Merivirta, Maija-Leena. (2017). The importance of commitment, communication, culture and learning for the implementation of the Zero Accident Vision in 27 companies in Europe. *Safety Science*. 96. 10.1016/j.ssci.2017.03.001.

CHAPTER 11

CRITICAL CHALLENGES IN CORPORATE SAFETY CULTURE - INDIAN SURVEY

Companies have given contract workmen a place to work, but not a place in their hearts. This disconnect creates a hurdle in safety culture transformation as well as business sustainability. Safety culture transformation doesn't get sustained until it is initiated by the safety professionals, adopted by the HODs, monitored by the site/top management, and reviewed by the Company Directors. Companies can assess as to where do they stand on this criteria of safety culture? This paper discusses the challenges of safety culture in terms of: managers deliver speeches on safety but don't visit the site, safety culture as workplace culture, role of site Head and HODs, lies in safety culture, minimum safety culture implementation, gaps in safety culture, Safety Criticalities, Role of Reward and Recognition in Safety Culture, Environment Focus, and Most companies adopt 'passing the buck' safety culture. Important recommendations are made to overcome the critical challenges in corporate safety culture based on the field visits to almost 48 site locations and interactions with 306 managers. Ground reality of safety culture is different from what is reflected in documents. Hence it is vital to visit site areas by each HOD daily and converse with employees and behavioural safety coordinators of each section/area/shift in organizations.

Keywords: Challenges, Safety, Culture, Organisations, Corporate

INTRODUCTION

Analysis of accidents and incidents shows that human failure contributes to almost all accidents and exposures to substances hazardous to health. Many major accidents such as Bhopal, and Chernobyl were initiated by human failure. In order to avoid accidents and ill-health, companies need to manage human failure or errors as robustly as the technical and engineering measures they use for that purpose (Health and Safety Executive, 2023). Human factors (positive or negative) are the organisational factors or situations that impact people's actions and mindset. Supportive factors would reinforce safety culture, whereas the negative /reactive factors impede the safety behaviours of the workers. Managers and supervisors need to be trained to positively deal with stress and mental health issues of the employees for augmenting safety culture. Similarly, the situational factors like time pressure, fear, lack of resources create a mindset that nobody takes safety decisions, and safety culture takes a back seat, and incidents creep in taking toll on people and property (Lal, 2023). How organisations' leadership respond in such situations, matters most in re-building positive safety culture.

The future of EHS would change hands for safety culture from EHS to non-EHS employees. Managements are terribly fast in business persuasions but terribly slow in matters of HSE implementation and decision-making. This differential thinking perspective makes a large space for incidents to settle in. Businesses are hard to sustain without tackling serious HSE issues, the people and businesses would get hit for sure, not coming to an end, failing all of us in our ambitious zero-harm goal. Efforts are there by some but it requires a deeper action orientation. For most organisations, change of safety culture is difficult to manage and confusing to know even how to begin. Passive management practice delays safety culture implementation at sites. The business as well as EHS leaders are not better informed on safety culture methodology. The safety officers in Indian industry are not much trained in positive safety culture implementation, which reflects on the institutions providing academic or skill safety training competency to them. At the same time, largely, the Indian industry is not focused to update their safety professionals except a few marginal organisations who are interested in their company safety culture for business reasons. The organisations, at large, are still struggling for PPE enforcement and barriers to safety.

Work Culture is a deep-rooted construct of a company's thought processes over the years going into daily practices. Any change in this work culture requires a well planned holistic intervention. If you wish to really become a global company for partnering into the harbour of international economies, you have to work internally on your behaviours, beliefs, practices and barriers. No business can afford delays in safety conflict management as it amounts to direct losses of people and property. Being silent is no solution. Lack of safety culture transformation has serious implications, on one side there are gaps in safety knowledge of SOP among employees, on other side, employees save their skin by wrong information that their organisation is best because they already kept awards and certifications in their pockets. Management always thought that safety is not their job, they have to do only management, hence safety culture suffered and business didn't get sustained as incidents continued due to lack of robustness in the positive safety culture.

A positive safety culture is a game changer. It requires two level teams, one on the topmost directors level leadership that is the review team, and the second team of the top management level that is the reinforcement team, to mobilise the safety culture down to all the levels till the last person at site. Both the teams should integrate positive safety culture in the workplace culture, which is essentially a long-term planned organisation-wide intervention. Both positive safety culture and positive work culture can not be separated as they are integral part of organisational performance and excellence. Positive work culture would require next level interventions such as psychological safety, cultural safety, human factors, human error, work life balance, systems improvements and their integration.

When employees are experiencing stress, they are reacting to a change in their work culture. Training alone can help create clouds of culture, but would not sustain it. The safety professionals must understand that the business results have to be fast-tracked and multiplied, hence safety culture transformational intervention also must be on same lines involving all in the organisation. The Psychology of Successful Positive Safety Culture is an internal locus of control of the company employees, which helps achieve the mission that no one would get injured at work sites. What employees do every day becomes part of their conscious work culture. The HSE Heads of companies such as Sembcorp Energy, ONGC, Torrent, Thermax emphasised that the leaders need to mentor the positive safety culture. If leaders do it, nobody can stop this best practice to be integrated with work culture. According to Asst. General Manager HSE of Afcons Infrastructure Limited, "Our efforts are always to enhance BBS techniques for HSE development and promote a culture of healthy and incident free environment across organisation and among neighbouring organisations / people at construction areas". Business leaders who don't mentor safety culture or just maintain lip safety culture would not be favouring sustainability.

It is particularly important that employees are well informed of the hazards, risks and control measures and are adequately trained to effectively perform their safety duties (Jain, 2022). Many companies try to establish a positive safety culture to ensure the well-being of their employees in hazardous environments. It is crucial that companies follow the four stages of behavioural safety culture development:

a. Risk assessment of behaviours;
b. Governance pattern (steering teams formation, observers);
c. Response preparedness (increased spot-corrections of behaviours and barriers);
d. Early warning management (observers development for all areas, monitoring by company directors).

The first challenge is that the safety culture is arguably a poorly articulated concept, with many different definitions (Louise, et al., 2023), indicate that there are several critical challenges in transformation of the safety culture for corporates as follows:

- Companies design safety culture intervention enthusiastically, why don't they continue?;
- Business contexts in India do not allow managers for stringent safety enforcement;
- Business safety or human safety in organisations is a critical concern for organisations;
- Are managers well aware of building a positive safety culture?;
- What are the big reasons for un-sustainability of safety culture in companies;
- Are we meeting standards of safety ethics in our industry?;
- Are organisations showing commitment for evolving positive safety culture?;
- What are the standards of a positive safety culture for an organisation?;
- How critical is it to introduce the culture of Psychologically Safe Environments (PSE);
- Are managements looking for 'just training' or safety culture transformation?;
- Is it developing positive safety culture or positive organization;
- Are there many bottlenecks in managements decisions for developing safety culture;
- How important is the history of safety of a company in building safety culture?;

- Is the emotional connect difficult for managers in building ethical safety culture?;
- How is the impact of perceived severity of incidents on business for safety culture response?;
- Are safety culture reviews and continuous improvement happening for life saving process?.

Another big challenge is that the psychological safety is going to be crucial for India Inc in 2023. 45% of all employers surveyed believe that psychological safety is a strong performance indicator and 47% believe it is a crucial need since it leads to higher employee retention and engagement, according to new data (Sarkar, 2023). The past 35 years have witnessed a shift away from safety monitoring solely based on 'lagging indicators' or retrospective data such as accidents and injuries, towards the measurement of 'leading indicators' or predictive measures such as safety culture (Key, et al., 2023). The safety culture in workplaces generally showed an acceptable level. However, workers with low safety behavior, safety leadership, communication, training and awareness exhibited higher rates of non-fatal accidents (Dendup and Wangchuk, 2023).

OBJECTIVES OF THIS SURVEY

- To explore the critical challenges in corporate safety culture.
- To explore ways to overcome the critical challenges in corporate safety culture

Figure 1: Site location example

METHOD

Field visits to almost 48 site locations (Figure 1) and interactions with 306 managers comprised sample of this research. Industry professionals participated in the study as part of an action field survey with the researcher. These research participants had been implementing behavioural safety compliance culture at their work sites. The research participants included, the Directors, Managers, Heads of Departments, EHS/HR Professionals belonging to the public and private industrial sectors, including chemicals, construction, gas, power and steel, across Indian locations. The sampling method used was a random sampling.

Both primary data (interviews, discussions) were collected. Interviews based on open-ended questions and personal in-depth discussions were conducted almost over 2 years (during 2021-23). The responses to the relevant questions were collated.

The study results and implications are reflected below from a rigorous review of safety culture literature and experiences / case studies shared by the industry leaders across Indian organizations.

RESULTS AND DISCUSSION

This paper dwells on ten aspects of the critical challenges in corporate safety culture as below.

1. Managers deliver speeches on safety but don't visit the site.
2. Safety culture as Workplace Culture.
3. Site Head and HODs.
4. Lies in safety culture.
5. Minimum safety culture implementation.
6. Gaps in safety culture.
7. Safety Criticalities.
8. Role of Reward and Recognition in Safety Culture.
9. Environment Focus.
10. Most companies adopt 'passing the buck' safety culture.

1. **Managers who deliver speeches on safety but don't visit the site for safety**, are false. And they impact this behavior down the levels, and others also do the same, this becomes the safety climate of an organization. It is just like firing without a bullet. They are not falsifying themselves but, others too. Walk the talk is key to any safety program in developing a good safety culture. HSE professionals say many views on this as follows. Daily Safety inspection is most important part for implementation of HSE by managers at sites. In our plant, plant head also give observations. Safety is just in their talk but not in action. He's not good observer and auditor who doesn't go to the site. It's again a part of the behavioural issue of an individual, needs constant hammering from the Director to ensure consistency. There is a scope for improvement in this. Nowadays management have no time to attend online safety meetings. It is absolutely true that those who give speeches have never worked by hand.They give lot of advises by going through articles. A business that has a poor safety culture won't just sacrifice its profits; it'll also put human lives at stake. A missing or lacking safety culture may lead to concerns such as increased injuries and deaths and more legal issues (RUPERT, 2023).

2. **Safety culture as Workplace Culture:** Safety culture is not just limited to individual 'my' work space, it is workplace culture for benefit of all workers. Effective implementation of positive safety culture requires meticulous planning, long-term commitment, and organization-wide support (Lal and Choueiri, 2023). Very few companies are focused on long-term safety culture intervention. The leaders need to aim decrease in the quantity and severity of incidents and injuries. Improving safety culture has demonstrated to reduce these events occurring, even if it doesn't follow a predictable path or happen overnight (Williams, 2023).

3. **Site Head and HODs** are naturally focusing more on production targets than safety implementation. This trending behaviors of leaders is disturbing and a warning for incidents to set in. The company's Directors need to act upon it immediately for business sustainability.

   Site Heads are generally not safety minded, they believe in delivering numbers of production and profits. At the same time, the HODs don't generally listen or respect the daily interventions of their unit Head. Site Head needs to review every month with HODs, corporate HSE

Head needs to monitor safety culture progress, and Director needs to reinforce quarterly with appreciation and gaps notification. Business leaders involvement is useful for creating a positive safety culture (Dahl, et al.,2022). It is worth mentioning that risk perception can serve as a mediator while safety culture can mediate the relationship between safety leadership and safety performance (Wei & Kuo, 2023).

4. **Lies in safety culture:** Most site Heads are not safety minded, they pretend so. Some safety officers lie often, they say something, do something, hide something. In most Indian organizations, safety is in files and walls, papers and policies, not in behavior of employees in corporates. A McKinsey Global report infers that organisations that do not guarantee psychological safety to their employees may have to face the flames of a toxic ecosystem and people tend to demonstrate safety behaviours for the fear of workplace victimisation (Umashankar, 2023). Indian workplaces face several challenges when it comes to workplace safety which can directly impact workers both physically and mentally. Up-skilling workers in health, safety and wellbeing can significantly help mitigate risks associated with these challenges (economic times, 2022).

5. **Minimum safety culture implementation:** It is observed that corporates follow minimum safety culture implementation just like safety laws. This survey research reveals the following:

   - Safety culture participation rate: 10% i.e. 50 observers out of 500 total manpower, which resulted in 70% safe behaviours, 30% at-risk behaviours and 100% spot-corrections.
   - Employees note down observations but don't talk with observees for correction.
   - HODs need to involve actively in BBS implementation for increasing participation rate.
   - Senior casual workmen should train new casual workers.
   - BBS review has made inactive employees active. Employees need training and retraining in BBS culture without which it gets slowed down.
   - Floor-wise, shift-wise, area-wise, section- wise observers names to be listed.

- Observers in the plant are just minimum.
- Inter-site quarterly review is recommended for BBS performance support.
- BBS is reviewed in MRM (monthly review meeting) by HODs.
- Annual review is too late for improvement. It should be quarterly or bi-annual.
- Divorce reactive/dependent safety culture and marry independent/interdependent safety culture.

Companies employees can have strong health and safety management systems through good communication, working together as a team and staff being involved on a daily basis with matters that affect their workplace (HSE, 2023).

6. **Gaps in safety culture include:** Client gives letter for non-compliance; Safety officer warns to cancel work permit; Supervisor give TBT, Consultant trains the trainer, But nobody sees that these trainers develop workmen as active observers, Nobody sees that after TBT, workmen are being observed or not. Resources are inadequate in terms of manpower and materials. Safety and caring are intended as company values. But no significance value addition is observed as it is limited to piece of paper.

When Project is delayed, there is significant stress on everyone from all sides, and then mostly, safety gets sidelined. How do we take care in this condition, is a serious concern? "We need safety culture, but we often neglect", an operations manager opened up during the training. Good workplace safety culture doesn't just happen, you need to take proactive steps to build it over time and to continually reinforce its importance in the workplace by setting standards and following through (Duncan, 2021).

Table 1 mentions the critical challenges in corporate safety culture that need special attention for night work, risk awareness to workers, banning reactive culture, and involvement of the Site Head and HODs in promoting the supportive safety culture. The sustenance of the safety systems management is possible only when the BBS - behaviour based safety has been transformed to be a culture of the organization (Pandi, et al., 2022).

Table 1: Critical challenges in corporate safety culture

1.	Safety is compromised at night work. At project sites, what can't be done with safety rules and regulations during the day, is delayed to night time and compromised without safety.
2.	Workers even don't know how much risk they are exposed to at projects site.
3.	Reactive culture returns as soon as there is a pressure of target especially when projects are delayed for its time line.
4.	Site Head and HODs are naturally focusing more on production targets than safety

7. **Safety Criticalities:** Do companies wait for safety criticalities and incidents before they act, or do they plan well to prevent any such harm to assets and manpower at workplaces? The success in delivering targeted programmes that help prevent injuries and harm depends on collective action by government, businesses, sector and business leaders, unions, and workers. A joint review of the 2019-22 Harm Reduction Action Plan shows good progress continues to be made toward reducing workplace harm through the initiatives we're undertaking together. We continue to strengthen and evolve our partnership. Together we identified key areas of collaboration to progress over the next 12 months to maximise our collective effort and reduce workplace harm (WorkSafe, 2022).

   People in organizations don't understand safety until it becomes critical. Workers follow what mindset is demonstrated by the management. Managers take safety only in critical sense which transpires into incidents and results in loss of mankind, assets, and delays in meeting projects deadlines. Practically, the industry is focused on cutting costs, savings, and profits, but these are not achieved without safety culture. More deeply people sense safety leadership, the clearer is their risk perception for achieving safety performance leading to safety culture.

8. **Role of Reward and Recognition in Safety Culture:** BBS culture development is restricted due to lack of information collected about the cultural background of an organization where BBS intervention is implemented. Moreover, BBS is not only about corrections of at-risk

behaviours and barriers, but it is a great deal about how an organization promotes, reinforces, and importantly celebrates safe behaviours through reward and recognition (R&R) system daily, weekly, and monthly basis. Quite often, organizations underestimate R&R, thinking that it is a waste of time activity, not realizing its strengths and positive consequences and influence on the organisational culture building process. The employers' practices must emphasise incentive programmes that aim to encourage and reward safe behaviour. Rewarding practices of large multinational companies should become more responsive to the individual employees and their specific socio-economic contexts and highlight the importance of employee involvement in reward programs (Houette, and Mueller-Hirth, 2022).

9. **Environment Focus:** If we don't save our environment, safety and health would fail automatically. Like climate change is impacting us today, as we failed to save our environment. Hence an equal emphasis is necessary for EHS aspects by all of us including governments, organizations, individuals etc. Organizations find their financial, social, and environmental risks, obligations, and opportunities better met when focused on safety in workplace culture. Occupational Safety and Health Administration (OSHA) says: "Sustainable organizations strive to balance the triple bottom line of people, planet, and profit to achieve long-term success and viability." EHS and sustainability are two sides of a coin (PULSE, 2021).

10. **Most companies adopt 'passing the buck' safety culture:** Good risk management means no buck-passing. Leaders must be trained to take responsibility for tough decisions rather than pass the buck. Companies must build safety by stop-passing the buck. It never helps to pass the buck. Leaders must accept total responsibility for the outcome.

Most companies adopt 'passing the buck' safety culture which means the directors or HODs pass responsibility of safety implementations down to the safety head, who in turn, shift their job to the managers, who pass it on to the safety officers, and safety marshall, supervisors, workers and so on. Due to which safety rules and procedures do not get implemented, and finally incidents appear. For example, in a three tier Work Permit System (WPS), the safety officer signs the work permit, but sheds responsibility on the receiver (sub-contractor), who in turn puts responsibility of safety to the executor, the worker. Hence the sense of three tier WPS gets lost, and the least capable worker handles safety job, the consequences of which are obvious.

Seniors pass on responsibility, not the decision making power. Hence the supportive safety culture never crops up. It remains a dependent safety culture. Since the seniors don't participate directly in safety culture activities, they are not aware of its benefits, so they neither take decisions, nor allow their juniors to decide for safety culture actions. Thus the progress is restricted in terms of wider implementation of safety support across the organisation.

In most companies, the corporate HR/EHS heads just initiate the safety intervention, and pass on entirely to the site heads, without sufficient monitoring or handholding or reviewing closely, which results in natural death of any best intervention to improve safety performance systems.

Passing-the-buck is to follow the dependent safety culture which is 2nd in the journey of safety management. Four levels of safety cultural maturity are followed in industry such as reactive, dependent, independent and interdependent. Higher officers depend upon the lower ones in organisational hierarchy. Obviously the best culture is the 4th one, i.e. interdependent, in which every one is active to care for safety of each other and connect, correct and converse daily about at-risk behaviours and barriers as an organisational intervention and a daily SOP to follow.

The heads of organisations need to be made aware of these four levels of culture, lack of daily culture monitoring by them and its implications in terms of business effects and sustainability.

Leaders effectiveness depends on how much they own what's on their plate. They usually reject responsibility out of self-protection from blame. It is recommended that companies must build safety by stop-passing the buck (CISA, 2023). It never helps to pass the buck. Accept total responsibility for the outcome. (Hyatt, 2023).

CONCLUSIONS AND RECOMMENDATIONS

Having seen significant improvements to accident rates in the last 40 years, companies in the industry now show a greater focus on the development of safety cultures throughout their organisations and workplaces. However, there is a lack of research examining the different safety initiatives and strategies practiced in the industry today. There is a need to explore the potential challenges and consequences on the development of safety cultures in the industry. However, it is important to emphasise the opportunities to approach safety culture from different perspectives than those common today (Sundström & Nygren, 2023).

ISO 45001:2018 mandates that human competence and behavioural elements need to be considered in risk assessment and as an internal issue for managing risks (SEIL, 2023). It is found that the progress in positive safety culture is going well at SEIL as they completed 6 years of journey and achieved 97% of safety behaviours. This means that the journey includes overcoming obstacles in health and safety practices requires a multi-faceted approach such as Behavioural Based Safety (BBS) Programs, Incentives and Recognition, Continuous Training and Education, Safety Culture Assessment, Management Commitment (Aslam, 2023).

Field visits to almost 48 site locations and interactions with 306 managers reflected the recommendations as below in order to meet with the challenges of safety culture among the corporates:

- Safety behaviours must reflect in company's HSE policy and banners displays at plant/site areas.
- Project sites which are delayed need more focus on safety implementation as people tend to take deviations in order to complete their work faster.
- Clients at project sites should not convey safety compliance by letters, but be a partner in daily observation and spot-correction. Client says, "when there is a correction, there is no need for letter to compliance."
- Include BBS in daily TBT with positive caring at sites.
- Have conversation with workmen after corrections of at-risk behaviours about importance of safe behaviours.
- BBS round to site is compulsory whether you are from office, operations, quality, maintenance, environment and so on.
- Workmen need to observe each other for actual safety culture transformation. Hence primary focus has to be on workers.
- Site Head needs to include 'daily BBS observation per employee/ workmen' in KRA/objective target.

- BBS culture has to be necessarily interdependent, as people observe cross functional more objectively.
- Company Director has signed the BBS policy which means all HODs would spread it down the levels. This policy needs to be displayed at all areas to build positive safety culture.
- Be polite, patient, and connected with the workforce to bring a revolutionary result.
- Safety culture means caring for each other with human connection.
- Corporate should include one slide on BBS in MIS to reflect on positive safety culture.
- BBS to be integrated with MIS, HSE policy, KPI and Directors' quarterly review.
- A mother can give birth to a few children, but a safety professional can give birth to unlimited safety brothers and sisters.

What we should be looking in best safety culture is the host of factors such as continual improvement in risk perceptions of employees and workmen, incremental quality assessment in at-risk behaviours and barriers, daily round and monitoring by steering team members/HODs, monthly review by site heads, and quarterly appreciation by directors.

Many insights on safety culture are experienced such as follows:

1. Organisations set in safety culture intervention, but did not continue as because they largely dwelt on individual behaviours not the organisational behaviours.
2. Teams can do miracles, like safety culture steering teams, if committed can really fetch zero-harm outcomes.
3. There seems to be a strong association between the severity of incidents and its business impacts, and correspondingly how much is the participation of employees in the safety culture development.
4. Business contexts in India, in general, do not allow managers for stringent safety enforcement.
5. Business safety and human safety are not the same in emphasis and focus. Unless managers understand the basic differences between the two, the imbalance shall prevail and incidents are most likely to occur.

6. It is crucial that companies follow the four stages of behavioural safety culture development:
   - Risk assessment of behaviours;
   - Governance pattern (steering teams formation, observers);
   - Response preparedness (increased spot-corrections of behaviours and barriers);
   - Early warning management (observers development for all areas, monitoring by company directors).
7. Studies unravel the relationship between safety performance and sustainable production performance.
8. Lack of steering team's inadequate qualitative leadership is a sole big reason for un-sustainability of safety culture.
9. Meeting standard of safety ethics is utmost essential as it drives by deep sense of commitment to ethical principles and values.
10. Are organisations doing their job of evolving positive safety culture, is a matter of real concern?
11. The qualities or standards of a positive safety culture for an organisation need to be discerned in order to decide the benchmarking, or directions that a company requires to take or drive towards.
12. Companies adopt a Psychological Safety (PS) policy and PS observers are trained to protect employees or workmen who are bullied, victimised or insulted by their managers/employees.
13. Are managements looking for 'just training' or safety culture transformation in the long run, is a matter of concern for companies before investing into it?
14. Positive safety culture or positive organization or both, as because the positive safety culture shall sustain only in positive organizations.
15. Top managements' decisions for behavioural safety culture in corporates can be either useful or harmful, they are never neutral and hence, can be very critical for employees, workmen, and the business sustainability.
16. The vision of any corporate management should be that no-one gets injured at any of their sites.

17. Emotional Connect for managers is crucial in building ethical safety culture.
18. Perceived severity of incidents on business has a great impacts in building safety culture response of employees and workmen.
19. Safety cultural reviews are of vital significance for continuous improvement for life saving process for organisations.
20. Are company directors really behaviourally awake about the safety culture approach implementation is a major concern, as they simply dump safety on top managements, and they in turn dump it on site management, who dump it on safety officers, and operational managers are hardly involved actively.

Government of India recognizes that safety and health of workers has a positive impact on productivity and economic and social development. It is very encouraging to see companies from India take the lead in setting new benchmarks for health safety and well-being. 123 Indian companies received the International Safety Award. Some of them are: Panchshil Realty, Larsen and Toubro India, Gail India, JSW Steel, Reliance Industries Ltd, Tata Projects, Sembcorp Green Infra Limited, and Godrej Properties, Nokia Solutions and Networks India Pvt. Ltd, NTPC, IOC Guwahati Refinery, Hindustan Petroleum Corp, and Ratnagiri Gas Ltd, among (Manufacturing Today, 2022).

India should push for a culture change in 2023 regarding the way that risks to workers' health, safety, and wellbeing are managed (Kamarajan, 2023). CEOs need to write and speak in a way that ensures their company's commitments to a strong safety culture as key strategic elements of their business model (Craig and Amernic, 2023). Behavioural decisions especially the formation of leadership steering team members, performance of these members in implementation of behavioural safety, strongly associate with the worker well-being and safety culture (Adair, et al., 2023). A study emphasized that 74% of employees believe a psychologically unsafe workplace can harm mental health. With the 2023 report, we are highlighting the enablers required for creating a nurturing environment that fosters psychological safety, allowing employees to thrive both professionally and personally (Deccan Chronicle, 2023).

According to K. K. Sharma Director EHS of DCM Shriram, "there is direct link of severity of incidents on business and employee participation as any accident results in tangible and non tangible costs impacting bottom line and adversely on moral of employees. A disengaged employee will not be interested in building safety culture with emotionally unstable mind with fear of getting hurt. Only a caring culture can be helpful in building safety culture."

Latest research indicates what next to follow for building safer world. Employee Well-Being and Psychological Safety are Key Concerns in the Workplace (Deccan Chronicle (2023). Safety culture goes a long way in ensuring the long-term sustainability of businesses (Times of India, 2023). Major focus has to be from safety behavioural changes to mindset transformation of employees.

Next emphasis needs from positive safety, health, environment culture to positive work culture.

Next attention is on safety culture from workplace to anyplace like your schools, roads, hospitals.

Safer World means Bharat Bane Surakshit for Vasudev Kutubhkam: safety efforts beyond company.

In a world where organizations constantly evolve, adapt and face new challenges, there is one constant that should never change: the unwavering commitment to safety, providing an essential aspects of safety culture, offering a unique perspective that spans across global standards, leadership attributes, and the critical differentiation between business and human safety. It is urgent to explore the challenges of maintaining a safety culture, understand why employees respond (or don't respond) to safety interventions, and discover the role that emotional connections play in building ethical safety cultures. Leaders need to be equipped with the knowledge, understanding, and inspiration needed to cultivate a corporate safety culture that transcends borders and safeguards the well-being of all (Ghabhane, 2023).

REFERENCES

Adair Kathryn C., Emily Levoy, Daniel S. Tawfik, Sofia Palassof, Jochen Profit, Allan Frankel, Michael Leonard, Joshua Proulx, J. Bryan Sexton. (2023). Assessing Leadership Behavior in Health Care: Introducing the Local Leadership Scale of the SCORE Survey. *The Joint Commission Journal on Quality and Patient Safety*, 49:166–173.

Aslam Sheraz. (2023, June 15). How to Overcome Challenges in the Health and Safety Field. https://www.linkedin.com/pulse/how-overcome-challenges-health-safety-field-sheraz-aslam

CISA. (2023, Feb 1). Companies Must Build Safety by Stop Passing the Buck. https://www.cisa.gov/resources-tools/resources/stop-passing-buck-cybersecurity

Craig Russell, Joel Amernic. (2023, May 25). Using "CEO-speak" to prioritize a safety culture. https://www.emerald.com/insight/content/doi/10.1108/SL-03-2023-0033/full/html

Dahl Ø, Rundmo T, Olsen E. (2022). The Impact of Business Leaders' Formal Health and Safety Training on the Establishment of Robust Occupational Safety and Health Management Systems: Three Studies Based on Data from Labour Inspections. *Int J Environ Res Public Health*. 2022 Jan 24;19(3):1269. doi: 10.3390/ijerph19031269. PMID: 35162292; PMCID: PMC8834684.

Deccan Chronicle. (2023, June 14). Employee Well-Being and Psychological Safety Key Concerns in the Workplace. https://www.deccanchronicle.com/lifestyle/health-and-wellbeing/140623/gi-group-holding-india-research.html

Dendup P, and Wangchuk P. (2023). Occurrence of Accident and Safety Culture in the Construction Industry of Bhutan. *Epidem Int*. 8(1):14-21.

Duncan, Caroline. (2021, Aug 31). Creating A Culture Of Safety In The Workplace. https://www.alert-software.com/blog/workplace-safety-culture

Economic times. (2022, March, 07). Workplace safety challenges: How safe are your workers?https://.indiatimes.com/news/company/corporate-trends/workplace-safety-challenges-how-safe-are-your-workers/articleshow/90044699.cms?utm_source=contentofinterest&utm_medium=text&utm_campaign=cppst

Ghabhane, L. (2023, Oct 12). Personal communication with DG-NSCI.

Health and Safety Executive. (2023). Human factors: Managing human failures. https://www.hse.gov.uk/humanfactors/topics/humanfail.htm

Houette, Beate and Mueller-Hirth, Natascha. (2022). Practices, preferences, and understandings of rewarding to improve safety in high-risk industries. *Journal of Safety Research*, Volume 80, 302-310, ISSN 0022-4375, https://doi.org/10.1016/j.jsr.2021.12.013.

HSE. (2023). SIMPL focus on. https://www.hse.gov.uk/plastics/simpl-focus-on.htm

Hyatt, Michael. (2023). Why It Never Helps to Pass the Buck. https://fullfocus.co/navy-seals/

Jain, Anil. (2022). Building_a_Sustainable_Safe_Culture. VP & Head – HSE, Essar Steel India Ltd. http://www.jcssi.com/seminar/isshrts1/3_Building_a_Sustainable_Safe_Culture_Dr.Anil_Jain.pdf

Kamarajan M. (2023, January 22). Improving construction safety in 2023. https://timesofindia.indiatimes.com/blogs/voices/improving-construction-safety-in-2023/

Key Kylie N., Peter T. Hu, Inchul Choi and David J. Schroeder. (2023, May). Safety Culture Assessment and Continuous Improvement in Aviation: A Literature Review. Civil Aerospace Medical Institute, Federal Aviation Administration, Oklahoma City, OK 73125.

Lal Harbans and Choueiri E.M. (2023). The integration of behavior-based safety (BBS) as a company value is advocated! *World Safety Journal* (WSJ), Vol. 32(2), 49-55. doi.org/10.5281/zenodo.8105788

Lal, H. (2023). Strengthening a positive safety culture despite underlying fear and peer pressure. *World Safety Journal*, 32(1), 57-64. https://doi.org/10.5281/zenodo.7770080

Louise A. Ellis, Falkland Emma, Hibbert Peter, Wiig Siri, Ree Eline, Schultz Timothy J., Pirone Christy, Braithwaite Jeffrey. (2023). Issues and complexities in safety culture assessment in healthcare. Frontiers in Public Health, Vol. 11, URL=https://www.frontiersin.org/articles/10.3389/fpubh.2023.1217542 DOI=10.3389/fpubh.2023.1217542

Manufacturing Today. (2022, July, 22). 123 Indian companies receive the International Safety Award https://www.manufacturingtodayindia.com/sectors/123-indian-companies-receive-the-international-safety-award

Pandi Ammavasi, P., Arumugam, K., & Meenakshi Sundram, A. (2022). Integrated Lean Safety Model to Develop Organizational Safety Culture. *IntechOpen*. doi: 10.5772/intechopen.107002

PULSE. (2021, Oct 28). Safety and Sustainability: The Emerging Pillars of Work Culture. https://www.pulsepro.ai/blog/safety-and-sustainability/

RUPERT JONES. (2023, APR 17). Understanding The True Cost of a Poor Workplace Safety Culture. https://ohsonline.com/articles/2023/04/17/understanding-the-true-cost-of-a-poor-workplace-safety-culture.aspx

Sarkar, B. (2023, Feb 15). Psychological safety to be crucial for India Inc in 2023. https://economictimes.indiatimes.com/news/company/corporate-trends/psychological-safety-to-be-crucial-for-india-inc-in-2023-and-beyond-survey/articleshow/97937736.cms?utm_source=contentofinterest&utm_medium=text&utm_campaign=cppst

SEIL. (2023). Behaviour Based Safety (BBS) Implemented at SEIL. https://www.sembcorpenergyindia.com/CSR/BBS

Sundström, E., Nygren, M. Safety Initiatives in Support of Safety Culture Development: Examples from Four Mining Organisations. Mining, Metallurgy & Exploration 40, 1007–1020 (2023). https://doi.org/10.1007/s42461-023-00809-y

Times of India. (2023, Feb 25). Build a safety culture to enhance safety performance. https://timesofindia.indiatimes.com/blogs/voices/build-a-safety-culture-to-enhance-safety-performance/

Umashankar K. (2023, Jan. 25). Safety behaviour and toxic work culture. https://www.deccanherald.com/supplements/dh-education/safety-behaviour-and-toxic-work-culture-1184471.html

WorkSafe. (2022, Oct 3). Our priorities: Our plan to reduce harm and injury at work. https://www.worksafe.govt.nz/about-us/who-we-are/our-priorities/our-plan

Wei Siao-Yun and Kuo Yen-Ku. (2023). The relationship among safety leadership, risk perception, safety culture, and safety performance: Military volunteer soldiers as a case study. Frontiers in Psychology,

14, https://www.frontiersin.org/articles/10.3389/fpsyg.2023.1000331 DOI=10.3389/fpsyg.2023.1000331

Williams Josh. (2023, April 27). WHY SAFETY CULTURE IMPROVEMENT MATTERS: CASE STUDIES. https://www.propulo.com/why-safety-culture-improvement-matters-case-studies/

ACKNOWLEDGMENT

Contribution of industry professionals is thankfully acknowledged.

CHAPTER

12 COMPANIES DESIGN SAFETY CULTURE INTERVENTION ENTHUSIASTICALLY, WHY DON'T THEY CONTINUE?

This chapter deliberates that the organisations set in safety culture intervention, but did not continue as because they largely dwelt on individual behaviours not the organisational behaviours. It is considered that the cluster of open conversations across levels over a variety of organisational factors (such as rewards and relationships, perceptions and passions, beliefs and barriers) would re-create a new pattern of organisational behaviour to follow on, implicitly put as Behaviour Based Safety (BBS) 2.0. There are challenges such as not giving up the dependent safety culture by leaders, passiveness in mentally stimulating people down the levels, lack of reinforcement from respective HODs/ leaders, lack of skills in mobilising and involving all employees/ associates. In this regard, the critical insights from a comprehensive literature review and 198 industry leaders are shared. Majorly, three aspects are discussed, firstly a host of 20 factors that need introspection by the EHS (environment, health, safety) and industry professionals. Secondly, how BBS 2.0 is implemented qualitatively/ conversationally at organisational levels? Thirdly, meeting the challenges of implementing BBS 2.0.

Keywords: Safety Culture, Organisation, BBS, Implementation, Intervention.

INTRODUCTION

Analysis of accidents and incidents shows that human failure contributes to almost all accidents and exposures to substances hazardous to health. Many major accidents such as Bhopal, and Chernobyl were initiated by human failure. In order to avoid accidents and ill-health, companies need to manage human failure or errors as robustly as the technical and engineering measures they use for that purpose (Health and Safety Executive, 2023). Human factors (positive or negative) are the organisational factors or situations that impact the people's actions and mindset. Supportive factors would reinforce safety culture, whereas the negative /reactive factors impede the workers' safety behaviours. Managers and supervisors need to be trained to positively deal with stress and mental health issues of the employees for augmenting safety culture. Similarly, the situational factors like time pressure, fear, lack of resources create a mindset that nobody takes safety decisions, and safety culture takes a back seat, and incidents creep in taking toll on people and property (Lal, 2023). How organisations' leadership respond in such situations, matters most in re-building positive safety culture.

The future of EHS would change hands for safety culture from EHS to non-EHS employees. Managements are terribly fast in business persuasions but terribly slow in matters of HSE implementation and decision making. This differential thinking perspective makes a large space for incidents to settle in. Businesses are hard to sustain without tackling serious HSE issues, the people and businesses would get hit for sure, not coming to an end, failing all of us in our ambitious zero-harm goal. Efforts are there by some but it requires a deeper action orientation. For most organisations, change of safety culture is difficult to manage and confusing to know even how to begin. Passive management practice delays safety culture implementation at sites. The business as well as EHS leaders are not better informed on safety culture methodology. The safety officers in Indian industry are not much trained in positive safety culture implementation, which reflects on the institutions providing academic or skill safety training competency to them. At the same time, largely, the Indian industry is not focused to update their safety professionals except a few marginal organisations who are interested in their company safety culture for business reasons. The organisations, at large, are still struggling for PPE enforcement and barriers to safety.

Work Culture is a deep-rooted construct of a company's thought processes over the years going into daily practices. Any change in this work culture requires a well-planned holistic intervention. If you wish to really become a global company for partnering into the harbour of international economies, you have to work internally on your behaviours, beliefs, practices and barriers. No business can afford delays in safety conflict management as it amounts to direct losses of people and property. Being silent is no solution. Lack of safety culture transformation has serious implications, on one side there are gaps in safety knowledge of SOP among employees, on other side, employees save their skin by wrong information that their organisation is best because they already kept awards and certifications in their pockets. Management always thought that safety is not their job, they have to do only management, hence safety culture suffered and business didn't get sustained as incidents continued due to lack of robustness in the positive safety culture.

A positive safety culture is a game changer. It requires two level teams, one on the topmost directors level leadership that is the review team, and the second team is of the top management level that is the reinforcement team, to mobilise the safety culture down to all the levels till the last person at site. Both the teams should integrate positive safety culture in the workplace culture, which is essentially a long-term planned organisation-wide intervention. Both positive safety culture and positive work culture can not be separated as they are integral part of organisational performance and excellence. Positive work culture would require next level interventions such as psychological safety, cultural safety, human factors, human error, work life balance, systems improvements and their integration.

When employees are experiencing stress, they are reacting for a change in their work culture. Training alone can help creating clouds of culture, but would not sustain it. The safety professionals must understand that the business results have to be fast-tracked and multiplied, hence safety culture transformational intervention also must be on same lines involving all in the organisation. The following guidelines would help in this direction. This manuscript describes varied aspects of the Psychology of a Successful Positive Safety Culture. Safety culture is an internal locus of control of the company employees, which helps achieve the mission that no one would get injured at work sites. What employees do every day becomes part of their conscious work culture.

HSE Heads of companies such as Sembcorp Energy, ONGC, Torrent, Thermax emphasised that the leaders need to mentor the positive safety culture. If leaders do it, nobody can stop this best practice to be integrated with work culture. According to Asst. General Manager HSE of Afcons Infrastructure Limited, "Our efforts are always to enhance BBS techniques for HSE development and promote a culture of healthy and incident free environment across organisation and among neighbouring organisations / people at construction areas". Business leaders who don't mentor safety culture or just maintain lip safety culture would not be favouring sustainability.

OBJECTIVES OF THE STUDY

- To explore that the safety culture intervention is designed well by the companies, but why not continued as a planned long-term policy?

- To explore, how BBS 2.0 is implemented qualitatively/ conversationally at organisational levels?
- To explore, how to meet the challenges of implementing BBS 2.0.

SAMPLE

198 industry professionals participated in the study as part of an action field survey with the researcher. These research participants had been implementing behavioural safety compliance culture at their work sites. The research participants included, the CEO, Directors, Managers, Heads of Departments, and Safety Professionals belonging to the public and private industrial sectors, including chemicals, construction, gas, power and steel, across Indian locations. Participants were selected from the researcher's contact list, invited by WhatsApp and e-mail to complete the online survey. The sampling method used was a non-random convenience sampling.

METHOD

Both primary data (interviews, discussions) and secondary data (incident and accident rates) were collected. Interviews based on open-ended questions and personal in-depth discussions were conducted through remote data collection techniques over 3 months (during Jan-March 2023) from diverse locations and organisations in India. This is a concept building, innovative and exploratory research design with an involvement of field professionals as study participants, using qualitative descriptive framework. This study is part of an ongoing interdisciplinary intervention of behavioural science, management and industrial safety disciplines and a national longitudinal action survey in India. Crucial element was the data collection conducted by means of controlled interviews and questionnaire surveys in the organizations. Their responses to the relevant questions were collated. The study results and implications are reflected below from a rigorous review of safety culture literature and experiences shared by the industry leaders across organizations.

RESULTS AND DISCUSSION

This paper dwells on three aspects as below.

1. Firstly, a host of areas that need introspection by the EHS and industry professionals to reflect that the safety culture intervention is designed

well by companies, but not continued as a planned long-term EHS policy?

2. Secondly, how BBS 2.0 is implemented qualitatively/conversationally at organisational levels?

3. Thirdly, meeting challenges of implementing BBS 2.0.

a. Safety culture intervention is designed well, not Continued as a Planned long-term EHS policy

The comprehensive review of EHS literature points out the following host of 20 areas that need introspection by the EHS and industry professionals to reflect on the safety culture intervention being designed well, but not continued as a planned long-term EHS policy. This helps us identify gaps and work on them as a robust EHS approach.

1. **Safety, Health and Environment:** What is Lacking in your organisation/site, and what is your action plan to fix the same? Please discuss the same with your team before answering. India should push for a culture change in 2023 regarding the way that risks to workers' health, safety, and wellbeing are managed, including during construction work. Although legislation is important in helping to improve the overall health and safety posture of an organisation, the project leaders in the construction sector should take the lead in championing the need for a good health and safety culture at every level of an organisation (Kamarajan, 2023).

2. **Future of Safety, Health and Environment:** What is the Future of EHS in your organisation. Critically review and discuss the same with your team and develop an action plan. The Future of EHS brings together EHS professionals, business leaders, researchers and solutions providers to discuss the latest in safety innovations (NSC, 2023).

3. **Psychological safety culture:** Empower workforce to speak up for safety of each other, deeper insight is that let them speak up otherwise as well, for building a psychologically safe culture. Discuss this concept with your team for implementation issues involved in Psychological safety culture for your company and reply. Psychological safety to be crucial for India Inc in 2023. 45% of all employers surveyed believe that psychological safety is a strong performance indicator and 47%

believe it is a crucial need since it leads to higher employee retention and engagement, according to new data (Sarkar, 2023).

4. **Effect of BBS on Safety Performance:** Discuss the Effects of BBS on Safety Performance with your team and reply with facts and data. SEIL has a target to reduce unsafe behaviour in increments. SEIL believes that most of the safety incidents are caused due to unsafe behaviour. A BBS steering committee led by the Business Heads Thermal and Renewable BU's, including Plant Heads, Senior HODs and Safety Heads guides and monitors implementation of the BBS implementation action plan at SEIL. As part of BBS, unsafe behaviour are being spotted and corrected on spot. Both safe and at-risk behaviours are being tracked, analyzed and displayed (SEIL, 2023).

5. **Risk Perceptions:** Discuss and explain the issues involved in Risk Perceptions of your employees at your sites, and how would you manage the same? Currently Manifesting Risks included Continued waves of COVID-19, Cost of living crisis, Cyberattacks on critical infrastructure, Debt crisis, Deployment of chemical and biological weapons on a catastrophic scale, Deployment of nuclear weapons on a catastrophic scale, Disruptions in global supply chains for non-food goods, Energy supply crisis, Failure to set and meet national net-zero targets, Food supply crisis, Rising inflation, Structural failures in health systems, Weakening of human rights, and Weaponisation of economic policy (World Economic Forum, 2023).

6. **To be a global company with positive safety culture:** Companies before becoming a global entity, need to understand first that a positive safety culture is all about implementing a consciousness among the workers about the sense of brotherhood, affection, affiliation, support and spot-correction of behaviours and barriers. Discuss your company scenario in this respect and reply after discussion with your team members. Companies that can convey care, compassion, and a desire for everyone to go home safe at night will have a better response than those that solely deliver a message of restrictions or punishment for missing the target mark (SSOE, 2021).

7. **Resilient Organisations and positive safety culture:** Developing resilient organisation and positive safety culture is meant to raise own implementation experience, data and information within the

organisation so that it can bounce forward in case of incidents, failure or uncertainty. Discuss and reply after discussion with your team members. Many of those leaders are stuck, not sure how to build a strong and resilient safety culture within their organization (Davey, 2021). Having a resilient safety culture means continuously improving processes by committed staff who systematically cope with the complexity and unpredictability of today's business environment (MDPI, 2023).

8. **Managements Prioritise on the safety Culture drive:** Discuss this with your team members. When employees feel safe at work, they are happier and perform better. Therefore, business leaders must prioritize creating a safe culture. Safety culture in the workplace is worth the investment, giving you and your employees a morale boost by fostering a sense of security (Catsavis, 2022).

9. **Passion for Safety Culture Transformation:** Having a passion for safety means really actively caring about your people and your operations. If you take care of your people, they will be more productive. How would you implement passion for Safety Culture Transformation amongst your employees? Almost 80% industry professionals observed a lack of management's will to support in safety culture, which amounts to a lag in business sustainability. Top managements need guidance about interventions leading to safety culture transformation (Kaila, 2022). How many Managing Directors review their company's safety culture every month or quarter?

10. **A Case on Positive Safety Culture:** Positive behaviour safety or big brother safety (BBS) provides the necessary components of care and timely intervention. However needs to be backed up by a robust Safety Management System. Discuss this in respect to your company scenario and reply in detail. Behaviour based safety has been practiced with all permanent and temporary employees working at Unit including those who have been at non-plant activities such as Admin, Commercial, Finance, IT etc.

11. **Safety culture suffers from disconnect and decision making:** Participation of employees in safety culture is less due to impaired felt leadership and dependent safety culture practiced by site heads, top leaders, site leaders and frontline engineers. Explain this frankly and openly in reference to your company. sustainable safety culture

considers contractual employees as 'own employees' with respect to safety. We strongly believe in it and strive to involve our critical mass, including contractors, in our transformation journey (Tata Steel, 2021).

12. **Digitalisation of positive safety culture:** Digitalising safety processes, checklists, training and implementations plays an essential role in driving your company's safety culture. Discuss your company practices in this regard for improvement to the next level. Digitalising safety processes, training and checklists plays an essential role in driving your company's safety culture (Branthonne, 2021).

13. **Success and Challenges of positive safety culture:** A successful safety culture connects everyone around a common goal to measurably reduce near misses and incidents, and have huge implications for business success. Critical review this for your company perspective. All our achievements and milestones in the last five years reflect our robust HSE management system and the true spirit in which it is implemented by all our staff. Management initiatives are massively improving staff commitment and participation in sustaining a positive Health & Safety culture (SEIL, 2023).

14. **Total Safety Culture (TSC) Interventions:** A safety professional's goal is to achieve a TSC in an organisation including a good balance of enforcement and reinforcements between the interventions such as behavioural safety, psychological safety, human factors, human errors, cultural safety, and robust safety systems. Explain the above in reference to your company. In a TSC, safety is not a priority that can be shifted depending on situational demands; rather, safety is a value linked with all other situational priorities (ProQuest, 2023).

15. **Linking Safety Behaviour to key performance indicators (KPI):** Like with one seed, we can grow thousands of fruits and more seeds, similarly with behavioural KPI of an Individual employee and actions, we save thousands of lives from incidents, and prevent injuries innumerable. How would you implement this for your sites? OHS KPIs must be Kept Short and Simple, realistic, observable, measurable, achievable and time-bound (Fouche, 2021).

16. **Human Factors and Human Error in Safety Culture:** How your organisation and leadership respond to the human factors and human

errors in building positive safety culture? Errors are broadly classified into two kinds: latent and active errors. While active errors need to be addressed at the individual level, latent errors indicate organisational inadequacies (Vattipalli, et al., 2021).

17. **Cultural Safety and Diversity (CSD):** How CSD is addressed to see that your workers at the lowest level are being listened to and understood with due respect to their cultural background, beliefs and language, for ensuring development of positive safety culture? Cultural safety is more than the absence of racism, it is the positive recognition and celebration of cultures that empowers people and enables them to contribute and feel safe to be themselves (NSW, 2023).

18. **Integrating Total Safety Culture Interventions with Organisational Behaviour:** Integrating and sustaining safety culture require a controlled focus on several levels of influence on worker safety and well-being, as the relationship between work and safety is never unidirectional. Explain this for your company scenario and implementation. Characteristics of Effective Integrated Interventions include the intervention development, implementation, and outcomes (Bradley, et al., 2016).

19. **Fixing Accountability Levels to Mobilise Positive Safety Culture:** Accountability, equality, encouragement, teamwork, and training are five elements of safety culture. All the five work in tandem for building best work culture. Discuss your company scenario in this regard. Accountability, equality, encouragement, teamwork, and training are the 5 elements of safety culture (Hanson, 2022). All the five work in tandem for building best work culture, and accountability becomes the function of the interaction of the other four elements.

20. **Rewarding Workers for Safety Cultural Change:** Most organisations remain passive in celebrating employee rewards for safety culture, some are regularly active and integrate it to their appraisal process. Explain your company practices in detail on the above. Boyce (2018) observed that reward behaviors, not outcomes, to Get the Most Value from Safety Incentives. Most organisations would be interested in safety outcomes which is achicvable by behavioural science approach implementation.

Though the positive safety culture is the responsibility of an individual employee /worker, as well as the organisation, it brings everyone together for an active HSE drive. During positive safety culture development, organisational hierarchies turn into brothers and sisters to actively care for the wellbeing of colleagues and the business workforce. Employees are trained with an objective that they are not the tools of safety rather a human chain to care for each other which promotes zero-harm culture at workplaces or elsewhere. When someone is cared for with human touch, it helps.

Table 1: Cluster of open conversations across levels

1.	Daily Conversation amongst observers and workers for empathic value addition of safe work. Each area/ section in-charge is accountable for critical review and success of these ongoing interactions.
2.	Weekly Each business level internal Conversation between HODs on the progress of safety culture. Each Business Head is accountable for critical review and success of these ongoing interactions.
3.	Weekly Each department level internal Conversation between HOD and observers. Each HOD is accountable for critical review and success of these ongoing interactions.
4.	Monthly Conversation amongst the HO steering team members for critically reading through the behavioural data trends very carefully, and acting on gaps and appreciating the progress milestones. The steering team chairperson is accountable for critical review and success of these ongoing interactions.
5.	Monthly Conversation between the HO steering team members and all sites management for providing resources, rectifying barriers, critically reviewing BBS progress, balancing enforcement and reinforcement when behavioural violations are too many, responding to the delays in decision making for safety implementation. The HO steering team chairperson is accountable for critical review and success of these ongoing interactions.
6.	Monthly Conversation between the expert and HO steering team members. The steering team chairperson and the expert are accountable for critical review and success of these ongoing interactions.

7. Monthly Conversation between site level steering team members and HODs. The site steering team chairperson is accountable for critical review and success of these ongoing interactions.
8. Monthly Site level town hall open mass-communication between site head and workers. The site head is accountable for critical review and success of these ongoing interactions.
9. Monthly HO level Conversations between HSE corporate head and entire HSE team. HSE corporate head is accountable for critical review and success of these ongoing interactions.
10. Quarterly Conversation between board of directors and top management of each business on the future directions, integration and critical reviews of safety culture interventions. The Managing Director is accountable for critical review and success of these ongoing interactions.

Safety culture arithmetic depends upon the two organisational indicators, one is the participation rate of workers, and the second is the monthly trends rate of at-risk behaviours. The accountability of leaders in safety culture at sites as well as the corporate level, is an independent factor which influences both these above indicators. Hence, people need to be not only made accountable, but also need to be evaluated on their accountability performance by their seniors.

b. How behaviour based safety (BBS) 2.0 is implemented qualitatively/ conversationally at organisational levels?

BBS 1.0 and 2.0 both together transform the safety culture into a positive work culture. BBS 2.0 focuses more on organisational culture factors, rather individual behaviour. BBS 1.0 is observational in nature, whereas BBS 2.0 is more conversational for developing response mechanisms to combat multi-faceted organisational barriers while evaluating the accountability of leaders for leading the positive safety culture intervention as a long-term roadmap for businesses.

How BBS 2.0 is implemented qualitatively and conversationally at organisational levels for establishing safety dialogues across the board from top to down, is described in 10 conversation levels (Table 1). It is important to fix accountability of each of these group level conversational interactions.

The above levels of conversations are categorised into themes/factors for time-bound corrections that culminate to an organisational progression of total positive safety culture in identifying issues concerning implementation of interventions as defined* below, such as behavioural safety, psychological safety, human factors, human errors, cultural safety, robust safety systems, integrating and critical reviews.

*Definitions of Interventions

- Behavioural safety: behavioural interventions with long term action plan / roadmap.
- Psychological safety: do people feel psychologically safe in an organisational context?
- Human factors in organisational cultural context: do people feel very strained with occupational stresses, workload, decision latitude issues?
- Human error in organisational cultural context: human cognition, decision making, fear, pressure. How companies handle group conflicts and differences that delay safety culture decisions. The Bhopal tragedy and the IOCL Jaipur fire incident were the result of top level dis-engagement with the safety culture of their respective companies effecting into human error and poor decision making for actions needed to correct unsafe antecedents at sites. Human error is not personal error but in organisational cultural context.
- Cultural safety and competency: Do people feel being understood with due respect to their cultural background and beliefs, and how companies respond to these factors effectively?
- Robust Safety systems with digital intervention: Positively reinforcing antecedents for managing all safety issues such as barriers, resources, safety controls.
- Integrating and Critical Reviews by the topmost leaders on all the above six interventions towards a goal of Vision Zero Harm.

Table 2 describes 20 organisational factors that need to be observed, discussed and corrected. During observation rounds and conversations, observers ask employees/ associates whether any of these factors are problematic with respect to creating positive safety culture. Employees go through each of these factors, tick mark and describe how any of these aspects are an obstacle or barrier in safety culture at their site, and how it can be resolved. These identified factors are tabulated and discussed in weekly/ monthly safety culture meetings for compliance. These twenty components need training and awareness to all employees as well as contractors workmen.

If an organization seeks to change its cultural state toward a just culture, there needs to be a purposeful alignment across all components or factors of the safety culture in terms of values, leadership strategies, attitudes, and behaviors. The time taken to change the culture depends on (a) effective articulation of the safety values and communication of the need (intensity and urgency) to change the culture and (b) the collective engagement at all levels of the organization to make the necessary changes in strategies, processes, and policies in order to align with the safety values. Safety culture is presented as a synthesis of safety culture components, methods and outcomes, and as a pyramid with components such as safety values, safety leadership strategies, safety attitudes, and safety performance. In order to truly and fully characterise safety culture, the state of each of the 20 factors/ components, the interconnection across these components, the dynamic balance between the four components, and the cumulative influence of values, safety leadership strategies, and safety attitudes on safety performance must be examined (Patnakar and Sabin, 2010).

There are several subcultures that contribute to the overall safety culture of an organization. Flexible culture, having a flexible culture means being able to reconfigure the system to deal with the pressures that are acting on it at the time. Reporting culture, people working in the organization feel completely comfortable to report threats, errors or undesirable conditions as well as any near-misses. Informed culture, the ability to respond, the components of the system know what they need to do and what is expected of them as part of the larger system. Learning culture, the ability to learn, the system can reconfigure itself based on what it has learned from past experience. Just culture, People working in the system trust that they will be treated fairly in the event of unsafe acts occurring. The key to a successful just culture is the acceptance of the new view of error (Moriarty, 2015).

Table 2: Organisational factors to be observed, described and corrected

1.	Safety, Health and Environment - What is Lacking?
2.	The Future of Safety, Health and Environment
3.	Psychological Safety Culture
4.	Effect of BBS on Safety Performance
5.	Risk Perceptions
6.	To be a global company with positive safety culture
7.	Resilient Organisations and positive safety culture
8.	Managements Prioritise on the safety Culture drive
9.	Passion for Safety Culture Transformation
10.	A Case on Positive Safety Culture
11.	Safety culture suffers from disconnect and decision making
12.	Digitalisation of positive safety culture
13.	Success and Challenges of positive safety culture
14.	Total Safety Culture (TSC) Interventions
15.	Linking Safety Behaviour to Key Performance Indicators (KPI)
16.	Human Factors and Human Error in Safety Culture
17.	Cultural Safety and Diversity
18.	Integrating Total Safety Culture Interventions with Organisational Behaviour
19.	Fixing Accountability Levels to Mobilise Positive Safety Culture
20.	Rewarding Workers for Safety Cultural Change

c. Meeting Challenges of implementing behaviour based safety (BBS) 2.0

Although, an accountability of each of the 10 group level conversational interactions are fixed (Table 1), there are challenges such as following dependent safety culture by leaders, passiveness in mentally stimulating people down the levels, lack of reinforcement from respective HODs/ leaders, lack of skills in mobilising and involving all employees/ associates. To deal with such challenges, the following insights are shared below by industry leaders.

1. Journey of safety culture - 'basics to core value by top management commitment' - opens benefits of BBS 2.0.

   Most companies plan safety culture intervention very scholarly but fail in driving it as a longterm change, due of lack of implementation of organisational factors. There are challenges such as not giving up the dependent safety culture by leaders, passiveness in mentally stimulating people down the levels, lack of reinforcement from respective HODs/ leaders, lack of skills in mobilising and involving all employees/ associates. To deal with such challenges, the following insights are shared below by industry leaders.

2. Core value of business: Most of the management don't have patience, actually there are no safety objectives in their business plans. Problem is when BBS is adopted as compliance-driven safety in place of commitment-driven safety. Then BBS becomes priority, not a core value of business. Priority can be changed due to dynamics of market conditions. Core value becomes a way of life. Still majority didn't understand what would be the BBS impacts on organisation culture. It is perceived as an audit tool for monitoring behaviour attributes. There is a need for more in-depth understanding of BBS to bring on the Table. Then only it can be a success. Initially when starting BBS journey, the speed is very fast (like 70-80 KMPH). Slowly, speed is very slow due to less interest of management. People leave the organisation, or involve in different activities. To change the behaviour, provide planned infrastructure, monitor and enforce the safe practices, training and awareness, motivation both positive and negative. Companies take good initiative but fail due to not getting right and strong leadership qualities in the team leader and line managers. Secondly, the process is not being watched, monitored as a long term benefit. After some time, the process gets dissolved due to less attention and diversified focus. Safety can implement effectively when it will be a line function responsibility and part of route activity. Management need to discuss the safety parameters along with other operations parameters in routine meetings. For any project, it requires consistency and involvement from top management, without which support such projects won't yield desired results.

3. Basic safety culture: Safety culture fails in driving as a longterm change because of lack of basic safety culture in the organisation, like owning safety as if it is in every employees' DNA. For that, basic need

is to be developed such as, use of PPE at site by all employees - top to bottom, every one has to know the safety policy, top management must involve in all safety activities, training is basic to develop safety culture, at least 3% of the man-hours should be consumed for employees training, employees feedback is very important, identification of hazard by execution or operation employees is the key, daily pre-job safety talk etc. After settling in these basics, if these processes continue on its own without pushing, then we can establish safety culture, otherwise it will fall anytime.

4. Top management: Unless the top management is committed, nothing can be done. Commitment from top decides the safety culture. Management commitment is required to monitor change as a boardroom practice. As long as, positive safety culture remains at doorstep of the boardroom, and doesn't find space and discussed sufficiently inside boardroom, it doesn't sustain. System works, but for long term change, system has to be a part of behaviour which must be carried forward. It doesn't work due to lack of company vision/ policy.
5. Organisational politics or human error (oh god they don't know what they are doing): Many companies begin well, but due to latent organisational conflicts and group errors, they don't continue the positive safety culture. Hence, the BBS 2.0 intends that the organisational issues be resolved and corrected simultaneously for developing positive work culture. Passive and silent leadership on supportive safety culture is risky for businesses: employees can not be trained unless they implement, learn, and experience what they are trained for. More than an observations, conversations about the at-risk behaviours with the workers is important. Success of safety culture does not mean a destination, but it is a roller coaster with ups and downs.

CONCLUSIONS AND IMPLICATIONS

This paper focused that organisations set in a safety culture intervention, but did not continue as because they largely dwelt on individual behaviours not the organisational behaviours. It is considered that the cluster of open conversations across levels (Table 1) over a variety of organisational factors (such as rewards and relationships, perceptions and passions, beliefs and barriers, broadly mentioned as 20 factors in Table 2) would re-create a new organisational behaviour pattern to follow on, implicitly put as BBS 2.0. The challenges of implementing BBS 2.0 are manifold as discussed in above section, but the chances of succeeding in safety culture would be maximised, as the focus is on the open conversations and dialogues about all the behaviours and antecedents related to safety culture in the organisation. If the employees feel that something new and positive in the organisation is going on, then it should continue over the years to become a norm, culture and a peoples' value. BBS, especially its more recent incarnations, such as so-called BBS 2.0, go beyond a strict focus on reducing injuries (and often times unfortunately blaming the victim) to take a more holistic approach that focuses not only on behaviours, but work environment, cultural antecedents, systems and employee attitudes to strengthen organisational cultures, values and performance (Johnson, 2021). The change in positive safety culture over the years and its sustainability need to be constantly explored. The management should continuously monitor and evaluate their strategies while delivering multifaceted interventions to be more specifically focused and to motivate workers to be enthusiastic in sustaining safety culture (Wong, et al., 2021). Sembcorp Energy India Limited (SEIL) manages Health, Safety and Environment (HSE) responsibility as its core value. To further strengthen the safety culture and secure a positive behavioural change within the work place, SEIL has implemented and integrated Behaviour Based Safety into its safety systems across all the assets. ISO 45001:2018 mandates that human competence and behavioural elements need to be considered in risk assessment and as an internal issue for managing risks (SEIL, 2023).

REFERENCES

Boyce, T. E. (2018, Apr 13). Safety Culture and Behavioral Safety. https://ehsdailyadvisor.blr.com/2016/08/reward-behaviors-not-outcomes-get-value-safety-incentives/

Branthonne, Denis. (2021, May 11). 5 ways technology is improving safety on construction sites. https://www.novade.net/5-ways-tech-can-improve-safety-construction/

Catsavis, Lindsay. (2022, April 28). How to Improve Safety Culture in the Workplace and the Company & Employee Benefits of Doing So. https://www.supplychain247.com/article/how_to_improve_safety_culture_in_the_workplace_and_the_benefits_of_doing_so

Davey, Tyler. (2021, July 14). Building a Strong and Resilient Safety Culture Starts with the C-Suite. https://www.safeopedia.com/building-a-strong-and-resilient-safety-culture-starts-with-the-c-suite/2/8991

Fouche Christel. (2021, Oct 13). Occupational Health and Safety KPIs. https://www.linkedin.com/pulse/occupational-health-safety-kpis-christel-fouche?trk=pulse-article_more-articles_related-content-card

Johnson, Dave. (2021, July 6). Breathing new life into Behavior-Based Safety (BBS) programs.https://www.ishn.com/articles/113027-breathing-new-life-into-behavior-based-safety-bbs-programs

Hanson, Eva Maria. (2022, Dec 21). Implementing a food safety culture in 2023. https://www.fooddocs.com/post/food-safety-culture

Health and Safety Executive. (2023). Human factors: Managing human failures. https://www.hse.gov.uk/humanfactors/topics/humanfail.htm

Kamarajan, M. (2023, Jan. 22). Improving construction safety in 2023. https://timesofindia.indiatimes.com/blogs/voices/improving-construction-safety-in-2023/?source=app&frmapp=yes

Kaila, Harbans Lal. (2020). TOP MANAGEMENT'S WILL to SUPPORT SAFETY CULTURE. International Journal of Research - GRANTHAALAYAH, Vol. 10 No. 4 (2022): Volume 10 Issue 4 : April 2022. DOI: https://doi.org/10.29121/granthaalayah.v10.i4.2022.4573

Lal, H. (2023). Strengthening a positive safety culture despite underlying fear and peer pressure. *World Safety Journal*, 32(1), 57–64. https://doi.org/10.5281/zenodo.7770080

MDPI. (2023). Special Issue Resilient Safety Culture. https://www.mdpi.com/journal/safety/special_issues/resilient_safety_culture

Moriarty, David. (2015). Practical Human Factors for Pilots, Academic Press, Pages 119-132, ISBN 9780124202443, https://doi.org/10.1016/B978-0-12-420244-3.00004-2

NSC. (2023). The Future of EHS 2023. https://www.nsc.org/workplace/safety-topics/work-to-zero/future-of-ehs?

NSW. (2023). What is cultural safety? https://www.safework.nsw.gov.au/safety-starts-here/our-aboriginal-program/culturally-safe-workplaces/what-is-cultural-safety

Patankar, Manoj S. Sabin, Edward J. (2010). Editor(s): Eduardo Salas, Dan Maurino, Chapter 4 - The Safety Culture Perspective, Human Factors in Aviation (Second Edition), Academic Press, Pages 95-122, ISBN 9780123745187, https://doi.org/10.1016/B978-0-12-374518-7.00004-3.

Sarkar, B. (2023, Feb 15). Psychological safety to be crucial for India Inc in 2023. https://economictimes.indiatimes.com/news/company/corporate-trends/psychological-safety-to-be-crucial-for-india-inc-in-2023-and-beyond-survey/articleshow/97937736.cms?utm_source=contentofinterest&utm_medium=text&utm_campaign=cppst

SEIL. (2023). Behaviour Based Safety (BBS) Implemented at SEIL. https://www.sembcorpenergyindia.com/CSR/BBS

SEIL. (2023). Safety at the Core. https://www.sembcorpenergyindia.com/AnnualReport2020/safety-at-the-core.php

SSOE. (2021, November 1). Creating a Positive Safety Culture. https://www.ssoe.com/creating-a-positive-safety-culture-2/

Tata Steel. (2021, March 15). Risk Profiling Turns Deep Shop Floor Experience into Enthusiastic Risk-Based Decision Making. https://www.consultdss.com/content-hub/risk-profiling-risk-based-decision-making/

ProQuest. (2023). Ten principles for achieving a total safety culture. https://www.proquest.com/docview/200347593

Vattipalli Sameera, Bindra A, Rath GP. (2021). Human errors and their prevention in healthcare. J Anaesthesiol Clin Pharmacol. 2021 Jul-Sep;37(3):328-335. doi: 10.4103/joacp.JOACP_364_19. Epub 2021 Oct 12. PMID: 34759539; PMCID: PMC8562433

Wong SY, Fu ACL, Han J, Lin J, Lau MC. (2021). Effectiveness of customised safety intervention programmes to increase the safety culture of hospital staff. BMJ Open Qual. 2021 Oct;10(4):e000962. doi: 10.1136/bmjoq-2020-000962. PMID: 34625426; PMCID: PMC8504354.

World Economic Forum. (2023, January 11) Global Risks Report 2023. https://www.weforum.org/reports/global-risks-report-2023/in-full/appendix-a-technical-notes-global-risks-perception-survey-2022-2023

ACKNOWLEDGMENT

Contribution of industry professionals is thankfully acknowledged.

CHAPTER 13

INTRODUCE THE CULTURE OF PSYCHOLOGICALLY SAFE ENVIRONMENTS (PSE)

Companies adopt a Psychological Safety (PS) policy and PS observers are trained to protect employees or workmen who are bullied, victimised or insulted by their managers/employees. The underlying principle of PS is that everyone at workplace has a right to respect and care from others, and organisation shall do everything to protect the same for creating a psychologically safe milieu.

The perception of psychological safety is shaped by the reactions of other employees in the positive /proactive behaviors. The level of psychological safety perception is low when other employees react negatively to the constructive suggestions and feedbacks of the employees. The perception of psychological safety is based on interpersonal trust and support in the organization. At times, employees have felt psychologically unsafe, alienated, helpless, psychological loneliness, and so on that can be measured accurately using psychological scales (Siddiqui and Sangwan 2022).

Fig. 1: Site location example

Psychological safety to be crucial for Corporate India in 2023 and beyond. Survey on Diversity, Inclusion and Belonging (DI&B) at Indian Workplaces' examines the need for psychological safety in Indian organisations.

Psychological safety refers to employees believing that they can take risks without being shamed by other members. 45% of all employers surveyed believe that psychological safety is a strong performance indicator and 47% believe it is a crucial need since it leads to higher employee retention and engagement (Sarkar, 2023). It is important that people of all cultures feel safe at work.

People should not only get injured physically, but also, they should not get psychologically injured. Employees need psychological care from each other. People should not only speak up for safety, they should speak up otherwise also without the fear of getting reprimanded or being criticised.

OBJECTIVES

Introducing the Concept and clarity about Psychological Safety.

Outcome of this article would be sensitization on the theme so that managers can initiate at their units or departments as a Psychological Safety mentor.

What is Psychological Safety at workplace and how to implement it.

Psychological safety intervention is an important part of the total safety culture.

Nobody wants to feel psychologically unsafe or at-risk. What are those psychological or psychosocial risks at work, when we feel threatened, harmed. Major question is: Is psychological safe place possible? In fact, psychologically safe work environments are rare.

Maslow called it a basic psychological need that motivates everyone to fulfil.

Freedom from hurt and harassment:

Are trust, interpersonal support the positive indicators of Psychologically Safe Environment (PSE), or is fear, pressure, burnout the negative indicator of PSE?

How do organisations, managers, leaders respond to these situations while employees experience these positive or negative aspects of PSE?

Empower workforce to speak up for safety of each other, but the deeper insight is that let them speak up otherwise as well, for building a psychologically safe culture.

Questions are - Who needs your psychological care or support? How do you give it everyday to people who work with you or who are with you in an organisation? How do organisations improve positive psychological connect amongst employees of all cultures?

In most meetings, people pick on someone or throw tantrums. In such humiliating conditions, someone who cares, empathises, speak up and saves the person from psychological injury before it takes place. Coming out of our comfort zones to support people from low profile like contract people is the concept of psychological safety.

Psychological Safety Observation checklist (Employees who need care):

1. Symptoms of stress, anxiety, fear,
2. Personal health issues
3. Aggressive behaviours
4. Hygiene / cleanliness
5. Career/ job concerns
6. Harassment
7. Interpersonal relations
8. Family care
9. Daily emotional care
10. New employees/workmen

Like in families, we abuse, blame, shout at each other or some times gang up against one member of a family, continue hurting at psychological level, which gradually turns into a serious conflict or relationship issue. The same way, we in an organisation behave to give psychological injuries to each other that go over months and years, if not resolved or intervened in a time frame by a manager or immediate supervisor. Sometimes people do not know how to resolve, they seek help of peers or a friend, or a OH / mental health practitioner.

People should not, get injured physically, but also, they should not get psychologically injured by their colleagues. "In my opinion, reprimanding or psychological injury amounts to an offence", Ex Director of Factories of Karnataka.

Physical injuries heal after some time whereas psychological injuries takes much longer time and sustained top management interventions. Actions matter more than words (Pavan Rao, Head HSE, Sembcorp Energy).

Employees need psychological care from each other at sites. "Prevent both Physical as well as psychological injuries", take care !! "Great concept for social well-being", a HSE Head of IOCL.

People should, not only speak up for safety, they should speak up otherwise as well, without the fear of getting reprimanded or being criticised.

How do develop psychological carers at company sites:

1. Develop psychological mentors in each section.
2. Develop positive listening skills among employees.
3. Remove negative behaviors: Don't react, blame, shout, reprimand.
4. Develop positive behaviors: appreciate, be a big brother and big sister.
5. In the long term, aim at developing everyone as psychological carer.
6. Define and help people understand what is psychological safety and psychological injury.
7. How do we injure or harm others psychologically with our words and actions?
8. Enquire colleagues daily about their Wellbeing, simply asking, how are you? Can I be of any help?
9. Connect with people emotionally especially new people at workplaces. Just smiling, talking to people at dining table, etc do help connecting.
10. Be support unconditionally daily at least to one person without any expectation.

As per WHO, Safe and healthy working environments are not only a fundamental right but are also more likely to minimize tension and conflicts at work and improve staff retention, work performance and productivity.

Psychological safety truly means everyone at site actively cares that no one hurts or harms or disrespects any one at any place. On the contrary, every one finds opportunity to protect the other person, known or known, if any one in office or meeting, tries to hurt or harm with words or action. A McKinsey Global report (2020) infers that organisations that do not guarantee psychological safety to their employees may have to face the flames of a toxic ecosystem and people tend to demonstrate safety behaviours for the fear of workplace victimisation (Umashankar, 2023).

REFERENCES

Sarkar Brinda. (2023, Feb 15). Psychological safety to be crucial for India Inc in 2023 and beyond: Survey. https://economictimes.indiatimes.com/news/company/corporate-trends/psychological-safety-to-be-crucial-for-india-inc-in-2023-and-beyond-survey/articleshow/97937736.cms?utm_source=contentofinterest&utm_medium=text&utm_campaign=cppst

Siddiqui, Shabnam and Sangwan, Ankur. (2022). The Catalytic Role of Perceived Psychological Safety on the Relationship Between 'Support from Supervisor' and 'Workplace Loneliness'. Journal of Positive School Psychology, Vol. 6, No. 6, 8401 – 8412.

Umashankar K. (2023, Jan. 25). Safety behaviour and toxic work culture. https://www.deccanherald.com/supplements/dh-education/safety-behaviour-and-toxic-work-culture-1184471.html

ACKNOWLEDGMENT

Contribution of industry professionals is thankfully acknowledged.

CHAPTER

14 BEHAVIOUR-BASED SAFETY (BBS) 2.0 - INTEGRATE IT AS COMPANY VALUE

INTRODUCTION

Analysis of accidents and incidents shows that human failure contributes to almost all accidents and exposures to substances hazardous to health. Many major accidents such as Bhopal, Chernobyl were initiated by human failure. In order to avoid accidents and ill-health, companies need to manage human failure or errors as robustly as the technical and engineering measures they use for that purpose (Health and Safety Executive, 2023). Human factors (positive or negative) are the organisational factors or situations that impact people's actions and mindset. Supportive factors would reinforce safety culture, whereas the negative /reactive factors impede the safety behaviours of the workers. Managers and supervisors need to be trained to positively deal with stress and mental health issues of the employees for augmenting safety culture. Similarly, the situational factors like time pressure, fear, lack of resources create a mindset that nobody takes safety decisions, and safety culture takes a back seat, and incidents creep in taking toll on people and property (Lal, 2023). How organisations' leadership respond in such situations, matters most in re-building positive safety culture.

HSE professionals emphasise on balancing the challenges and issues while integrating the safety systems and positive safety culture. The elements of the total safety culture interventions must not exist as disjointed form in the organisation for best results of manpower safety as well as business prosperity. Safety systems provide nothing more than the safety climate. People need to feel psychological safe for giving optimum performances. The complicated human factors of safety and the complex human error in safety must be addressed by the corporates. Cultural safety and equitable care require workers migrated from diverse cultural backgrounds to be understood in their own cultural backdrop, language and communication, so that any kind of racism or inequity is ruled out. Total safety culture framework integrates information across disjointed conceptualisations to clearly portray the dynamic nature of safety culture and specific drivers of its development.

BBS 1.0 & 2.0 is a journey from Individual behaviours to organisational transformation. This chapter briefs on how behaviour based safety (BBS) 2.0 is implemented qualitatively / conversationally at organisational levels?

BBS 1.0 and 2.0 both together transform the safety culture into a positive work culture. BBS 2.0 focuses more on organisational culture factors, rather than individual behaviour. BBS 1.0 is observational in nature, whereas BBS 2.0 is more conversational for developing response mechanisms to combat multi-faceted organisational barriers while evaluating accountability of leaders for leading the positive safety culture intervention as a long-term roadmap for businesses.

How BBS 2.0 is implemented qualitatively and conversationally at organisational levels for establishing safety dialogues across the board from the topmost level to the down-most/ last person. It is important to fix accountability of each of the BBS steering teams interactions.

Defining BBS 2.0 Interventions

- Behavioural safety: behavioural interventions with long term action plan / roadmap.
- Psychological safety: do people feel psychologically safe in an organisational context? Psychological safety to be crucial for India Inc in 2023. 45% of all employers surveyed believe that psychological safety is a strong performance indicator and 47% believe it is a crucial need since it leads to higher employee retention and engagement, according to new data (Sarkar, 2023).
- Human factors in organisational cultural context: do people feel very strained with occupational stresses, workload, decision latitude issues?
- Human error in organisational cultural context: human cognition, decision making, fear, pressure. How companies handle group conflicts and differences that delay safety culture decisions. The Bhopal tragedy and the IOCL Jaipur fire incident were the result of top level dis-engagement with the safety culture of their respective companies effecting into human error and poor decision making for actions needed to correct unsafe antecedents at sites. Human error is not personal error but in organisational cultural context. Errors are broadly classified into two kinds: latent and active errors. While active errors need to be addressed at the individual level, latent errors indicate organisational inadequacies (Vattipalli, et al., 2021).

- Cultural safety and competency: do people feel being understood with due respect to their cultural background and beliefs, and how companies respond to these factors effectively? Cultural safety is more than the absence of racism, it is the positive recognition and celebration of cultures that empowers people and enables them to contribute and feel safe to be themselves (NSW, 2023).
- Robust Safety systems with digital intervention: positively reinforcing antecedents for managing all safety issues such as barriers, resources, safety controls.
- Integrating and Critical Reviews by the topmost leaders on all the above six interventions towards a goal of Vision Zero harm (Nambudiri & Ghulyani, 2018). Integrating and sustaining safety culture require a controlled focus on several levels of influence on worker safety and well-being, as the relationship between work and safety is never unidirectional. Explain this for your company scenario and implementation. Characteristics of Effective Integrated Interventions include the intervention development, implementation, and outcomes.

BASIC DIFFERENCE BETWEEN BBS 1.0 & 2.0 (BBS 2.0 DOES NOT REPLACE BBS 1.0 BUT BOTH ARE COMPLEMENTARY TO EACH OTHER)

Culture building - Broad Focus of BBS 1.0 is on:	Perspective building - Focus of BBS 2.0 is on:
Observations and corrections	Increased open and empathic conversations across levels, critical reviews, mass-communications
Employees as observers at all levels/ areas	Integrating contractors, customers, stakeholders
Individual Behaviours	Organisational barriers/antecedents, resources provision
Corporate Steering teams	MD level, Board of Directors reporting, Challenge management's passionate involvement
Behavioural safety culture	Total safety culture:Psychological safety, human factors, human error, cultural safety, digitalising, integration

Culture building - Broad Focus of BBS 1.0 is on:	Perspective building - Focus of BBS 2.0 is on:
Steering teams commitment for months/years	Accountability evaluation of leaders/ managers, performance & policy based commitment for long-term
Actively caring with empathy	HSE as core value and zero-harm, corporate rewards and reinforcements (digital and non-digital)
Quantitative score-board/ measurement	Qualitative Site steering team/HODs monitoring
Safety and business perspective	Health, Safety, Environment, Well-being, Sustainability
Monthly monitoring and recognitions	Weekly monitoring and spot-rewards at sites

MEETING CHALLENGES OF IMPLEMENTING BEHAVIOUR BASED SAFETY (BBS) 2.0

Although, an accountability of BBS steering teams at Corporate and Site location levels are fixed, there are challenges such as managers lacking challenges for long-term safety culture involvement. To deal with many such challenges, the following insights are shared below by industry leaders (Kaila, 2020, 2020a).

1. Journey of safety culture is 'from basics to core value by top management commitment' which opens benefits of BBS 2.0. Most companies plan safety culture intervention very scholarly but fail in driving it as a longterm change, due of lack of implementation of organisational factors. There are challenges such as not giving up the dependent safety culture by leaders, passiveness in mentally stimulating people down the levels, lack of reinforcement from respective HODs/ leaders, lack of skills in mobilising and involving all employees/ associates (Lal, 2023).

2. Core value of business: Most of the managements don't have patience, actually there are no safety objectives in their business plans. Problem is when BBS is adopted as compliance-driven safety in place of commitment-driven safety. Then BBS becomes priority,

not a core value of business. Priority can be changed due to dynamics of market conditions. Core value becomes a way of life. Still majority didn't understand what would be the BBS impacts on organisation culture. It is perceived as an audit tool for monitoring behaviour attributes. There is a need for more in-depth understanding of BBS to bring on the table. Then only it can be a success. Initially when starting BBS journey, the speed is very fast (like 70-80 KMPH). Slowly, speed is gone down due to less interest of management. People leave the organisation, or involve in different activities. To change the behaviour, provide planned infrastructure, monitor and enforce the safe practices, training and awareness, motivation both positive and negative. Companies take good initiative but fail due to not getting right and strong leadership qualities in the team leader and line managers. Secondly, the process is not being watched and monitored as a long term benefit. After some time, the process gets dissolved due to less attention and diversified focus. Safety can implement effectively when it will be a line function responsibility and part of routine activity. Management need to discuss the safety parameters along with other operations parameters in routine meetings. For any project, it requires consistency and involvement from top management, without which support such projects won't yield desired results (CPCL, 2021).

3. Basic safety culture: Safety culture fails in driving as a longterm change because of lack of basic safety culture in the organisation, like owning safety as if it is in every employees' DNA. For that, basic needs is to be developed such as, use of PPE at site by all employees - top to bottom, every one has to know the safety policy, top management must involve in all safety activities, training is basic to develop safety culture, at least 3% of the man-hours should be consumed for employees training, employees feedback is very important, identification of hazard by execution or operation employees is the key, daily pre-job safety talk etc. After settling in these basics, if these processes continue on its own without pushing, then we can establish safety culture, otherwise it will fall anytime.

4. Top management: Unless the top management is committed, nothing can be done. Commitment from top decides the safety culture. Management commitment is required to monitor change as a boardroom practice. As long as, positive safety culture remains at

doorstep of the boardroom, and doesn't find space and discussed sufficiently inside boardroom, it doesn't sustain. System works, but for long term change, system has to be a part of behaviour which must be carried forward. It doesn't work due to lack of company vision/ policy (Kaila, 2022, 2022a).

5. Organisational politics or human error (oh god they don't know what they are doing): Many companies begin well, but due to latent organisational conflicts and group errors, they don't continue the positive safety culture. Hence, the BBS 2.0 intends that the organisational issues be resolved and corrected simultaneously for developing positive work culture. Passive and silent leadership on supportive safety culture is risky for businesses. Employees can not be trained unless they implement, learn, and experience what they are trained for. More than an observations, conversations about the at-risk behaviours with the workers is important. Success of safety culture does not mean a destination, but it is a roller coaster with ups and downs (Tata Steel, 2021).

CONCLUSION

Ten big reasons for un-sustainability of safety culture are that the companies are lacking in:

- Understanding workplace and psychological safety challenges, sharing of learnings.
- HODs and all employee's understanding concepts deeply resulting in lots of unlearning.
- Steering team's adequate qualitative leadership for sustainability of safety culture.
- KPI for BBS to be added in management monthly presentation.
- Following timeframes of safety culture phases such as first 6 months in building BBS awareness, observation and structure. Next 6 months in strengthening reviews and accountability etc.
- Maturity on part of organisation to promote Psychological Safety, particularly for leadership.
- Sowing the seeds of brotherhood: the foundation of safety culture which needs further manure.
- Feedback from all members in positive and constructive ways.

- Motivating self-regulations, Observing self and mentoring, Timely follow-ups.
- Linking BBS culture to safety systems, like consequences management, enforcement, etc.

Most companies take safety implementation as a face saving exercise to suit business perspective, because, the longterm commitment is a bit harder for them. Thus, they do their bit and sit back, to wait and watch for incidents. Some organisations set in a safety culture intervention, but did not continue as because they largely dwelt on individual behaviours, not the organisational behaviours. It is considered that the cluster of open conversations across levels over a variety of organisational factors (such as rewards and relationships, perceptions and passions, beliefs and barriers, would re-create a new organisational behaviour pattern to follow on, implicitly put as BBS 2.0. The challenges of implementing BBS 2.0 are manifold as discussed in above section, but the chances of succeeding in safety culture would be maximised, as the focus is on the open conversations and dialogues about all the behaviours and antecedents related to safety culture in the organisation. If the employees feel that something new and positive in the organisation is going on, then it should continue over the years to become a norm, culture and a peoples' value. BBS, especially in its more recent incarnations, such as so-called BBS 2.0, go beyond a strict focus on reducing injuries (and often times unfortunately blaming the victim) to take a more holistic approach that focuses not only on behaviours, but work environment, cultural antecedents, systems and employee attitudes to strengthen organisational cultures, values and performance (Johnson, 2021). The change in positive safety culture happens over the years and its sustainability need to be constantly explored. The management should continuously monitor and evaluate their strategies while delivering multifaceted interventions to be more specifically focused and to motivate workers to be enthusiastic in sustaining safety culture (Wong, et al., 2021). Sembcorp Energy India Limited (SEIL) manages Health, Safety and Environment (HSE) responsibility as its core value (SEIL,(2023a). To further strengthen the safety culture and secure a positive behavioural change within the work place, SEIL has implemented and integrated Behaviour Based Safety into its safety systems across all the assets. ISO 45001:2018 mandates that human competence and behavioural elements need to be considered in risk assessment and as an internal issue for managing risks (SEIL, 2023).

REFERENCES

CPCL. (2021). CPCL kickstarts Behaviour Based Safety in Refinery at Chennai. https://cpcl.co.in/events-updates/cpcl-kickstarts-behaviour-based-safety-in-refinery-at-chennai/

Health and Safety Executive. (2023). Human factors: Managing human failures. https://www.hse.gov.uk/humanfactors/topics/humanfail.htm

Johnson, Dave. (2021, July 6). Breathing new life into Behavior-Based Safety (BBS) programs.https://www.ishn.com/articles/113027-breathing-new-life-into-behavior-based-safety-bbs-programs

Kaila, Harbans Lal. (2020). Behaviour-Based Safety in Organizations: Life Before the Accident' I.K International Publishing House Pvt Ltd, New Delhi. ik_publishers@ikinternational.com

Kaila, Harbans Lal. (2020a). Top management will to support safety culture. International Journal of Research - GRANTHAALAYAH, Vol. 10 No. 4 (2022): Volume 10 Issue 4 : April 2022. DOI: https://doi.org/10.29121/granthaalayah.v10.i4.2022.4573

Kaila, Harbans Lal. (2022). Long term safety culture implementation. Prints Publications, New Delhi. ISBN-13: 9788192769462, https://www.printspublications.com/book/long-term-safety

Kaila, Harbans Lal. (2022a). https://store.pothi.com/book/ebook-dr-harbans-lal-kaila-behaviour-based-safety-2-0/

Lal, H. (2023). Strengthening a positive safety culture despite underlying fear and peer pressure. World Safety Journal, 32(1), 57–64. https://doi.org/10.5281/zenodo.7770080

Nambudiri, Ranjeet & Ghulyani, Swati. (2018). GAIL (India) Limited: Transforming Safety Culture (Management Case: Ivey Publishing).

NSW. (2023). What is cultural safety? https://www.safework.nsw.gov.au/safety-starts-here/our-aboriginal-program/culturally-safe-workplaces/what-is-cultural-safety Sarkar, B. (2023, Feb 15). Psychological safety to be crucial for India Inc in 2023. https://economictimes.indiatimes.com/news/company/corporate-trends/psychological-safety-to-be-crucial-for-india-inc-in-2023-and-beyond-survey/articleshow/97937736.cms?utm_source=contentofinterest&utm_medium=text&utm_campaign=cppst

SEIL. (2023). Behaviour Based Safety (BBS) Implemented at SEIL. https://www.sembcorpenergyindia.com/CSR/BBS

SEIL. (2023a). Safety at the Core. https://www.sembcorpenergyindia.com/AnnualReport2020/safety-at-the-core.php

Tata Steel. (2021, March 15). Risk Profiling Turns Deep Shop Floor Experience into Enthusiastic Risk-Based Decision Making. https://www.consultdss.com/content-hub/risk-profiling-risk-based-decision-making/

Vattipalli Sameera, Bindra A, Rath GP. (2021). Human errors and their prevention in healthcare. J Anaesthesiol Clin Pharmacol. 2021 Jul-Sep;37(3):328-335. doi: 10.4103/joacp.JOACP_364_19. Epub 2021 Oct 12. PMID: 34759539; PMCID: PMC8562433

Wong SY, Fu ACL, Han J, Lin J, Lau MC. (2021). Effectiveness of customised safety intervention programmes to increase the safety culture of hospital staff. BMJ Open Qual. 2021 Oct;10(4):e000962. doi: 10.1136/bmjoq-2020-000962. PMID: 34625426; PMCID: PMC8504354.

CHAPTER 15

ORGANIZATIONAL COMPLIANCE CULTURE IMPLEMENTATION: BEHAVIOUR BASED SUPPORTIVE INTERVENTION

The researches indicate that there is a wide gap between compliance and non-compliance at Indian workplaces which can ultimately decay the organization. This study explored a basic query from 303 Indian industry professionals whether a culture of work compliance is lacking in India, and how can it be implemented? More than 90 percent of the professionals affirmed that a culture of compliance is lacking. The study explored the basic questions on longterm supportive safety culture, observers' collective voice on at-risk behaviours, and whether the companies are empowering their workforce for performing safety implementation.A host of recommendations as received from the study participants are discussed in this paper for developing a better business culture scenario. Also, a caring safety culture can increase the organizational citizenship behavior (OCB). This paper has added an in-depth sense of qualitative data on the topic.

Keywords: Business, Compliance, Behaviour, Safety, Culture, Qualitative, OCB.

INTRODUCTION

Several researches investigated the influence of safety compliance on Organizational Citizenship Behavior (OCB) indicating that safety compliance is a significant predicator of OCB (Lee et al., 2007). Organizational citizenship behaviors are one of the factors, which can develop organizational culture including safety culture (Jafarpanah and Rezaei, 2020).

Corporate compliance and economic development go hand to hand (Zee News, 2022). Compliance helps organizations to act responsibly and obey regulations related to labor, work safety, finance, operations, and accounting standards (VComply Technologies, 2022). A lack of culture, not compliance, is the primary cause of India's safety woes, as observed by the British Safety Council, India (2020). Work compliance culture transformation for industry is the need of hour for achieving business excellence. Over the years, workplace culture, company ethics, values and mission, rules and regulations are challenged or under examination. Work culture includes all areas of the company such as safety, quality, production, maintenance etc. Compliance is not only limited to safety, but also applicable to an entire work organization concerns. Though compliance training is an integral part of companies, still compliance in all aspects of a company lacks in practice by almost 30 percent of the manpower. Business disruption and productivity losses are the most expensive consequences of non-compliance. The least expensive consequences are fines, penalties and other settlement costs (Ponemon Institute, 2011). Government is trying to eliminate or reduce compliances, which have an adverse impact on time and cost of businesses (Business Standard, 2021).

The traditional safety approach has failed to develop a stronger safety culture at sites, hence it is crucial for top management to innovate on the new safety culture transformational methodology. The leaders build cultures of empowerment (Baumgartner, 2020). Lack of empowerment to employees in building safety culture amounts to a lag in business sustainability. A Successful Safety Culture begins with Leadership's Commitment and Engagement. Sometimes leaders are committed, but not engaged with safety culture (Prescient National, 2021). Corporate top managers influence the safety culture through their decision-making on budgets and policies, their daily actions and attitudes (Räisänen, 2008). GAIL's top management decided to implement the Behavioural Safety Organizational Longterm Planned intervention across all of the company's work sites, and transformed the safety culture of the company successfully (Nambudiri and Ghulyani, 2018) and managed significant reductions in lagging indicators, and increased the compliance levels at sites.

The relationship with OCB by linking compliance with commitment and job satisfaction, are the established antecedents of OCB. It is observed that the socially responsible human resource management (SR-HRM) are positively related with the employees' organizational commitment . labour-related legal compliance HRM and general corporate social responsibility facilitation HRMs have a significant positive relationship with affirmative commitment, continuance commitment and normative commitment (Shen Jie & Jiuhua, 2011). A study indicated that after 17 years, there is considerable improvement in the compliance among employees, though there are still non-compliances that could not manage to be at par with leading compliant offices. It is interesting to know that the organizational commitment and the organizational also maturity impact the level of compliance (Nelson, 2020). Boudlaie, et al., (2020) examined that social responsibility and internal marketing have a positive and significant effect on organizational commitment, and organizational commitment has a significant negative impact on employee turnover intentions. Also, organizational commitment completely mediates the negative impact of social responsibility and internal marketing on the employee turnover intentions.

RESEARCH QUESTION

The Economic Times (2019) raised a query as to why has Compliance Culture suddenly being spoken about and assuming importance? In the present research, the Indian industry professionals were asked to reflect on the Work Culture Compliance. Whether, in general, a culture of compliance is lacking in India at sites/plants, and how can it be implemented?

METHODOLOGY

Sample

303 HSE, medical, education, management, mental health professionals. For this research a total of 700 people were approached out of which 303 completed an action field survey with the researcher. These research participants had been implementing behavioural safety compliance culture at their work sites. The research participants included, the CEO, Directors, Managers, Heads of Departments, Safety Professionals belonging to the public and private industrial sectors, including chemicals, construction, gas, power and steel, across Indian locations.

Types of Data & Data Collection Method

Both primary data (interviews, discussions) and secondary data (incident and accident rates) were collected. Interviews based on open-ended questions and personal in-depth discussions were conducted through remote data collection techniques over 2-months (during Jan-Feb 2022) from diverse locations and organisationsin India. The sampling method used was a non-random convenience sampling. Participants were selected from the researcher's contact list, invited by WhatsApp, and email to complete the online survey.

Research Design

This is a concept building, innovative and exploratory research design at the behest and involvement of field professionals as being study participants, using qualitative descriptive framework.

Data Analysis Techniques

This study is part of an ongoing interdisciplinary intervention of behavioural science, management and industrial safety disciplines, and part of a national longitudinal action survey in India. Crucial element in this research was data collection conducted by means of controlled interviews and questionnaire surveys in the organizations. Their responses to the relevant questions were collated.

THE RESULTS

The multiple perspectives came out from the responses of study participants as described below. More than 90 percent of the professionals affirmed that yes, a culture of compliance is lacking, which can be achieved through the top management commitment and continual interventions. The leaders from 54 countries are struggling to create and communicate a strong and effective culture of integrity within their business. There is a growth in compliance programs, yet failure to address unethical behavior, whichis an internal disconnect (EY, 2022). Also remarked a new employee, this is the employers fault. Employers treat their employees as temporary workers who can be replaced easily. They don't believe in investing in the employees safety compliance to build a culture for the same reason. The moment we change the treatment from ritual to necessity, the compliances increase, as quoted by the Head of executions of a large multi-locational construction company. A corporate safety head of pharmaceutical units from south India discerned that the compliance culture is lacking in India as there is no curriculum in studies. We can implement only through top management leadership. A seasoned HSE professional stated that it is the Poor Operational Discipline. A west Bengal HSE professional retired from a public sector large organization with 30 years experience demanded to imposing huge penalty due to non-compliance of compliance rules. The professionals focused on zero tolerance. An executive Director of an ONGC expressed that a culture of compliance is lacking very much. Culture and values are top driven. Top managements should hold exclusive sessions on compliance supportive culture. In India, an absence of punishment due to laxity in compliance needs to be addressed, it should be taught at graduation level. A plant HSE Head of a multinational organization clarified that the problem is not of compliance but in understanding that the associates completely trust the orders, and orders are often given without proper risk assessment and consideration that it is responsibility of senior employees to have enough controls in place to ensure zero harm. So this is the gap in Indian scenario,. A young manager explained that all are having a skill to developing the compliance culture. But we fail to implement due to nearby working environment/willpower/and lack of resources. Sometime, we see that worker doing unsafe and we do not ask to do safe because we knew that there is low potential hazard, but when the worker comes to know that we have seen him doing wrong, yet ignored him, his morale to do wrong boosts up. If we want a 100% culture, then we have to train our employees first, then we can go with worker. If our site/plant executive are trained, then only he can teach another one and then we can achieve compliance more than 90%. A factory medical officer recommended that the best compliance is to conduct awareness sessions in factories on applicable laws/rules and advice each one to do right things always. A culture of compliance can be implemented through audits, work permits, SOP, plans. What was safe workplace yesterday, is not safe today due to changes in antecedents, manpower and technology. Hence the compliance definition needs to be revisited. We visited religious places in the past when there was not much crowd, but now these places are overcrowded with less planning, and incidents are happening and fatalities took place. So are these places safe, we need to rethink and improve our actions to be on safer side. Heads of locations alongwith leadership of directors and HODs achieve work compliance culture while spreading it to all down the levels for developing observers to observe compliance and non-compliance behaviours and spot-correct the same as a big brother, not big boss, so that employees take it positively to integrate it on their job. Behavioural safety supportive culture training has to be essentially very authentic from the mentors side to touch the heart of the observers so that they become active in their observation and spot-correction of at-risk behaviors daily.

Sometimes, even seniors or your colleagues, take it as an offence or insult, when observers ask for compliance to safe behaviours. For various reasons in India, safety and health is at low preference in our families. Though some change is visible due to COVID-19 with lives lost.

Companies aimed to satisfy only legal / compliance requirements. Companies are made to understand by HR professionals that safety is a common subject, everyone can talk about it, that safety is to be managed. Law is to be complied. It's always the HR / IR team which handles compliance with authorities. So they satisfy them with numbers (as per law).

Basic questions on longterm supportive safety culture

In India, the employers' pocket size decides the safety size for employees. Whether employees deserve safety system or culture or no safety is decided by how much profit comes to the company. Care comes second, it is money first, not safety first. That is the bottom line. So the future of businesses is at risk, as without safety, the business does not get sustained. The at-risk behaviours at site are life threatening to employees and business threatening for employers. It is preventable with BBS culture. Switch to a new culture for sustainable future of our businesses caring employees' safety right. Let's change the OSH scene together. Sometimes, it is great difficulty for even leaders to convince some people due to certain contingencies at sites that HSE violations are not acceptable to practice. It is to be realised that at-risk behaviours in industries are unsafe to the citizens in the civil societies, sometimes disabling, injurious, even fatal. Safety is a moment of spot-correction, Rest is in scope of an incident. Spot-correction is a function of one and all to achieve safety culture. There seems to be a bleak future of businesses if they are not establishing longterm supportive safety culture at their sites. Though a large number of companies believe in this, yet they do not appear to be acting accordingly.

Basic 12 Questions on longterm safety cultures that emerged during discussions were:

1. Does investing in Supportive Safety Cultures Pay? How would observers respond in a split-second when an incident can take place, or how would national safety culture impact at-risk behaviors of people at site?
2. Why ideologies on safety cultures vary across the industries in terms of practices?
3. Why industry is confused between the mental safety and behavioural safety?

4. What are the Periodical Impact Assessments for Safety Culture in Organisations for Improvement?

5. How to understand the features of companies that do not empower and enable their workforce for performing safety implementation, and to provide a framework for facilitating plants to performing safety implementation by their workforce?

6. Why do not the corrections of at-risk behaviours become permanent safety culture after few observations, how long would it take? What is the involvement of HODs in this aspect? What is the response of the corporate on this issue? What is inter-relationship between corporate, plant management, HODs, observers for achieving permanent safety culture?

7. A well-planned BBS approach opens ones' mind 360 degree about how safety is redefined, measured, and achieved as a company culture. But some people at site do not wish, a reactive safety culture to go away, why?

8. Why people do not understand the difference between safe and unsafe behaviour? Why managers do not get involved in safety implementation?

10. Why safety observations are not discussed at sites?

11. Why there are competencies gap amongst the safety professionals to convince their own managements for longterm safety culture solutions? Why HR departments did not realise and fill up this competency gap? Are our training colleges or institutions insufficient to train the safety professionals for the required competencies?

12. How human factor and safety culture are related? Is it that the exponential value of human factor reflects in safety culture?

The major question, the corporates need to ask themselves is: are you ready to develop a long term interdependent safety supportive culture: just find out below:

1. It should take between 1-4 years depending upon your workforce size.

2. It would transform safety culture from reactive to interdependent safety culture.

3. The journey would involve everyone from top to the last person at site.
4. This would involve everyone to become an active BBS observer.
5. This would help measure at-risk behaviors at site.
6. This would involve HODs to drive the safety culture.
7. This would help create a structure to monitor BBS score over weeks/months.
8. This would need to link safety culture with EHS policy and PMS in the organization.
9. It would require expert guidance to handhold, support and review progress.
10. It would need continued management engagement.

The above questions of industry delve upon the critical concerns that impact safety culture in organisations.

At-risk behaviours, Observers' collective voice and Leadership

The influence of group collective voices is greater than the fear of any form of punishment. At-risk behaviours are the wake up call just before incidents occur. BBS Observers' collective voice at site are an epitome of corporate safety culture which needs to prevail in positive sense. Observers training is most important, and they need to understand their daily observation in terms of company's safety culture. Moreover, Safety at site would not suffer, even when safety officers are on leave, as long as our BBS trained observers are active to care for at-risk behaviors. "Yes, we are moving towards this", a plant head said. In this regard, some experiences by the study participants are expressed below:

Peer group implementation of BBS would be helpful by support from companies that implemented supportive safety culture successfully mentoring other plants to give them online guidance and handholding in order to fast track culture of safe behaviours across sites.

Regulated Surprise Monthly BBS rounds by the individual steering team members across the site would help support and strengthen the longterm safety culture. The visible leadership observation daily rounds are important in reinforcing supportive safety culture at sites.

Personal and organizational safety behaviors are significant in building safety culture. We are reducing our personal risk by adopting BBS and being a part of it actively, people would observe and look after you. In terms of gaining increased risk control, train everyone as observer. 77 percent HSE professionals agreed that it takes only one observation to stop any incident, it may be of yours! Isn't it, so why not train everyone for the same at site.

Consider plants, sites, corporates for behavioural safety awards that have trained 100 percent of their manpower including contractors staff as active observers who are correcting at-risk behaviors on daily basis for developing supportive safety culture.

Nearly 90% of this study participants expressed that be careful, in India, we don't measure well. It doesn't support zero-harm policy, if you don't measure at-risk behaviours at site work areas. If you don't measure, you don't understand it well. Beware, it may give you surprise. Then the question arises, whether a BBS intervention is useful without its measurement aspect. The answer is yes, but it is useful in a limited way, and the risk control is not covered fully, as it is not understood without measurement.

89 percent HSE professionals agreed that we need corporate safety leaders more than the safety professionals who can lead safety implementation passionately as a core value. This reflects that the dependent safety culture exists at sites to a greater extent. We introduced leader member exchange quality as a central predictor of leaders' support for employees' ideas for constructive change (Urbach and Fay, 2020).

It is noticed that leaders rarely do observation rounds by themselves rather they present observations done by their observers down the levels. Also the hot-spots of at-risk behaviors trigger incidents, and spot-correction of at-risk behaviors is done, but behavior needs to be changed by regular Risk Based Conversations (RBC). This is a serious feedback to sustain safety culture at work sites. Successful longterm safety culture management essentially requires a sustained untiring leadership to guide and direct the involvement of all concerned from top to the last persons at sites. Dedicated leaders could see the vision of transformed safety culture in terms of safe behaviours being reinforced by everyone, and reflecting its vibrations into business excellence.

Companies not empowering their workforce for performing safety implementation

Companies can ensure success in their safety procedures by building a culture of safety (Vos, 2021). If you really wished to create a strong safety culture, you must listen to every observer who developed an emotion into the heart of every observee to behave safe who was behaving unsafe (Kaila, 2021).

The subject needs to be addressed as how to conduct BBS process as a "longterm planned intervention of applied behavioural science." When you don't spend on safety, you spend on incidents. Low safety budget is equal to high incidents budget. It is important to know the pitfalls on the journey of turning around the sick safety culture by mentors addressing the safety culture engagement reflecting on the real-world experiences with measurable safety culture transformations (ISHN, 2021).

There is a need to include safety culture in personal life of leaders for effectively implementing behavioural safety at sites. If you do not emphasise or spend on safety and health in personal life, you tend to do the same at workplaces in corporate decision making for HSE aspects. If you leave safety to chance and complacency, it would lead to incidents. There are managers who encourage employees when they complete their tasks with unsafe approach and save time. Negative encouragement produces resistance and barriers for safe behaviours at sites. Justifying unsafe behaviour is an anti for safety culture, which is demonstrated to manage target pressures without adequate pre-planning.

Ten Features (Table: 1) would help measuring and building the action plan for companies in empowering their workforce for performing safety implementation.

Table 1: Ten Features of companies not empowering their workforce for performing safety implementation (mark each item Yes or No)

Low on the concept of of psychological safety for workforce.
Low on the values of human compassion and empathy.
Low on corporate social responsibility.
Low on corporate care as a core value.
Low on international business operations.

Low on leading indicators but high on lagging indicators.
High on reactive, and dependent safety culture.
Low on independent and interdependent safety culture.
Low on their leadership safety consciousness.
Low on safety implications on business and employees.
Scoring: The number of Yes means, the company is not empowering their workforce for performing safety implementation. Indicate action plan for improvement based on number of Yes.

MANAGERIAL IMPLICATIONS

Definitely the culture of compliance is lacking badly, reason is time pressure and cost pressure. Above all, the safety compliance education is missing among the management. Economic Times (2021) noted that at small companies, compliance is not taken seriously. A HSE professional described, "Even few who worked with reputed organization like L&T, when we join a new organization, we fail miserably to take the culture forward. In my site, I still see many workers are not provided with minimum PPEs. Safety compliance cost must be part of tender documents. Contractor selection based on compliance records, but not only L3 or L4, must be looked in. Safety compliance has become a ritual, but not seen as a value. Government shall make a mandatory 3 days session on safety for all CEOs, and isolate them completely from gadgets those 3 days." A study indicated that top management must consistently reinforce a culture of compliance and integrity, lest it decays throughout the organization (Jennifer, et al., (2021). It was suggested that an organization views meeting legal and regulatory requirements as more important than meeting compliance with internal policies and procedures (Ponemon Institute, 2011).

Culture comes from upbringing. Hence it is strongly suggested to include compliance as subject from standard 3 in schools, this will not only make compliance a basic adherence but it will be as necessity like water, food and clothes, This will make great working places and India will grow bounds. Let us focus on our present generation, children need to be educated about what is hazard and what are its consequences? How would they deal to comply it?

Also we should meet across companies and share implementation ideas, same as IPL teams, compliance teams from each organization can meet many teams across India. We should have State and National trophies for best out of box ideas for implementing compliance at work place, home or anywhere we go. We should organize compliance tour for each Organization, where top management or HOD level persons should be part of this tour. Each organization shall keep some 25% marks for appraisals for compliance implementation. Moreover, motivation on the job for engineers those who consider compliance as priority for their job. High reward and monetary assistance, job continuity, all these are the main motivators.

For present situation the laws of enforcement on job supervisors and project managers need to be implemented strictly. They have to be accountable for compliance lapses. As a top industry professional said, "Let them go to jail." Respect for ethical business from owners and fear of law for the workmen can save from these lapses. Though there are improvements of HSE compliances over last two decades in India, still there are lot of major gaps. It probably happens due to dual stand and policies of the management. Safety compliances can't be negotiated, neither it should be compromised. This attitude is expected from the leaders and industry must demand that. First of all, we need to make them understand the importance of compliance. As compliance is part of real requirement of Working Environment, Health, Safety of employees, Society, statutory bodies, local public at large. Need to make them understand the repercussions if deviated. Need to initiate Behavioural Based Supportive program and develop champions by empowerment through CEO of the company, tracking effectiveness before company CEO, and Gap assessment and corrections on continual basis and its reflection in company's annual report. IIFL (2022) noted that the risk management, compliance, and audit strategies will need to be, reprioritized and to balance global operations, hybrid workforces, growth goals, regulatory demands, and stakeholder relationships.

Supportive work culture means one cares for all, all care for one. Company develops a procedure on this concept to make everyone aware to practice it. Behavioural research highlights multiple situational antecedents of non-compliance. Hence the correction is needed in the cultural antecedents by employees under a planned intervention to achieve compliance (Feldman and Kaplan, 2019). At the end of the day, its humanity what matters and delivers in every way, that is what is referred as behavioural safety supportive culture in true sense to practice.

Company also cares that employees and associates do not practice what is unsupportive, negative, fault-finding, blaming, shouting, being reactive etc. Daily shop-floor brief meeting in departments is held to demonstrate the regularity of Compliance procedure. There is a least paper documentation encouraged, instead an evidence is shown by way of meeting's photographs and put on the notice board or social media specifically maintained for this compliance culture.

A supportive work culture compliance checklist is described below (Table 2) for implementation. Employees conduct daily compliance observations and spot-corrections tour in their respective department, area, section for ease and understanding. Spot-correction is a way of work culture transformation. All leaders, HODs, and everyone would focus and value spot-correction of any work compliance. This would enhance business excellence. Every employee/ associates would do minimum one or two spot-correction of 12 observation categories. If there are 1000 workforce, we shall achieve 1000 spot-corrections in every single day. A culture of compliance is implementable as a planned behavioural intervention in any organization.

Finally, a senior EHS professional from a mega construction company shelled out that a work compliance culture can be achieved by stopping bluffing and rewards on Safe-Man-hours, which is one way out of many ways. One has to be straightforward. Now people perceiving compliance means cosmetic, this field must erase that impression. One can truly work towards this goal. Unless everyone is made responsible and accountable, everyone feels that it is not their job. Everyone should believe in compliance to make it happen. Compliance has always been a challenge, but this challenge is becoming greater than ever. Firms need a tech-enabled human approach to compliance, making reporting as easy as possible for employees to do, can help firms close the compliance gap (NASSCOM, 2021). Any compliance gap is to be viewed by every employee as a responsible care for immediate compliance in his/her supportive role. Company HODs empower and enable each employee for daily achieving minimum one correction of non-compliance in their respective department or site, and leaders appreciate this initiative. These are easy behavioural solutions to bridge the gaps and develop a culture of compliance. A project manager stated that "We have changed mindset of most of the working people though behavioural based supportive compliance culture implementation especially for who are not following safety at site." Compliance training does not bring change, unless it is a part of a longterm planned compliance culture intervention for implementing the sustainable culture of compliance at the corporates, to be strengthened and supported by the company directors to ensure that the collaborative intentions and delivery are turned into results to become an integrated process (Bob et al., 2019). It is imperative that the top leaders walk the talk in behavior and communication, and make compliance easy to understand and practice by the employees (Compliance Quest, 2022). Moreover, compliance effectiveness largely depends on successful detection and management of non-compliance, which means characterising non-compliance, its categories, consequences. Solely relying on enforcement-led deterrence can fail to identify and mitigate nuanced non-compliance (Collins et al., 2021). Moreover, safety compliance increases the organizational citizenship behavior (OCB) as an outcome of a caring safety culture (Parke, 2021).

Table 2: Supportive work culturecompliance tour Checklist for Observers

Name of observer/Area/ Dept/Date:	**No. of Persons (Lacking Compliance)**	**No. of spot-corrections**	**Remarks**
***Observation* Categories**			
1. Safety, Health, Environment 2. Quality 3. Instrumentation 4. Marketing 5. Production/Operations 6. Materials/Stores 7. Maintenance 8. Contractors 9. Security/HR/Canteen 10. R&D 11. Packing/Despatch 12. Legal /Finance			

REFERENCES

Baumgartner, Natalie. (2020, April, 08). Build a Culture That Aligns with People's Values. Retrieved on 2 April 2022. https://hbr.org/2020/04/build-a-culture-that-aligns-with-peoples-values

Bob Hudson, David Hunter & Stephen Peckham. (2019). Policy failure and the policy-implementation gap: can policy support programs help?, Policy Design and Practice, 2:1, 1-14, DOI: 10.1080/25741292.2018.1540378

Boudlaie Hasan, Nik Behrouz, Kenarroodi Mohammad Hosein. (2020). The Impact of Corporate Social Responsibility and Internal Marketing on Employee Turnover Intentions with the Mediating Role of Organizational Commitment. *Technium Social Sciences Journal*. 4. 121-134. 10.47577/tssj.v4i1.104.

British Safety Council, India. (2020, August, 17). Why a lack of culture—not compliance—is the primary cause of India's safety woes. Retrieved on 20 March 2022. https://www.britsafe.in/publications-and-blogs/blogs/read-all-blogs/why-a-lack-of-culture-not-compliance-is-the-primary-cause-of-india-s-safety-woes/

Bryan, Jordan. (2019, April 04). Create a Culture of Integrity to Improve Corporate Compliance. Retrieved on 20 March 2022. https://www.gartner.com/smarter withgartner/create-a-culture-of-integrity-to-improve-corporate-compliance

Business Standard. (2021, March, 10). Centre, states to remove 6,000 compliance norms by Aug 15, 2022: DPIIT Secy. Retrieved on 22 March 2022. https://www.business-standard.com/article/economy-policy/centre-states-to-remove-6-000-compliance-norms-by-aug-15-2022-dpiit-secy-121030901463_1.html

ComplianceQuest. (2022). Minimizing non-compliance. Retrieved on 21 March 2022. https://www.compliancequest.com/blog/minimizing-non-compliance/

Collins, Claire. (2021, May, 10). Understanding Persistent Non-compliance in a Remote, Large-Scale Marine Protected Area. Front. Mar. Sci. https://doi.org/10.3389/fmars.2021.650276

Economic Times. (2021, May, 05). Leave aside ESG India's bigger problem is EHS. Retrieved on 21 March 2022. https://m.economictimes.com/markets/stocks/news/leave-aside-esg-indias-bigger-problem-is-ehs/articleshow/82394008.cms

EY. (2022, Jan, 12). Businesses must review compliance programs: lack of improvement in integrity standards, according to EY survey. Retrieved on 21 March 2022. https://www.ey.com/en_gl/news/2022/01/businesses-must-review-compliance-programs-lack-of-improvement-in-integrity-standards-according-to-ey-survey

Feldman, Yuval and Kaplan,, Yotam. (2019, Dec, 06). A Behavioural Ethics Approach to Legal Compliance. https://www.law.ox.ac.uk/business-law-blog/blog/2019/12/behavioural-ethics-approach-legal-compliance

Financial Express. (2021, March, 11). Importance of behavioural-based safety in workplaces during the pandemic. Retrieved on 20 March 2022. https://www.financialexpress.com/jobs/importance-of-behavioural-based-safety-in-workplaces-during-the-pandemic/2210560/

IIFL Securities. (2022). 2022 - An Outlook on Corporate Governance & Compliance of BFSI Industry. Retrieved on 20 March 2022. https://www.indiainfoline.com/article/general-others-factiva/2022-an-outlook-on-corporate-governance-compliance-of-bfsi-industry-121122000049_1.html

Jafarpanah, M., Rezaei, B. (2020). Association between organizational citizenship behavior and patient safety culture from nurses' perspectives: a descriptive correlational study. *BMC Nurs* 19, 24 (2020). https://doi.org/10.1186/s12912-020-00416-y

Jennifer L. M. Altamuro,John V. Gray, Haiwen (Helen) Zhang. (2021, August, 14). Corporate Integrity Culture and Compliance: A Study of the Pharmaceutical Industry. Contemporary Accounting Research, Volume 39, Issue 1 p. 428-458. https://doi.org/10.1111/1911-3846.12727

Lee, Tzai-Zang & Wu, Chien-Hsing & Hong, Chih-Wei. (2007). An Empirical Investigation of the Influence of Safety Climate on Organizational Citizenship Behavior in Taiwan's Facilities. *International journal of occupational safety and ergonomics*. JOSE. 13. 255-69. 10.1080/10803548.2007.11076726.

Macht, Betsy and Davis, Annie. (2018) Strategies to Influence a Quality and Compliance Culture. IJAMT, Vol. 17 (1), 68-82. https://doi.org/10.5590/IJAMT.2018.17.1.06

Nambudiri, Ranjeet and Ghulyani, Swati. (2018, August 30). GAIL (India) Limited: Transforming Safety Culture. Ivey Publishing. https://store.hbr.org/product/gail-india-limited-transforming-safety-culture/W18522

NASSCOM. (2021, April, 04). How to combine people & tech to bridge growing gaps in compliance. Retrieved on 21 March 2022. https://community.nasscom.in/communities/tech-good/how-combine-people-tech-bridge-growing-gaps-compliance

Nelson, Celis. (2020). Compliance Theory A Case Study Approach in Understanding Organizational Commitment. 88-118. https://www.researchgate.net/profile/Nelson-Celis-2/publication/344712535_Compliance_Theory_A_Case_Study_Approach_in_Understanding_Organizational_Commitment/links/5f8aed09299bf1b53e2c514c/Compliance-Theory-A-Case-Study-Approach-in-Understanding-Organizational-Commitment.pdf

Nungchim, Bridget & Leihaothabam, Jibon. (2022). Impact of Organizational Culture on the Effectiveness of Organizations: A Case Study of Some Service Sector Organizations in Manipur. *Jindal Journal of Business Research*. 227868212210825. 10.1177/22786821221082592.

Parke, Michael. (2021, October 04). Employees can become better organizational citizens. http://knowledge.wharton.upenn.edu/article/employees-can-become-better-organizational-citizens/

Ponemon Institute. (2011). The true cost of compliance: Benchmark Study of Multinational Organizations. Retrieved on 20 March 2022. https://www.ponemon.org/local/upload/file/True_Cost_of_Compliance_Report_copy.pdf

Prescient National. (2021, July, 30). Creating a Successful Safety Culture Begins with Leadership's Commitment, Engagement. https://www.prescientnational.com/creating-a-successful-safety-culture-begins-with-leaderships-commitment-engagement

Räisänen, Pekka. (2008). Influence of corporate top management to safety culture - A literature survey. Turku University of Applied Sciences, www.merikotka.fi

Shen Jie & Jiuhua Zhu Cherrie. (2011). Effects of socially responsible human resource management on employee organizational commitment, *The International Journal of Human Resource Management*, 22:15, 3020-3035, DOI: 10.1080/09585192.2011.599951

The Economic Times. (2019). Compliance Culture – its importance and how to prevent it from becoming just a buzzword? Retrieved on 19 March 2022.https://cfo.economictimes.indiatimes.com/news/compliance-culture-its-importance-and-how-to-prevent-it-from-becoming-just-a-buzzword/70224217

VComply Technologies. (2022). Impact of Non-compliance on Organizations. Retrieved on 20 March 2022. https://www.v-comply.com/impact-of-non-compliance-on-organizations/

Yohn, Denise Lee. (2021, February 08). Company Culture Is Everyone's Responsibility. Retrieved on 19 March 2022. https://hbr.org/2021/02/company-culture-is-everyones-responsibility

Zee News. (2022). Corporate Compliance: Here's how it will become a pathway to economic development. Retrieved on 19 March 2022. https://zeenews.india.com/economy/corporate-compliance-here-s-how-it-will-become-a-pathway-to-economic-development-2436187.html

ACKNOWLEDGMENT

Contribution of industry professionals is thankfully acknowledged.

CHAPTER

16

BALANCING ORGANISATIONAL SAFETY SYSTEMS AND SAFETY CULTURE - ISSUES AND CHALLENGES

HSE professionals emphasized balancing the challenges and issues while integrating the safety systems and positive safety culture. The elements of the total safety culture interventions ought not exist as disjointed forms in the organization for best results for safety of manpower as well as business prosperity. Safety systems provide nothing more than the safety climate. At the same time, the safety culture interventions must move on with fast-tracking safety culture decisions. People need to feel psychological safe to give optimum performances. The complicated human factors of safety and the complex human error in safety must be addressed by the corporates. Cultural safety and equitable care require workers migrated from diverse cultural backgrounds to be understood in their own cultural backdrop, language and communication, so that any kind of racism or inequity is ruled out. Total safety culture framework integrates information across disjointed conceptualisations to clearly portray the dynamic nature of safety culture and specific drivers of its development.

Keywords: Balancing, Safety, Systems, Safety culture, Challenges.

INTRODUCTION

The Total Worker Health approach prioritizes a hazard-free work environment for all workers. It also brings together all aspects of work in integrated interventions that collectively address worker safety, health, and well-being (NIOSH, 2022). Integrating safety interventions is crucial and a long-term commitment. There is a challenge especially, in the beginning when a company launched the safety culture intervention, how to balance the two entities while the safety systems are weak and in the hands of a few safety and management staff. Safety culture presupposes that everyone from CEO till the last worker at the site is involved in the safety culture of caring for each other. As one has to become a child to interact well with children, likewise manager has to stoop to level of a worker to interact with workmen to understand them. A large number of factors affect the development and maintenance of a safety culture including: communication (explicit and tacit) on safety within an organization, including incident reporting systems; apportionment of blame, managing and learning from incidents, investment in safety systems, and emergency management procedures; training and awareness of human factors (e.g., teamwork, effect of stress, and fatigue on performance); cultural influences, such as societal acceptance of open comment and a willingness to speak out (Arblaster, 2018).

Organizations with strong safety culture will be recognized by having an effective safety standard for integrated management systems. If the safety culture is weak it will show in the poor design, poor strategies to achieve good production results, lack of systematic approach of the work processes and so on (IAEA, 2015). It is crucial to understand safety culture ties in with an HSE management system, for example, an appropriate balance between the production and safety issues? (SaferMe team, 2019). The most successful types of interventions were those related to the importance of safety, leadership style and behavioural monitoring (Aburumman, et al., 2019).

Organizations with strong safety cultures are not characterized by a complete absence of adverse events, but by their commitment to capturing and responding to these events, recognizing how each one gives valuable insight for further system improvement. Unsafe cultures, in contrast, can be highlighted by a lack of trust, fear of speaking up, absence of transparency, incivility, or even workplace violence. A robust safety culture includes several fundamental elements: Psychological safety: In a psychologically safe environment, individuals feel comfortable, even obligated, to discuss adverse events and near misses in an open and transparent manner, with the goal of improving safety and quality of care. Just Culture: Just Culture guides an organization's response to accountability for errors based on a central belief that most adverse events reflect complex interactions of human factors within imperfect systems. Reporting, learning, transparency, and feedback: All team members recognize the value of reporting errors and near misses. Events are analysed and learning is transparent and shared with all team members (ASA, 2022).

The presence of safety culture at workplace has potential to influence negative safety outcomes. In addition, safety compliance and safety participation as mediation paths would be the strengthening addition to an integrated robust safety model (Hafeez, et al., 2022). Occupational safety interventions directed at the corporate group or organizational level are more effective for improving safety and behaviour and reducing accidents at work than interventions directed solely at the individual level. Multifaceted measures are particularly effective, but Safety regulation and enforcement contribute to the prevention of accidents at work, but with lesser effect (Dyreborg, et al., 2022).

OBJECTIVES OF THE STUDY

- To explore the challenges and issues while integrating and balancing the safety systems and positive safety culture.
- To explore the Total Safety Culture (TSC) Interventions.
- To explore the how to achieve a good balance between safety systems and safety culture.

SAMPLE AND SAMPLE SIZE

252 industry professionals participated in the study as part of an action field survey with the researcher. These research participants had been implementing behavioural safety compliance culture at their work sites. The research participants included, the CEO, Directors, Managers, Heads of Departments, Safety Professionals belonging to the public and private industrial sectors, including chemicals, construction, gas, power and steel, across Indian locations.

Participants were selected from the researcher's contact list, invited by WhatsApp and e-mail to complete the online survey. The sampling method used was a non-random convenience sampling.

RESEARCH METHODOLOGY

Both primary data (interviews, discussions) and secondary data (incident and accident rates) were collected. Interviews based on open-ended questions and personal in-depth discussions were conducted through remote data collection techniques over 3-months (during Oct-Dec 2022) from diverse locations and organisations in India. This is a concept building, innovative and exploratory research design with an involvement of field professionals as being study participants, using qualitative descriptive framework. This study is part of an ongoing interdisciplinary intervention of behavioural science, management and industrial safety disciplines and part of a national longitudinal action survey in India. Crucial element in this research was data collection conducted by means of controlled interviews and questionnaire surveys in the organizations. Their responses to the relevant questions were collated. Eeckelaert et al., (2011) suggested that the safety culture can be assessed using questionnaires, interviews, focus groups and observations. In practice, quantitative questionnaires are the simplest and cheapest assessment method and the most widely implemented in industry.

The study results and implications are reflected below from a rigorous review of safety culture literature and experiences shared by the industry leaders across organizations.

RESULTS AND DISCUSSION

The results are categorised in three themes and discussed here below.

- Challenges and issues in balancing the safety systems and positive safety culture.
- Total Safety Culture (TSC) Interventions.
- How to achieve a good balance between safety systems and safety culture?

Challenges and issues in balancing the safety systems and positive safety culture

HSE professionals emphasized on balancing each of the challenges and issues in percentages while integrating the safety systems and safety culture (Table 1). Though safety culture and systems compliment each other to be effective, both have unique core operatives and distinct aspects to function that cannot be compromised. Aligning safety culture with performance analysis is important for bringing all operations people together. Not following safety culture intervention, organizations are almost three times backward to the global practices, and just focusing passively on the safety systems. By following safety cultural practices as long-term intervention, this gap is closed, and organizations are almost at par with the world practices. The efficient safety management system ought to be based on safety awareness that should then become a culture in the industry. Efficient safety culture should be demonstrated to the public as a good value business (Misnan, 2007). The Plan, Do, Check, Act approach achieves a balance between the systems and behavioural aspects of safety management (HSE, 2022).

Table 1: Percentages of HSE professionals emphasising the challenges and issues in balancing the safety systems and positive safety culture (N=252).

1. Enforcement and soft peddling culture transformation - 89%.
2. Involvement of all workforce by regular training - 84%.
3. Safety systems are weak such as SOP, work permit system - 81%.
4. Safety Resources are insufficient - 75%.
5. Management will to safety is poor - 70%.
6. Clarity of safety culture roadmap - 63%.
7. Need to Strengthening safety procedures - 55%.
8. Resolve Safety budgeting issues - 52%.
9. Willing to continue the long-term safety culture - 50%.
10. Meeting time of Directors for safety - 46%.

There is a need to check the pros and cons of each of these challenges while balancing safety systems and safety culture. Enforcement and reinforcement are both part of the soft-peddling culture transformation with involvement of all workforce. Most companies have safety systems, but they are passive and weak. Safety resources are insufficient, and the management will to safety is poor. Clarity of safety culture roadmap is inadequate. There is a dire need to strengthening safety procedures and resolve safety budgeting issues. Organizations willing to continue the long-term safety culture is an issue and meeting time of directors for safety is scarce. When employees see that leadership truly cares for them, the relationship is strengthened, and safety is more assured (Sears and Sullivan, 2022).

Safety should be more than just the focus of a few designated roles within an organization. Instead, a successful safety program requires creating a culture of safety that permeates all departments and all levels of a company. Organizations that embrace worker safety in a holistic way strengthen employee loyalty and build trusted relationships between workers and management, ultimately increasing productivity, helping attract and retain top talent, and reducing costly turnovers. A culture focused on safety directly correlates with business performance. "When workers are getting hurt, it's a sign that things aren't going right," says David Michaels, eight-year OSHA Assistant Secretary of Labor, whose work focuses on helping companies be "safe, productive, and profitable at the same time." In other words, safety isn't a discrete issue for companies: it's actually a key performance indicator of an organization's overall operational effectiveness (Blackline Safety, 2021). Safety is an emotional trigger that employees receive from each other.

Total Safety Culture (TSC) Interventions

Corporates need to take insights beyond the safety culture and safety systems. A positive safety culture helps organizations achieve their ultimate goal of achieving better safety performance However, the process of understanding and improving a safety culture can be way much beyond for achieving vision zero. The best way to do this is by tracking the right data efficiently, which is best achieved by using an automated safety data management system (Easton, 2011). Many organizations are not able to resolve human factors of safety such as teamwork, group dynamics, groupthink, relationships, stress, pressure, fear, fatigue, mental health, sub-group cultures and so on. While the safety culture refers to the overall culture of an organisation as a whole, safety culture is just one aspect of the total work culture values and virtues. Promoting a positive safety culture can reduce stress at work (Pearson, 2021).

Total safety culture is a long and continuous journey strengthening and consolidating each of the elements involving everyone from top to bottom. Many organizations leave the safety culture interventions in-between at some stage. Table 2 reveals the percentage of HSE professionals favouring each of the TSC interventions that must be implemented by the organisations.

Table 2: Percentages of HSE professionals emphasising Total Safety Culture (TSC) Interventions (N=252)

1.	Robust Safety systems with digital intervention: positively reinforcing antecedents for managing all safety issues such as barriers, resources, safety controls - 92%.
2.	Safety culture: long term behavioural interventions with fast-tracking action plan - 90%.
3.	Psychological safety: do people feel psychologically safe in an organisational context? - 88%.
4.	Human factors in organisational cultural context: do people feel very strained with occupational stresses, workload, decision latitude issues? - 86%.

5.	Human error in organisational cultural context: human cognition, decision making, fear, pressure. How companies handle group conflicts and differences that delay safety culture decisions. The Bhopal tragedy and the IOCL Jaipur fire incident were the result of top level dis-engagement with the safety culture of their respective companies effecting into human error and poor decision making for actions needed to correct unsafe antecedents at sites. Human error is not personal error but in organisational cultural context - 80%.
6.	Cultural safety and competency: do people feel being understood with due respect to their cultural background and beliefs, and how companies respond to these factors effectively? - 78%.
7.	Integrating and Reviews by the topmost leaders on all the above six interventions towards a goal of Vision Zero harm - 75%.

These above-said seven elements ought not exist as disjointed form in the organization for best results for safety of manpower as well as business prosperity. Safety systems though provide only and nothing more than a safety climate, must be handled with a single window for closing all safety issues. At the same time, the safety culture interventions must move on with fast-tracking safety culture decisions. Thereon, the people need to feel psychological safe for giving optimum performances. The complicated human factors of safety and the complex human error in safety must be addressed by the corporates. Cultural safety and equitable care require workers (Figure 1) at the last rank and file, or less educated, contract staff, migrated from diverse cultural backgrounds or locals to be understood in their own cultural backdrop, language and communication, so that any kind of racism or inequity is also ruled out. Integration of all these above elements of the total safety culture is absolutely crucial and holistic over a period of time. The recommendations for industry is in terms of implementing safety climate as a form of social control over safety performance. The most compelling rationale for including safety climate and culture within systems models is the notion of bottom-up control. Bottom-up control is likely to be more effective and sustainable under the types of conditions faced by high hazard organizations in the modern age, where uncertainty, interdependence, and dynamic environments are encountered routinely (Casey, et al., 2017).

Eliminating indigenous and ethnic inequities require addressing the determinants of health and safety inequities which includes an institutionalised racism and ensuring a system that delivers appropriate and equitable care. To do this, we must be prepared to critique the taken for granted power structures and to challenge the cultural systems rather than prioritise becoming competent in the culture of others. A move to cultural safety rather than cultural competency is recommended (Curtis, et al., 2019). The management should continuously monitor and evaluate their strategies while delivering multifaceted interventions to be more specifically focused and to motivate staff to be enthusiastic in sustaining safety culture. The change in positive safety culture over the years and its sustainability need to be further explored (Wong, et al., 2021).

Figure 1: Workers safety with tool box talk (TBT)

How to achieve a good balance between safety systems and safety culture?

Table 3 revealed how to achieve a good balance between safety systems and safety culture, as expressed by the HSE heads of companies who implemented safety culture interventions over the years. Robust Safety Management System firmly implemented with human touch and care with an intent of learning and improving is necessary. This will help build an Interdependent and Learning culture with commitment to continually improve. We should develop culture of 100% compliance of the system developed otherwise hefty fines. If seat belt is provided in the car, it must be used by the passenger, otherwise no point of talking systems. Good safety systems (adherence) drive good safety culture and vice versa. Relation between safety systems and safety culture is like mother and child. Safety culture always takes care of safety systems like a mother taking care of her child. We should imbibe safety systems in our culture which will be part of our life and generations to come, by providing behavioural trainings as well as regular review of system effectiveness by involving people. Safety system and culture are two sides of a coin. To develop safety culture, organisation should have strong safety system. It can be good balance through the involvement of the top management and development of positive safety culture. The system and culture are 70:30 ratio. Behavioural safety is the right approach. But without a positive health and safety culture, you're never going to get the best results (Haspod, 2020). Developing a strong safety culture has the direct greatest impact on the incident and accident reduction of any workplace (Schonscheck, 2021).

Table 3: Percentages of HSE professionals emphasising how to achieve a good balance between safety systems and safety culture? (N=252).

1.	Robust Safety Management System firmly implemented with human touch and care with an intent of learning and improving is necessary. This will help build Interdependent and Learning culture with commitment to continually improve - 90%.
2.	We should develop culture of 100% compliance of the system developed otherwise hefty fines. If seat belt is provided in the car, it must be used by the passenger, otherwise no point of talking systems - 87%.
3.	Good safety systems (adherence) drive good safety culture and vice versa - 86%.
4.	By providing behavioural trainings - 85%.
5.	Regular review of system effectiveness by involving people - 81%.
6.	It can be good balance through the involvement of the top management and development of positive safety culture. The system and culture are 70:30 ratio. Behavioural safety is the right approach - 79%.
7.	Good Relations rather good balance. Relation between safety systems and safety culture is like mother and child. Safety culture always takes care of safety systems like a mother taking care of her child. - 70%.
8.	Safety system and culture are two sides of a coin. To develop safety culture, organisation should have strong safety system - 66%.
9.	We should imbibe safety systems in our culture which will be part of our life and generation to come - 60%.

CONCLUSIONS AND SUGGESTIONS

Balancing organisational safety systems and safety culture underlines that the Total Safety Culture (TSC) framework synthesizes information across fragmented conceptualizations to clearly depict the dynamic nature of safety culture and specific drivers of its development. TSC development may depend on employee learning from behavioural outcomes, conducive enabling factors, and consistency over time (Bisbey, et al., 2019). The total system safety integration approach not only delivers a positive safety culture but also enhances other performance metrics such as increased organizational citizenship behaviours, reduced employee turnover, enhanced engagement, organizational learning, and creativity and so on (Institute of Organisational Psychology NZ, 2021). Safety perceptions differ significantly among groups within an organization. An integrated approach in the development of an organisation's safety culture may result useful for an in-depth analysis of the criticality and the adoption of appropriate improvement strategies (Tocco, et al., 2022).

A safety professional's ultimate goal is to achieve a total safety culture (TSC) within his/her organization. In a TSC, everyone feels responsible for safety and pursues it on a daily basis; employees go beyond the call of duty to identify unsafe conditions and behaviors, and intervene to correct them; safe work practices are supported via rewarding feedback from peers and managers; people actively care on a continuous basis for safety; safety is not a priority that can be shifted depending on situational demands, rather safety is a value linked with all other situational priorities (ProQuest, 2023).

Industries are fast increasing in numbers, so are the risks, fires, fatalities, incidents and accidents. Organizational safety is to be treated more than its celebrations and certifications. The elements of total safety culture interventions ought not exist in disjointed form for best results of safety for manpower as well as business prosperity (Lal, 2023).

REFERENCES

Aburumman, Mohammed & Newnam, Sharon & Fildes, Brian. (2019). Evaluating the effectiveness of workplace interventions in improving safety culture: A systematic review. *Safety Science*. 115. 376-392. 10.1016/j.ssci.2019.02.027.

Arblaster, Margaret. (2018). Safety Regulation of Air Traffic Management, Editor(s): Air Traffic Management, Elsevier, 2018, 5, 87-115, ISBN 9780128111185, https://doi.org/10.1016/B978-0-12-811118-5.00005-9.

ASA. (2022 October 26). Statement on Safety Culture. https://www.asahq.org/standards-and-guidelines/statement-on-safety-culture

Bisbey TM, Kilcullen MP, Thomas EJ, Ottosen MJ, Tsao K, Salas E. Safety Culture: An Integration of Existing Models and a Framework for Understanding Its Development. Hum Factors. 2021 Feb;63(1):88-110. doi: 10.1177/0018720819868878. Epub 2019 Aug 19. PMID: 31424954.

Blackline Safety. (2021, August 24). A Guide to Integrating Safety Throughout Your Oil and Gas Organization. https://www.blacklinesafety.com/blog/integrating-safety-throughout-your-oil-and-gas-organization

Casey, Tristan & Griffin, Mark & Flatau Harrison, Huw & Neal, Andrew. (2017). Safety Climate and Culture: Integrating Psychological and Systems Perspectives. *Journal of Occupational Health Psychology*. 22. 10.1037/ocp0000072.

Curtis, E., Jones, R., Tipene-Leach, D. et al. Why cultural safety rather than cultural competency is required to achieve health equity: a literature review and recommended definition. *Int J Equity Health* 18, 174 (2019). https://doi.org/10.1186/s12939-019-1082-3

Dyreborg, J., Lipscomb, H. J., Nielsen, K., Törner, M., Rasmussen, K., Frydendall, K. B., Bay, H., Gensby, U., Bengtsen, E., Guldenmund, F., & Kines, P. (2022). Safety interventions for the prevention of accidents at work: A systematic review. Campbell Systematic Reviews, 18, e1234. https://doi.org/10.1002/cl2.1234

Easton, John. (2011, April 01). A Solution to Measure (and Improve) Safety Culture. https://ohsonline.com/articles/2011/04/01/a-solution-to-measure-safety-culture.aspx?m=1

Eeckelaert, Lieven, Starren, A., van Scheppingen, A., Fox, D. & Brück, C. (2011). Occupational safety and health culture assessment - a review of main approaches and selected tools. Working environment information working paper. EU-OSHA, https://osha.europa.eu/en/ publications/occupational-safety-and-health-culture-assessment- review-main-approaches-and-selected/

Hafeez, H., Abdullah, M.I., Zaheer, M.A. and Ahsan, Q. (2022), "Organizational resilience process: integrated model of safety culture", *Organization Management Journal*, Vol. 19 No. 1, pp. 2-21. https://doi.org/10.1108/OMJ-03-2020-0893

Haspod. (2020, June 18). How To Grow A Positive Health And Safety Culture. https://www.haspod.com/blog/management/how-to-grow-positive-health-safety-culture

HSE. (2022). A brief summary of Plan, Do, Check, Act. https://www.hse.gov.uk/managing/plan-do-check-act.htm

IAEA. (2015). Basic Professional Training Course, Module XXI, Management system, leadership and safety culture.

Institute of Organisational Psychology, NZ. (2021, March 8). Developing safety culture through integrated high performance work systems. https://organisationalpsychology.nz/uncategorized/developing-safety-culture-through-integrated-high-performance-work-systems/

Lal, H. (2023). Strengthening a positive safety culture despite underlying fear and peer pressure. *World Safety Journal*, 32(1), 57–64. https://doi.org/10.5281/zenodo.7770080

Misnan, Mohd Saidin & Mohammed, Miswan abdul hakim & Mohammad, Izran Sarrazin & Nesan, L. (2007). Problem and Issues in Developing Safety Culture in Construction Industry. *Malaysian Journal of Real Estate*. 2. 61-69.

NIOSH. (2022). What Is Total Worker Health? https://www.cdc.gov/niosh/twh/totalhealth.html

ProQuest. (2023). Ten principles for achieving a total safety culture. https://www.proquest.com/docview/200347593

Pearson, Nicola. (2021, May 14). What is safety culture and where is it going today. https://www.ideagen.com/thought-leadership/blog/safety-culture-today

SaferMe team. (2019, December 2). how does safety culture tie in with an HSE management system? https://www.safer.me/blog/safety-culture-tie-hse-management-system/

Schonscheck, Daniel. (2021, Jan 13). Creating A Strong Safety Culture. https://www.mcclone.com/blog/creating-a-strong-safety-culture

Sears, Don and Sullivan, Julie. (2022). To integrate safety culture, focus on changing behaviour. https://www.mscdirect.com/betterMRO/safety/integrate-safety-culture-focus-changing-behavior

Tocco Tussardi, I, Moretti, F, Capasso, M, et al. Improving the culture of safety among healthcare workers: Integration of different instruments to gain major insights and drive effective changes. *Int J Health Plann Mgmt*. 2022; 37(1): 429- 451. doi:10.1002/hpm.3348

Wong SY, Fu ACL, Han J, Lin J, Lau MC. Effectiveness of customised safety intervention programmes to increase the safety culture of hospital staff. BMJ Open Qual. 2021 Oct;10(4):e000962. doi: 10.1136/bmjoq-2020-000962. PMID: 34625426; PMCID: PMC8504354

ACKNOWLEDGMENT

Contribution of industry professionals is thankfully acknowledged.